# FINALS

# CRIMINAL LAW

## CORE CONCEPTS AND KEY QUESTIONS

**Second Edition**

**T. Leigh Hearn, Esquire**
**Series Editor**

© 2009 by Kaplan, Inc.

Published by Kaplan Publishing, a division of Kaplan, Inc.
1 Liberty Plaza, 24th floor
New York, NY 10006

Printed in the United States of America

10   9   8   7   6   5   4   3   2   1

ISBN13: 978-1-60714-094-8

Kaplan Publishing books are available at special quantity discounts to use for sales promotions, employee premiums, or educational purposes. Please email our Special Sales Department to order or for more information at kaplanpublishing@kaplan.com, or write to Kaplan Publishing, 1 Liberty Plaza, 24th floor, New York, NY 10006.

# TABLE OF CONTENTS

KAPLAN **pmbr**

**IV. PARTIES TO CRIME: ACCOMPLICE LIABILITY** ..........27
  **A. COMMON LAW CLASSIFICATIONS** ..........27
   1. Principal in the First Degree
   2. Principal in the Second Degree
    a. Insufficient bases
    b. Punishment
   3. Accomplice
    a. Definition
    b. Mental state requirement
    c. Scope of liability
    d. Ability to act alone
    e. Victims
    f. Members of legislatively protected class
    g. Defenses
    h. False accomplices
    i. Necessary parties
   4. Accessory Before the Fact
    a. Definition
    b. Punishment
    c. Conviction of the principal—majority view
    d. Conviction of the principal—common law
   5. Accessory After the Fact
    a. Definition
    b. Accomplice distinguished
    c. Misdemeanor required

**V. CRIMES AGAINST THE PERSON** ..........31
  **A. MURDER** ..........31
   1. Common Law Definition
   2. Actus Reus Requirement
   3. Person Requirement
   4. Actor Requirement
    a. Suicide
    b. Aiding in suicide
   5. Causation Requirement
    a. Cause-in-fact requirement
    b. Proximate cause requirement
    c. Timing requirement
    d. Simultaneous acts
    e. Pre-existing condition
   6. Mercy Killing
   7. Justification or Excuse
   8. Mens Rea Requirement
   9. Intent to Kill Murder
    a. Definition
    b. Deadly weapons doctrine
    c. Specific-intent crime

**KAPLAN) pmbr**

## I. GENERAL PRINCIPLES

### A. INTRODUCTION AND GENERAL CONSIDERATIONS

1. **Classification of Crimes**

   a. **Felonies.** A felony is a crime punishable by death or by imprisonment exceeding one year. At common law, *burglary, arson, robbery, rape, larceny, murder, manslaughter,* and *mayhem* were considered felonies.

   b. **Misdemeanors.** A misdemeanor is a crime punishable by imprisonment for less than one year or by a fine only. At common law, crimes not considered felonies were deemed misdemeanors.

   c. **Malum prohibitum.** A crime termed a *malum prohibitum* is a wrong which is legislatively prohibited (e.g., speeding, failing to register a firearm).

   d. **Malum in se.** On the other hand, a crime *malum in se* is one evil in itself (e.g., murder) involving an element of general criminal intent (e.g., battery), or involving moral turpitude (e.g., disbarment of an attorney).

   e. **Infamous crimes.** An infamous crime at common law involves fraud or dishonesty.

   f. **Modern statutes.** Presently, states enforce the criminal law primarily by legislative statutes or codes. Common law is used in the absence of such statutes. Because there is no federal common law of crimes, federal statutory criminal law is used. The Model Penal Code is widely used in influencing the scope of state statutory criminal law but is itself not a source of criminal law. *The Multistate Bar Examination (MBE) follows common law unless there are specific instances where the MBE question directs you to follow the Model Penal Code or modern view.*

      (1) **Void-for-vagueness doctrine.** Under the due process clause of the Fifth and Fourteenth Amendments of the United States Constitution, persons must be on notice that certain conduct is forbidden. Therefore, the Supreme Court has required that criminal statutes be specific, and give a person of ordinary intelligence "fair notice" of what conduct is prohibited. Furthermore, the void-for-vagueness doctrine also requires that statutes are fair and consistent in their enforcement; they may not be arbitrarily or eradically enforced.

      (2) **Ex post facto laws.** Under the Constitution, ex post facto laws are also prohibited. An ex post facto law is one that:

      (a) retroactively makes conduct criminal;

(b) retroactively enforces a stricter punishment for the same conduct; or

(c) retroactively alters procedural or evidentiary rules in a way that makes conviction of the criminal defendant easier.

(3) **Bills of attainder.** A bill of attainder is the legislative punishment of a named person or group without the benefit of a judicial trial. The Constitution also prohibits pass age of bills of attainder.

(4) **Statutory interpretation issues.** Criminal statutes may be difficult to interpret. Therefore, the courts are consistent in applying certain interpretation rules.

(a) **Plain meaning.** Where the language of a statute is clear and unambiguous, the court must apply the statute as written even where it feels that, in doing so, an undesirable result would occur. However, where the court feels that injustice or oppression would result, the court may decline to apply the statute as written. *Note that this is a rare occurrence and probably will not occur on the MBE.*

(b) **Ambiguous statutes.** Where a statute is ambiguous, the court must give the benefit of the doubt to the defendant. The statute must be construed in favor of the defendant. Note that an ambiguous statute is one where there are at least two possible meanings for the wording of a statute. It is important to distinguish ambiguity from vagueness, because vagueness occurs when language of a statute is so unclear that there is no way to reasonably ascertain a meaning for the statutory language.

(c) **Specificity.** Occasionally, there will be a conflict between statutes. Where this situation arises, a more specific statute will govern over a more general statute.

(d) **Recency.** Similarly, where two statutes address the same criminal conduct, the more recent statute will trump the earlier statute.

(e) **Repeal.** Where a statute is repealed or invalidated, no new prosecutions may take place under that statute. This rule also applies to pending prosecutions where there has not been a final judgment. However, where someone has already been convicted, a repeal of the statute will have no effect on that person, because there has already been a final judgment in the case.

g. **General-intent crimes.** A general-intent crime requires commission of an unlawful act (e.g., non-consensual intercourse) without a specific mens rea. A general bad state of mind will suffice.

   (1) **Mental state required.** Negligence or recklessness is sufficient for general-intent crimes. Criminal negligence involves conduct creating an unreasonable risk of harm, viewed by the objective test (tort standard), plus either a greater risk of harm or a subjective awareness of the risk by the defendant or both (i.e., recklessness). The concept of "motive" is substantively immaterial to the determination of intent to commit a criminal act.

   (2) **Listing of general-intent crimes**

      (a) Rape

      (b) Battery

      (c) Arson

      (d) Kidnapping

      (e) False imprisonment

      (f) Involuntary manslaughter

      (g) Depraved-heart murder

h. **Specific-intent crimes.** A specific-intent crime involves more than the objective fault required by merely doing the proscribed **actus reus.**

   (1) **Mental state required.** In addition, *a specific-intent crime includes an actual subjective intent to cause the proscribed result.* Specific-intent may be indicated by the use of such words as intentionally, knowingly, purposely, or willfully.

   (2) **Listing of specific-intent crimes**

      (a) Attempt

      (b) Solicitation

      (c) Conspiracy

      (d) Larceny

  (e) Larceny by trick

  (f) Forgery

  (g) Burglary

  (h) Assault

  (i) Robbery

  (j) Intent to kill or Murder

  (k) Voluntary manslaughter

i. **Malicious crimes.** To be guilty of a malice crime, the defendant must act with a reckless disregard of a high risk that harm will occur.

 (1) **Listing of malicious crimes**

  (a) Malicious destruction of property

  (b) Arson

j. **Strict liability crimes.** Under strict liability crimes, culpability is imposed on a defendant for ***doing the act*** which is prohibited by statute.

 (1) **Mental state.** No particular mental state is required for strict liability crimes.

 (2) **Defenses.** A reasonable mistake of fact is no defense to a public welfare offense (such as sale of liquor to a minor).

 (3) **Constitutionality.** Strict liability statutes have generally been held constitutional where the penalty is minor and excludes imprisonment.

 (4) **Listing of strict liability crimes**

  (a) Regulatory offenses (e.g., traffic violations, vehicle offenses, administrative statutes)

  (b) Public welfare offenses (e.g., regulation of firearms, food and drugs)

  (c) Morality crimes (e.g., statutory rape, bigamy)

| CLASSIFICATION OF CRIMES | | | | |
|---|---|---|---|---|
| | **General-intent Crimes** | **Specific-intent Crimes** | **Malicious Crimes** | **Strict Liability Crimes** |
| **List** | • Battery<br>• Rape<br>• Kidnapping<br>• False imprisonment<br>• Involuntary manslaughter<br>• Depraved-heart murder | • Attempt<br>• Solicitation<br>• Conspiracy<br>• Larceny<br>• Larceny by trick<br>• False pretenses<br>• Embezzlement<br>• Forgery<br>• Burglary<br>• Assault<br>• Robbery<br>• Intent to kill or murder<br>• Voluntary manslaughter | • Arson<br>• Malicious destruction of property | • Regulatory offenses<br>• Public welfare offenses<br>• Morality crimes (such as statutory rape, bigamy)<br>• Selling liquor to minors |
| **State of Mind Required** | Negligence, recklessness. Only intent to do the act, not intent to do the crime. | Intentional, knowing, purposeful, willful or wanton. Intent to do the crime. | Reckless disregard of a known risk. | Irrelevant. |

2. **Burden of Proof**

   a. **Elements of crimes.** The prosecution has the burden of persuasion to prove each and every element of a crime *beyond a reasonable doubt.*

   b. **Affirmative defenses.** The defendant has the burden of persuasion to prove affirmative defenses *by a preponderance of the evidence (majority rule).*

   c. **Directed verdict of guilty.** A directed verdict of guilty may *never* be issued against a defendant in a jury trial in accordance with principles of due process.

3. **Theories of Liability**

a. **Direct liability.** Usually, a criminal is directly liable for his criminal conduct because he personally participates in commission of the crime.

b. **Vicarious liability**

(1) **Definition.** The doctrine of vicarious liability in criminal law is similar to the doctrine of **respondeat superior** in tort law, in that one person (usually an employer) who is without fault, is made liable for the criminal conduct of another person (usually an employee). However, in criminal law vicarious liability often applies in situations other than employer/employee.

(2) **Punishment.** Because no **actus reus** is committed by the vicariously liable party, legislatures generally limit liability to minor punishment in the form of fines and santions that do not include incarceration, to avoid due process conflicts.

(3) **Application—serving liquor to a minor.** A legislative intent to impose vicarious liability on a tavern owner for the strict liability offense of his bartender serving liquor to a minor should *not* be inferred where the employee's actions were unauthorized.

c. **Enterprise liability**

(1) **Modern view.** Under modern statutes, unlike at common law, a corporation can be held criminally liable for strict liability crimes committed by an agent of the corporation acting on its behalf within the scope of employment.

(2) **Superior agent rule.** Under the "superior agent" rule, corporate liability is limited to situations in which the criminal conduct is performed or participated in by corporate agents of such authority as to imply that their actions reflect the policy of the corporate body.

**Note:** Where provided by statute, as in the case of regulatory offenses, partnerships may be held criminally liable; however, in the absence of such statutes, the partnership is not liable for crimes of individual partners because at common law the partnership had no legal existence apart from its individual members. Where an individual partner participates in or authorizes criminal conduct, he will be liable for the crimes committed by other partners.

B. **ELEMENTS OF CRIMES**

1. **In General.** Generally, the prosecution must prove the following elements: (1) *actus reus* (or guilty act); (2) *mens rea* (or guilty mind); (3) *concurrence in time* between the act and the requisite mental state; (4) *causation* between defendant's act and the harm suffered (both actual and proximate causation required); and (5) *harm* to victim resulting from defendant's criminal conduct.

2. **Actus Reus.** The defendant must act voluntarily. Acts which are reflexive, convulsive, performed while unconscious, or otherwise involuntary, are insufficient, as are mere bad thoughts unaccompanied by action.

3. **Omission to Act.** Criminal liability can be imposed on a defendant for an omission to act where:

   a. there is a legal duty to act *and*

   b. the defendant can physically perform the act.

4. **Such a Legal Duty to Act May Arise in the Following Ways:**

   a. *by statute* (e.g., failure to file a tax return);

   b. *by contract* (e.g., failure of a lifeguard, a nurse, or a guide on a hiking or river-rafting expedition to rescue);

   c. *based upon relationship* (e.g., a parent for a child, a spouse for a spouse);

   **MBE Exam Tip:** If two people, though not closely related, live together under one roof, one may have a duty to act to aid the other who becomes helpless.

   d. *where a voluntary undertaking is begun* (e.g., unreasonable abandonment of a rescue which could worsen victim's plight is sufficient even if done by a good samaritan); or

   e. *where the defendant created the victim's peril* (e.g., D pushes V into the path of an oncoming car which D did not see and then fails to take steps to assist V).

   **MBE Exam Tip:** Also, it is important to note that these same situations give rise to a duty to act under tort law as well!

5. **Mens Rea.** In determining a defendant's culpability for general-intent and specific-intent crimes, the jury must look to the defendant's state of mind at the commission of the crime.

   a. For strict liability crimes, the defendant's state of mind is irrelevant.

   b. Definitions of types of mental states:

      (1) **Intentionally.** One acts intentionally when he desires that his acts cause certain consequences or knows that his acts are substantially certain to produce those consequences.

      (2) **Knowingly.** Traditionally, intent has been defined to include knowledge. One acts knowingly when he knows that the nature and/or result of his conduct exists as he thinks it to be. Lack of knowledge can often excuse criminal liability under the defense of mistake of fact.

(3) **Purposely.** One acts purposely when there exists a conscious objective to engage in such conduct or to cause such a result.

(4) **Willfully.** The term "willfully" encompasses the concepts of "intentionally" and "purposely," as opposed to accidentally or negligently, and has been used to imply evil purpose in crimes involving moral turpitude.

(5) **Wanton Conduct.** Wantonness is greater than criminal negligence. It is akin to recklessness in that both a high degree of risk of harm and an awareness of such harm is required. In the area of depraved-heart murder, a standard of wanton conduct is used, because a form of unintentional killing is involved.

6. **Concurrence of Mens Rea with Actus Reus.** It is not only necessary that the defendant's criminal intent occur at the time he commits the criminal act, but the mental state should also actuate, or put into action, the act or omission.

   **EXAMPLE:** In burglary, the intent "to commit a felony or larceny therein" must exist at the *time (or moment) of the breaking and entering.*

7. **Causation**

   a. **Rule.** The defendant's conduct must be both the actual and the proximate cause of the specified criminal result.

   b. **Proximate cause.** To find proximate cause, the resultant harm must be within the risk created by defendant's conduct in crimes involving negligence or recklessness, or sufficiently similar to that intended in crimes requiring intent, so as not to hold the defendant liable for extraordinary results (such as acts of nature, or grossly negligent or intentional bad acts of third parties, including intentional medical mistreatment, but not negligent medical care).

   **Question:**

   The state of Newton has the following hit and run statute in effect:

   > "Any driver of a motor vehicle (including but not limited to automobiles, trucks, buses, or motorcycles) involved in an accident or collision resulting in injury or death to a human being shall immediately stop his or her vehicle at the scene of such accident or collision, render necessary aid to the injured victim and furnish the police or other person(s) at the scene with his or her name, address and driver's license. Any violation or noncompliance with said statute shall be punished by imprisonment for not less than 3 years nor more than 7 years."

   At 3:30 P.M. on the afternoon of January 13, 2002, nine-year-old Goldie Hand was riding her bicycle along Pacific Coast Highway. As

Goldie swerved into the southbound lane, a car driven by Ellen Brennan struck her bicycle. Goldie was knocked off her bike and thrown onto the sidewalk adjacent to the highway. Although Goldie received some minor scrapes and bruises, she was not seriously injured. Following the accident, the car driven by Brennan sped away.

Moments later, however, a tractor-trailer crashed into the rear of a Ford Pinto about 30 feet from where Goldie was lying. The Pinto almost instantly caught fire as its gas tank exploded. Goldie, who was engulfed in the flaming wreckage, burned to death.

If Brennan is charged with involuntary manslaughter for the death of Hand, the defendant should be found

(A) guilty, because she unlawfully fled the scene of an accident in violation of her statutory duty
(B) guilty, because her failure to render aid to Hand would make Brennan criminally responsible for the victim's death
(C) not guilty, because under the circumstances her failure to aid Hand cannot be a basis for imposing criminal responsibility for the victim's death
(D) not guilty, because there was not a sufficient causal connection between her actions and Hand's death to impose criminal responsibility

**Answer:**

(D) As a general rule, most crimes require the following elements: (1) an act, (2) mental fault (or "guilty mind"), (3) concurrence (of act + mental state), (4) harm, and (5) causation. With crimes so defined as to require not merely conduct but also a specified result of conduct, the defendant's conduct must be the "legal" or "proximate" cause of the result. In the example provided herein, the fact that Brennan fled the scene of the accident (in violation of the hit and run statute) was not the "legal" cause of Hand's death. Rather, Hand's death resulted from the Pinto's gas tank exploding, which was caused by the collision with the tractor-trailer. Note that, although choice (C) is also conceivably correct, alternative (D) is preferred because it refers to the requirement of *a causal connection* which is a material element in both criminal and tort law.

## II. DEFENSES

### A. RESPONSIBILITY

1. **Insanity**

    a. **M'Naghten test.** Under this test, a defendant is relieved of criminal responsibility upon proof that at the time of commission of the act, he was laboring under such a defect of reason from a disease of the mind, as not to know the nature and quality of the act he was doing, or, if he did know it, he did not know that what he was doing was wrong.

(1) **Majority rule.** The majority of jurisdictions follow the M'Naghten test.

(2) **Disease of the mind.** "Disease of the mind" includes all mental abnormalities, but not a psychopathic personality.

b. **Irresistible impulse test.** Under the "irresistible impulse" test, a defendant will be found not guilty where he had a *mental disease* which keeps him from *controlling his conduct.*

(1) In almost half of the jurisdictions following the M'Naghten test, the "irresistible impulse" test has also been adopted such that if a defendant is found to meet the requirements of either test, he will be found insane.

c. **Durham (or New Hampshire) test.** Under the Durham rule, or the "product" rule, a defendant is not criminally responsible *if his unlawful act was the product of mental disease or defect.*

(1) A crime is a product of a mental disease if it would not have been committed "but for" the defect or disease.

(2) **Note:** The Durham test has been criticized as being overly broad.

d. **The Model Penal Code test—"substantial capacity."** Under this test, a person is not responsible for criminal conduct if, at the time of such conduct, as a result of mental disease or defect, he lacked substantial capacity to appreciate the criminality (wrongfulness) of his conduct or to conform his conduct to the requirements of law.

(1) Developed by the American Law Institute (ALI), *this test combines the M'Naghten and the irresistible impulse tests.*

(2) Hereafter, "mental disease or defect" does not include abnormalities manifested only by repeated criminal or otherwise antisocial conduct.

(3) Note that this test considers both a cognitive and a volitional capacity.

e. **Procedural issues**

(1) **Burden of proof.** A defendant is *presumed sane* until such time as he goes forward by raising either a scintilla of evidence or evidence sufficient to raise a reasonable doubt as to his sanity, depending on the particular jurisdiction. Then some states require the defendant to prove insanity by a preponderance of the evidence, while other states require the prosecution to prove sanity beyond a reasonable doubt.

**MBE Exam Tip:** The defendant has the initial burden (of production) to present evidence raising a reasonable doubt of his/her mental responsibility for the criminal act. Once the defendant has met this burden, then the burden of persuasion shifts to the prosecution to prove responsibility beyond a reasonable doubt.

**Note:** In the federal court system, the defendant has the burden of proving his insanity defense by "clear and convincing evidence."

(2) **Effect of "not guilty" plea.** A "not guilty" plea at arraignment does not waive the right to raise the insanity defense at a later time.

(3) **Psychiatric examination.** Upon pleading insanity, a defendant has no right to refuse examination by a court-appointed psychiatrist; however, there is no constitutional right of an indigent defendant to a psychiatric examination.

(4) **Commitment.** Following a finding of "not guilty by reason of insanity," some jurisdictions automatically commit the defendant to a mental institution, while the majority of jurisdictions order commitment only where the defendant's insanity is presently existing or he is found (usually by the trial judge) to be dangerous.

    (a) Where found incompetent (by a *jury* determination in many jurisdictions), commitment usually results for a reasonable time until recovery.

    (b) Similarly, a defendant found incapable of understanding the nature and purpose of the punishment may not be executed until such time as he has recovered. Generally, only the warden may raise this issue.

f. **Diminished capacity.** Some jurisdictions allow the defense of diminished capacity, which is short of insanity, to prove that as a result of a mental defect the defendant did not have a state of mind that is an element of the offense.

(1) When pleading diminished capacity, the defense is used to negate a specific mental state required for the particular crime.

**EXAMPLE:** In negating the premeditation and deliberation requirement of first degree murder, the defense of diminished capacity can mitigate murder to voluntary manslaughter by negating the element of malice.

2. **Intoxication.** Voluntary or involuntary intoxication (whether brought about by alcohol or by narcotic drugs) is a defense to crime when *it negates the existence of an element of the crime.*

a. **Voluntary intoxication.** Under the prevailing view, voluntary intoxication maybe a valid defense for a specific-intent crime if it negates the requisite

# CRIMINAL LAW

mental state. However, ***voluntary intoxication is no defense to crimes involving malice, recklessness, negligence, or strict liability***.

b. **Involuntary intoxication.** Involuntary intoxication is a defense to a crime, even though it does not negate an element of the crime, under the same circumstances as insanity.

c. **Excessive use.** The excessive use of alcohol or drugs may bring about real insanity, in which case the rules concerning insanity as a defense to crime govern.

d. **Specific versus general-intent crimes.** Intoxication is a valid defense for specific-intent crimes if it negates the mens rea, but it is not a valid defense for general-intent crimes, because they do not require a specific mens rea.

**Question:**

Kyle was charged with attempted rape of Meredith. The crime allegedly occurred at a party at Kyle's home. During the party, Kyle invited Meredith into his bedroom to show her some of his etchings. When she entered his bedroom, Kyle ripped off her blouse and threw Meredith onto his bed. He then jumped on Meredith and tried to pull off her skirt. When Meredith began to scream, some of the guests rushed into the bedroom and pulled Kyle off the victim. At trial, Kyle testified that he wanted to have sexual intercourse with Meredith but he believed that she was consenting. Kyle further testified that he had consumed a pint of whiskey earlier in the evening and was intoxicated at the time the incident occurred.

If the jury believes that Meredith did not consent but also believes that Kyle in his intoxicated state honestly believed that she was consenting, the defendant should be found

(A) guilty, because consent is determined by the objective manifestations of the victim and not the subjective beliefs of the defendant
(B) guilty, because voluntary intoxication is no defense
(C) not guilty, because he honestly believed that she was consenting
(D) not guilty, unless his belief that she was consenting was unreasonable

**Answer:**

(C) It should be noted that the crime of attempt consists of (1) an intent to do an act or to bring about certain consequences which would in law amount to a crime; and (2) an act in furtherance of that intent which goes beyond mere preparation. Remember that intoxication is a defense to a crime if it negates a required element of that crime; this is so whether the intoxication is voluntary or involuntary. Generally speaking, intoxication (when it negates an element of the crime) does so by negating some mental element (i.e., intent or knowledge) which the crime requires. Choice (C) is correct because ***intoxication (whether voluntary or involuntary) negates the element of intent*** required for the crime of attempt to commit rape. This is a classic Multistate example because the test maker is aware that many students will incorrectly choose choice (B). Note that, if Kyle were charged with the crime of rape, then choice (B) would be correct (because intoxication is not a valid defense for the "general-intent" crime of rape). In this example, however, ***Kyle is not charged with the crime of rape, but, rather, he is being charged with the crime of attempt to commit rape*** (which is a "specific-intent" crime). In sum, intoxication is a valid defense for "specific-intent" crimes (if it negates the mens rea) but not for "general-intent" crimes (which do not require a specific mens rea).

3. **Infancy**

   a. **Common law.** At common law, a complete defense, due to incapacity, existed for children under seven years of age. Children between the ages of seven and 14 were rebuttably presumed to lack criminal capacity. Children over age 14 were held responsible as adults.

   b. **Modern statutes.** Many states have abolished the common law presumptions and established a specific minimum age required for a criminal conviction. For rehabilitation rather than punitive purposes, juvenile courts have been provided in all states to exercise either exclusive or concurrent jurisdiction with criminal courts, depending on the offense committed and the age of the offender.

4. **Competency.** An accused may not be tried, convicted, or sentenced if he lacks the capacity to assist counsel and rationally defend himself by understanding the nature of the proceedings being brought against him. ***Note that competency speaks not to the defendant's mental state at the time the criminal act was committed, but rather to the defendant's mental state at the time of trial.***

## B. JUSTIFICATION

1. **Self-Defense.** If a person has a reasonable belief that he is in imminent danger of unlawful bodily harm, he may use that amount of force which is reasonably necessary to prevent such harm, unless he is the aggressor.

   a. **Deadly versus non-deadly force**

      (1) **Deadly force—definition.** Deadly force is that which threatens death or serious bodily harm.

      (2) **Non-deadly force—definition.** Non-deadly force threatens only bodily harm.

b. **Rights of the aggressor**

An aggressor is one who strikes the first blow or commits a crime against the victim. The aggressor can regain the right of self-defense in either of two ways: (1) upon complete withdrawal perceived by the other party, or (2) escalation of force by the victim of the initial aggression.

c. **Duty to retreat**

(1) **Majority view.** The majority view is that *there is no duty to retreat.*

(2) **Minority view.** In jurisdictions that do follow a retreat rule, one need not retreat unless it can be done in complete safety, and retreat need not be made in one's home.

2. **Defense of Others**

A defendant is justified in defending another person with reasonable force only if he reasonably believes the victim had a right to use such force. Some jurisdictions limit this defense to situations where a special relationship exists between the defendant and the victim, while other jurisdictions view the defendant as "standing in the shoes" of the person defended.

3. **Defense of Property**

a. **Non-deadly force**

(1) **Justification**

(a) *Reasonable non-deadly force is justified in defending one's property* from theft, destruction, or trespass where the defendant has a reasonable belief that the property is in immediate danger and no greater force than necessary is used.

(b) Non-deadly force is also proper when used to re-enter real property or regain possession of wrongfully taken personal property upon *immediate pursuit.*

(2) **Lack of justification.** The use of non-deadly force is improper where a request to desist would suffice.

b. **Deadly force**

(1) *Deadly force may never be used merely to defend property.*

(2) However, by virtue of other defenses (self-defense, defense of others), deadly force may be used where unlawful interference with property is accompanied by a threat of deadly force or where the defender reasonably

believes an entry will be made or attempted in his dwelling by one intending to commit a felony therein.

4. **Law Enforcement Defenses**

   a. **Police**

      (1) A police officer may use that amount ***of non-deadly force*** that he reasonably believes necessary to effect a lawful arrest or prevent the escape of the arrestee.

      (2) Deadly force may not be used to arrest or prevent the escape of a misdemeaner offender. A police officer may use ***deadly force to prevent the commission of a dangerous felony*** or to effectuate an arrest where it is reasonably believed the person has committed a felony and the force is reasonably necessary to effectuate the arrest.

   b. **Private citizens**

      (1) A private citizen is privileged to use that amount of ***non-deadly force that reasonably appears necessary to prevent the commission of a felony or a misdemeanor amounting to a breach of the peace.***

      (2) A private citizen may use ***non-deadly force to make an arrest if the crime was in fact committed*** and he reasonably believes the person against whom he uses the force committed the crime.

      (3) A private citizen may use the same amount of ***deadly force as a police officer only if a dangerous felony is involved and the person against whom he used the force is actually guilty of the crime.***

5. **Resisting Unlawful Arrest**

   a. A defendant may use reasonable non-deadly force to resist an ***unlawful arrest.***

   b. An individual may only resist ***a lawful arrest by a police officer where the individual does not know that the other person is a police officer*** (because this presents a situation of self-defense).

6. **Necessity**

   a. **Justification.** Even deadly force is justified to avoid imminent injury resulting from natural (non-human) forces or where an individual reasonably believes that his criminal conduct ***is necessary to avoid a "greater harm"*** (e.g., A kills B to save C and D) that would result from compliance with the law.

   b. **Lack of justification.** There is no defense of necessity where the defendant is at fault in creating the perilous situation.

## 7. Duress

a. **Definition and application.** The defense of duress justifies criminal conduct where the defendant reasonably believes that the only way to avoid unlawful threats of great bodily harm or imminent death is to engage in conduct proscribed by law. For duress, the threat comes from human forces rather than from forces of nature.

b. **Belief requirement.** The defendant must possess a reasonable belief that the threat will be carried out.

c. **Murder.** *Duress, or coercion, is not available as a defense to murder.*

**Question:**

> After waiting in line for two hours to gain entry into Studio 69, a popular discotheque, Calvin was denied admission because his attire failed to conform to the club's dress code. When he was refused admittance, Calvin angrily shouted to the club's doorman, "You'll be sorry for this. After I'm through, Studio 69 will be reduced to rubble." Later that same evening, Calvin returned to the disco with two Molotov cocktails in his possession. He noticed Homer leaving the disco and followed him into a nearby parking lot. As Homer was about to enter his car, Calvin grabbed him, pointed a gun and said, "Follow me, you disco punk, or I'll blow your brains out." Calvin led Homer to the rear of the disco, handed him the Molotov cocktails, and directed him to throw the firebombs through an open window of the club. In fear of his life, Homer tossed the Molotov cocktails into the club causing an inferno which killed 25 patrons.

> If Homer is charged with felony-murder for the death of the patrons, he will most likely be found

> (A) guilty, under the felony-murder rule
> (B) guilty, since duress is not a defense to murder
> (C) not guilty, since duress is a defense to arson
> (D) not guilty, since Homer was justified under the circumstances

**Answer:**

(C) It has been recognized that duress may be a valid defense to arson under the holding of *Ross v. State,* 82 N.E. 781 (1907). In addition, duress has been held a good defense to kidnapping and the lesser crimes of robbery and burglary. Keep in mind that even though **duress is not a defense to murder**, it may be a defense to felony-murder if it negates the underlying felony.

8. **Public Duty.** A public officer, policeman, or private citizen offering assistance, is justified in using reasonable force against another or in taking the property

of another, ***provided*** the officer is acting within his authority pursuant to a law, court order, or process which is valid or which he reasonably believes to be valid.

9. **Domestic Authority**

   a. **Minor children.** The parents of a minor child, or one "in loco parentis," may justifiably use reasonable force to promote the child's welfare.

   b. **Reasonableness.** "Reasonableness" is determined in light of the child's age, sex, health, and particular misconduct based on the totality of the circumstances.

   c. **Availability of defense in other situations.** This defense is available in some other situations where similar responsibility lies—a ship captain for his crew, a warden for his prisoners, but not a husband using force on his wife.

10. **Entrapment**

   a. **Application.** The defense of entrapment exists where the criminal plan is the product of creative activity originating with law enforcement officials and the defendant is in no way predisposed to commit the crime.

   b. **Absence of entrapment.** Government officials can, however, encourage criminal activity by providing the opportunity or the equipment for the commission of a crime.

   c. **Unavailability of defense.** Procedurally, a defendant may not raise the issue of entrapment if he has denied his participation in the crime.

   d. **Past criminal record.** A defendant's past criminal record is relevant in proving predisposition, even though such potentially damaging evidence may prejudicially affect the judge.

11. **Mistake of Fact or Ignorance**

   a. **Mistake of fact.** Mistake of fact is a defense where it negates the existence of a mental state required to establish a material element of the crime. In other words, there would be no crime if the facts were such as defendant thought them to be.

      (1) **General-intent crimes.** To negate the existence of a general-intent, ***a mistake of fact must be reasonable*** to the extent that under the circumstances a reasonable person would have made that type of mistake.

      (2) **Specific-intent crimes.** To negate the existence of a specific-intent, a mistake of fact need not be reasonable. ***It may be unreasonable, provided it is honest.***

**Question:**

Viceroy is on trial for rape. April, the alleged victim, testified that she went out to dinner with Viceroy. Afterwards, he invited her to his apartment for coffee. Upon entering the apartment, he violently assaulted her. Although she tried to resist, he overpowered and raped her.

Viceroy testified that during dinner he and April drank two bottles of champagne. When they returned to his apartment, he was so intoxicated that he honestly believed that she consented to the intercourse.

The jury determined that April did not consent to the intercourse. The jury also found that Viceroy as a result of his intoxication honestly but unreasonably believed that she was consenting. As a consequence, the defendant should be found

(A) not guilty, because he honestly believed that April consented
(B) not guilty, because his intoxication negated his criminal intent
(C) guilty, because rape is a general-intent crime
(D) guilty, because she did not consent and his belief that she was consenting was unreasonable

**Answer:**

(D) This Criminal Law question involves a two-step approach. First, it is important to point out that rape is a "general-intent" crime. Second, mistake of fact may be a valid defense for a "general-intent" crime if it is reasonable. On the other hand, mistake can be a valid defense for a "specific-intent" crime (such as larceny or burglary), whether it is reasonable or unreasonable as long as it is honest. Since Viceroy's mistake was unreasonable, it will ***not provide a valid defense for the crime of rape.*** Choice (C) is not the best answer because it does not address the reasonableness of Viceroy's mistake. In other words, if Viceroy's mistake had been reasonable, then he would not be guilty of rape despite the fact that it is a "general-intent" crime.

(3) **Strict liability crimes.** Mistake of fact or ignorance is no defense to a strict liability crime which itself requires no mental state. Thus, it is no defense to statutory rape that the defendant thought the victim was of age.

b. **Mistake of law**

(1) **General rule.** Generally, where the defendant is unaware that his acts are criminally proscribed, such ignorance of the law is no defense.

(2) **Knowledge or awareness.** However, where some element of a crime involves knowledge or awareness by the defendant, a mistake of law as to this element may provide a valid defense.

(3) **Exceptions**

    (a) Mistake of law is a valid defense where a statute proscribing the defendant's conduct has not been reasonably made available, or where the defendant has reasonably relied on a statute or judicial decision that is later overruled or declared unconstitutional.

    (b) Mistake of law is also a valid defense where a defendant relies in good faith upon an erroneous official statement of law contained in an administrative order or in an official interpretation by a public officer or department.

12. **Consent**

    a. **General rule.** Consent of the victim is no defense to a crime.

    b. **Exception.** Consent is a defense to a crime where it negates a specific element of the offense, such as in rape or kidnapping.

13. **Condonation**

    a. **Subsequent forgiveness.** Subsequent forgiveness by the victim is generally no defense to commission of a crime.

    b. **Guilt of the victim.** Neither is guilt of the victim a defense to the criminal conduct of the defendant.

## III. INCHOATE CRIMES

### A. SOLICITATION

1. **Definition.** Solicitation was a common law misdemeanor consisting of *enticing, advising, inciting, inducing, urging, or otherwise encouraging another to commit a felony or breach of the peace.*

    **Model Penal Code:** The MPC defines solicitation broadly to include requesting another to commit any offense (which would include misdemeanors as well as felonies).

    **MBE Exam Tip:** As a general rule, students are instructed to answer MBE questions based on the common law unless instructed otherwise.

2. **Timing of crime.** The offense is complete at the time the solicitation is made.

3. **Agreement unnecessary.** It is unnecessary that the person solicited enter into an agreement to commit the requested crime. Indeed, a person solicited to do a crime may not even respond, but the solicitor will still be guilty of solicitation.

4. **Underlying crime.** The completion of the crime solicited is unnecessary for a conviction.

5. **Defenses.** At common law, there were *no defenses* to solicitation.

   a. **Impossibility.** Even where it would be impossible for the soliciting person to carry out the crime, such impossibility is no defense to the crime of solicitation. What matters is how the solicitor believes the circumstances to be, not how they actually were.

   b. **Withdrawal.** Because the crime of solicitation is complete as soon as the solicitation is made, *withdrawal can be no defense to the crime of solicitation.* Even where the solicitor later changes her mind, such will be a defense to the underlying crime, but not to the solicitation crime.

6. **Merger.** The crime of solicitation, unlike conspiracy, *merges with the target felony* upon completion of the latter.

   **Question:**

   Jasmine and Zeke were good friends who lived in the same apartment building. Jasmine approached Zeke and asked him for a favor. She told Zeke that she had loaned her stereo to Fabian and now wanted it back. Jasmine said that Fabian had left town and had given her permission to go to his house and retrieve the stereo. Since the stereo was heavy, she asked Zeke to go to Fabian's house and pick it up for her. She told Zeke that he could enter Fabian's home through the back door which would be kept unlocked.

   Unknown to Zeke, Jasmine was lying. The stereo was really owned by Fabian and he did not give Jasmine permission to enter his home and remove it. Zeke agreed to get the stereo as Jasmine requested. Zeke went to Fabian's house and found the back door unlocked. He entered the dwelling and removed the stereo which was located in the living room. When he brought the stereo to Jasmine, she laughed and said, "You idiot, I lied to you. This isn't my stereo, it really belongs to Fabian." Angered, Zeke took the stereo to his apartment intending to return it to Fabian. Zeke did not report the incident to the police and the next day he decided to keep the stereo.

   Jasmine is guilty of

   (A) burglary and larceny
   (B) solicitation and burglary
   (C) solicitation, conspiracy, burglary and larceny
   (D) conspiracy and larceny

**Answer:**

(A) Choices (B) and (C) are wrong because solicitation merges with the target offense. Likewise, choice (D) is incorrect because at common law conspiracy requires an agreement between two or more guilty parties (the so-called "plurality" requirement). By process of elimination, alternative (A) is the best of the given choices.

7. **Specific-intent crime.** Solicitation is a specific-intent crime in that the person soliciting ***must specifically intend the other party commit the crime*** and not merely show approval.

## B. ATTEMPT

1. **Elements of the Crime.** The crime of attempt consists of two elements:

   a. a *specific-intent* to bring about a criminal result, and

   b. a *significant overt act* in furtherance of that intent.

2. **Merger.** Once the target crime is committed, ***the attempt merges into the target crime.***

3. **Specific-Intent Crime.** Attempt is a specific-intent crime. The specific-intent for attempt can apply to both specific and general-intent crimes, as well as strict liability crimes.

   **EXAMPLE:** Although rape is a general-intent crime, attempt to commit rape is a specific-intent crime.

4. **Overt Act Requirement.** The overt act required must render the defendant significantly close enough to actual perpetration that he unequivocally intends to commit the crime.

   a. **Approaches.** Several approaches are used to determine what constitutes a sufficient overt act.

      (1) **Common law.** At common law, a defendant was required to have performed the "last act" necessary to achieve the intended result.

      (2) **Modern view.** Today, acts prior to the last act are often sufficient, as long as the act is a *substantial step* toward commission of the crime.

      **Note: *The MBE follows the substantial step requirement for attempt.***

      (3) **Preparation.** Mere preparation is not enough for attempt.

5. **Defenses**

   a. **Abandonment**

      (1) **Common law standard.** At common law, abandonment is no defense to attempt once the attempt is complete.

      (2) **Model Penal Code standard.** Under the Model Penal Code, a voluntary and complete abandonment can operate as an affirmative defense of renunciation.

   b. **Legal impossibility.** *Legal impossibility is traditionally regarded as a defense to attempt* and involves the situation where the defendant did all those things he intended to do, but these acts did not constitute a crime.

   **Question:**

   Wright is charged with attempted arson. In this jurisdiction, arson is defined as the unlawful or intentional burning of the dwelling of another. One night, Wright decided to set fire to his own home intending to collect the insurance proceeds. Wright, who was an electronics expert, put together an explosive device and lit the fuse that was supposed to detonate after a ten-minute interval. After lighting the fuse, Wright left the dwelling and drove to a local bar. Unknown to Wright, the fuse became disjointed and did not trigger the explosive device. In fact, none of the structure was burned or damaged.

   At the time Wright carried out his plan, he believed that setting fire to one's home constituted arson. Previously, Wright's lawyer erroneously advised him that he would be guilty of arson if he were to set fire to his own home for purposes of defrauding the insurance company.

   If Wright is subsequently prosecuted for the crime of attempted arson, he should be found

   (A) not guilty, because of legal impossibility
   (B) not guilty, because there was no damage to the structure
   (C) guilty, because mistake of fact is not a valid defense
   (D) guilty, because he performed an overt act that constituted a substantial step in the commission or attempted commission of the crime

   **Answer:**

   (A) At common law arson was defined as (1) the malicious (2) burning (3) of the dwelling house (4) of another. One could not be guilty of arson for setting fire to her own home. This would be an example of legal impossibility that constitutes a valid defense to the inchoate crime of attempt. Under the traditional or common law view, legal impossibility but not factual impossibility is a defense to a charge of attempt.

c. **Factual impossibility.** Factual impossibility is ***no defense to attempt*** where the defendant intends a criminal act but cannot accomplish it because of facts unknown to him at the time of the act. Examples of factual impossibility include: where the defendant attempted to steal from an empty pocket, an empty receptacle, or an empty house; where the defendant shot with intent to kill a certain person but failed because the intended victim was not where the defendant believed he was or because the victim was too far away to be killed by the weapon employed; where the defendant attempted to kill with an unloaded or defective gun or by use of poison or a bomb with was incapable of producing death; where the defendant attempted rape but was impotent; where the defendant attempted an abortion but the woman was not pregnant or the drugs or instruments were incapable of producing an abortion; where the intended victim of false pretenses had no money or was not deceived; where the intended victim of extortion was not put in fear; and where an attempt at bribery was unsuccessful because the employee who was to offer the bribe instead went to the police or because the other party was unwilling to take a bribe.

d. **Inherent impossibility.** Where a defendant uses means that a reasonable person would view as being extremely inadequate to fulfill the requisite criminal act, inherent impossibility may be used as a valid defense to attempt.

## C. CONSPIRACY

1. **Elements.** A conspiracy is:

   a. an unlawful criminal combination

   b. ***between two or more persons***

   c. who enter into ***an agreement***

   d. ***with the specific-intent to commit an unlawful act or***

   e. ***a lawful act by unlawful means.***

2. **Agreement.** The essence of the conspiracy is the ***agreement***. Feigned agreement (as in the case of an undercover police officer) is insufficient. Actual agreement is required.

   a. **Meeting of the minds.** To form a conspiracy, the parties must act together and agree to accomplish the same crime.

   b. **Express agreement not required.** An agreement may be evidenced by conduct where the conspirators demonstrate over time that they intended to achieve the same objective and agreed to work together toward that end.

3. **Overt Act—Traditional View.** Traditionally, no "overt act" is required for conspiracy. At common law, ***the agreement itself constitutes a crime.***

4. **Overt Act—Modern View.** In about half of the states, modern statutes require ***an overt act in furtherance of the conspiracy.***

5. **Merger.** Unlike attempt, ***conspiracy is a separate and distinct offense that does not merge*** upon completion of the target crime, because criminal combinations are deemed to be dangerous apart from the underlying crime itself.

6. **Scope of the Conspiracy.** Each co-conspirator is liable for the crimes of all the other co-conspirators where the crimes were both:

   a. ***a foreseeable outgrowth of the conspiracy and***

   b. ***were committed in furtherance of the conspiratorial goal.***

7. **Single or Multiple Conspiracy.** It is the nature of the agreement which determines whether there is a single or a multiple conspiracy.

   a. **Single.** In a "chain" relationship where several crimes are committed under one large scheme in which each member knows generally of the other parties' participation and there exists a community of interest, one single conspiracy results.

   b. **Multiple.** Alternatively, in the so-called "hub-and-spoke" relationship, where one common member enters into agreements to commit a series of independent crimes with different individuals, multiple conspiracies exist.

8. **Mental State.** Conspiracy is a specific-intent crime.

9. **Termination.** Once the target crime has been committed, the conspiracy terminates.

   **Note:** The timing of termination is very important because statements of co-conspirators are only admissible if they were made in furtherance of the conspiracy! Statements made after a conspiracy terminates are not admissible.

10. **Procedural Issues**

    a. **Acquittal of one.** An acquittal of one co-conspirator results in the acquittal of a single remaining co-conspirator, because at least two guilty parties are required for a conspiracy conviction.

    b. **Wharton Rule.** The ***Wharton Rule*** states that in crimes where two or more people are necessary for the commission of the offense, ***there is no conspiracy*** unless the agreement involves an additional person who is not essential to the definition of the crime.

       **EXAMPLE:** If A and B engage in a duel, they are guilty of the crime of dueling but not conspiracy to duel. Likewise, if A and B are guilty of adultery, they cannot be criminally liable for conspiracy as well.

      (1) **Wharton rule crimes include:**

          (a) dueling

          (b) bigamy

          (c) adultery

          (d) incest

          (e) gambling

          (f) giving and receiving of bribes

  c. **Application of conspiracy to corporations.** Because a corporation and its agent are considered one person, no conspiracy can exist between them.

  d. **Legislatively protected classes.** A member of a legislatively protected class likewise cannot be guilty of conspiracy to commit that crime (a minor female cannot conspire with a male to commit statutory rape) or of being an accessory to that crime.

  e. **Inability to commit crime oneself.** A person can be guilty of conspiracy to commit a crime she could not commit herself.

    **EXAMPLE:** Sara, a quadrapleigic, conspires with Suzy to kill Sara's husband. Although Sara has no use of her arms and legs and cannot stab or shoot her husband herself, where she conspires with Suzy to carry out the crime, Sara can be guilty of conspiracy.

11. **Defenses**

  a. **Impossibility.** Impossibility is no defense to conspiracy.

  b. **Withdrawal:**

      (1) **Common law rule.** At common law, withdrawal was not recognized as a valid defense to conspiracy. Because the conspiracy was complete as soon as the parties agreed to commit the crime. Withdrawal may be a valid defense, however, to crimes committed in furtherance of the conspiracy.

          **EXAMPLE:** Oscar and Fernando on Monday enter into an agreement to rob the Wells Fargo Bank on the following Friday. On Wednesday Oscar gets "cold feet" and tells Fernando that he is withdrawing from the felony. On Friday Fernando (without Oscar's involvement) commits the bank robbery. During the course of the robbery, Fernando shoots and kills a bank security guard. Oscar is guilty of conspiracy but not guilty of robbery or felony-murder.

(2) **Model Penal Code rule.** Under the Model Penal Code, withdrawal by a co-conspirator may be a valid affirmative defense where the renouncing party *gives timely notice of his plans to all members of the conspiracy and performs an affirmative act to "thwart" the success of the conspiracy.* In this case, note that withdrawal serves as an affirmative defense to a conspiracy charge.

| INCHOATE CRIMES | |
|---|---|
| **SOLICITATION** | **CONSPIRACY** |
| 1. Defendant entices, advises, encourages, orders, or requests another to commit a crime. | 1. Consists of (a) an agreement between two or more persons to commit a crime and (b) an intent to achieve the criminal objective. |
| 2. The crime solicited need not be committed. | 2. The agreement is the "essence" or "gist" of the crime. |
| 3. The crime requires no agreement or action by the person solicited. | 3. Unlike attempt, the crime does not require a "substantial step" in the commission of the crime. |
| 4. Defenses: at common law no defenses were recognized; under Model Penal Code, however, renunciation is an affirmative defense. | 4. Defenses: at common law withdrawal was not a valid defense; under the Model Penal Code, however, withdrawal is recognized as an affirmative defense if the defendant "thwarted the success of the conspiracy." |
| | 5. Solicitation merges into conspiracy; if the conspiracy is successful, a conspirator may be subject to conviction for both the conspiracy and the completed crime. |
| **ATTEMPT** | |
| 1. Consists of (a) an intent to commit a crime and (b) an act in furtherance or a "substantial step" toward the commission of the offense. | |
| 2. The act in furtherance of the crime must go beyond mere preparation. | |
| 3. "Specific-intent" crime, i.e., the defendant must have the specific-intent to commit the designated crime. | |
| 4. Defenses: at common law legal impossibility but not factual impossibility was a defense to a charge of attempt; under the modern view, however, impossibility is no defense when the defendant's actual intent (not limited by the true facts unknown to him) was to do an act proscribed by law. | |

## IV.  PARTIES TO CRIME: ACCOMPLICE LIABILITY

### A.  COMMON LAW CLASSIFICATIONS

1. **Principal in the First Degree.** *The actual perpetrator who performs the criminal act* with the requisite mental state is known as the principal in the first degree. More than one person can perpetrate the same crime.

2. **Principal in the Second Degree.** One who is present at the scene of the felony and aids, abets, or otherwise encourages the commission of the crime with the requisite intent is guilty as a principal in the second degree (e.g., get away car driver who awaits outside during a bank robbery).

    a. **Insufficient bases.** Mere presence without assistance or assistance without intent are insufficient.

    b. **Punishment.** A principal in the second degree may be punished to the same extent as the perpetrator.

3. **Accomplice**

    a. **Definition.** An individual is criminally liable as an accomplice *if he gives assistance or encouragement* or fails to act where he has a legal duty to oppose the crime of another (actus reus), and *purposefully intends* to effectuate commission of the crime (mens rea).

    **Question:**

    Davis was a 17-year-old dropout who lived in Oakland and belonged to a neighborhood gang called the Raiders. One day Parcells was walking along a street in Oakland. Davis saw Parcells and knew he was a member of the Jets, a rival gang based in Berkeley. Davis accosted Parcells and pushed him to the ground. Davis then pulled out a knife, held it to Parcells' throat and said, "Who gave you permission to enter our turf?" Before Parcells could respond, Simpson, who was Davis's friend and a fellow Raiders gang member, approached and asked what was happening.

    Davis told Simpson that Parcells belonged to the Jets and came to Oakland looking for trouble. Simpson then said to Davis, "Why don't you show him what happens to Jets who come to Oakland looking for trouble?" Davis then stabbed Parcells in the throat, killing him.

    Simpson will most likely be

    (A) guilty of murder because Simpson had the purpose of shouting words of encouragement to Davis
    (B) guilty, if Davis would not have stabbed Parcells but for Simpson's words of encouragement

(C) guilty, if Simpson had the purpose of shouting words of encouragement to Davis and Davis would not have stabbed Parcells but for his encouragement

(D) guilty, if either Simpson had the purpose of shouting words of encouragement, or, but for Simpson's actions Davis would not have stabbed the victim

**Answer:**

(A) This question deals with accomplice liability. In order to be subject to accomplice liability two requirements must be satisfied: (1) the accomplice must have the *specific-intent* that the crime be committed and (2) the accomplice *must aid, abet, or encourage* the perpetrator in the commission or attempted commission of the crime. Choice (A) addresses both of these elements. Note that choices (B), (C), and (D) are wrong because the courts do not employ a "but for" test but rather whether the alleged accomplice intended to give aid or encouragement to another.

b. **Mental state requirement**

(1) **Common law.** At common law, the person must have had the intent to help or to encourage the principal to commit the crime charged.

(2) **Modern view.** Some modern statutes create accomplice liability with a lower mental state, that of knowingly assisting or encouraging a crime, such as in supplier cases where a seller, knowing of the buyer's intent to commit arson, sells him an explosive device.

c. **Scope of liability.** A defendant is responsible for the criminal acts of another whom he aided, abetted, or facilitated, provided the criminal consequences are *reasonably foreseeable* in terms of the acts defendant intended to aid or abet. In other words, an accomplice can be guilty of not only the crimes he personally performs or encouraged another to perform, but also for any crimes committed by another that occurred as the other was in the process of committing the contemplated crime.

d. **Ability to act alone.** A defendant may be guilty as an accomplice for crimes he could not commit alone.

e. **Victims.** A victim cannot be liable as an accomplice.

f. **Member of legislatively protected class.** Similarly, members of legislatively protected classes may not be liable as accomplices.

g. **Defenses.** Withdrawal may be a valid defense where an accomplice makes a timely repudiation and takes sufficient steps to neutralize any assistance or material he has provided before the commission of the crime can no longer be prevented.

h. **False accomplices.** An individual is not liable as an accomplice for the acts of a "false accomplice" (secret agent).

i. **Necessary parties.** Some statutes provide a definition for crimes so that the crime must involve more than one actor. However, some of the statutes only hold one actor liable for the crime. In this situation, the court presumes that the legislature did not intend to hold the other actor liable (i.e., that actor is granted immunity under the statute). Note that this situation often arises in drug sale cases, where the seller of the drugs may be held liable but the buyer is not an accomplice to the sale, even though the buyer is a necessary party to the crime.

4. **Accessory Before the Fact**

a. **Definition.** One who aids, abets, counsels, or otherwise encourages the commission of a felony, but is not present at the scene, is guilty as an accessory before the fact.

b. **Punishment.** An accessory before the fact may be punished to the same extent as a principal for all crimes committed within the scope of the conspiracy.

c. **Conviction of the principal—majority view.** Under the majority view, the principal need not be convicted for the accessory before the fact to be convicted.

d. **Conviction of the principal—common law.** At common law, conviction of the principal was required for conviction of an accessory.

5. **Accessory After the Fact**

a. **Definition.** The following three requirements must be met for one to be an accessory after the fact:

(1) a completed felony must have been committed;

(2) the accessory must have known of the commission of the felony;

(3) the accessory must have personally given aid to the felon to hinder the felon's apprehension, conviction, or punishment.

**Question:**

Jesse was the leader of the notorious "Hole in the Wall Gang" which consisted of a group of thugs who committed a string of robberies, burglaries, and thefts in the Sheepsmeadow section of Brownsville. After committing a number of smaller crimes mostly in the residential section of town, Jesse decided to go "bigtime" and rob the First National Bank in the heart of downtown Brownsville.

As part of the plan, Jesse and James would enter the bank while Raven, the only female member of the gang, would drive the getaway car. As they were driving to the bank on the morning of the robbery, Jesse saw a hitch-hiker thumbing a ride. He ordered Raven to stop the car and pick up the hitchhiker. When the hitchhiker named Mitch entered the car, Jesse asked him where he was going. Mitch responded that he was going to Baytown which was located about 5 miles north of Brownsville. Jesse told Mitch that they were going in that direction and would drop him off there but first they had to "take care of some business" in Brownsville.

A few minutes later, the car pulled up in front of the bank and Jesse turned to Mitch and said, "Listen, buddy, we're going inside to rob this place. I want you to stay in the car with Raven and help her keep a lookout for any cops." Startled by the chain of events Mitch feigned agreement by shaking his head.

Jesse and James then entered the bank and brandishing their weapons ordered everyone on the floor. They went to the nearest counter and com-manded the teller to fill up a bag with all the cash she had in the register. After they were handed the loot, Jesse and James fled to the car and made a hasty getaway. While the bank robbery was in progress, Mitch remained in the car and sat silently in fear.

The group then sped toward Baytown where their hideout was located. Upon reaching Baytown, they drove Mitch to his destination. As he was leaving the vehicle, Jesse gave him a $100 bill and thanked him for his help.

With respect to Mitch's criminal liability, which of the following statements is most accurate?

    (A)  Mitch is guilty of bank robbery as an accomplice.
    (B)  Mitch is guilty of bank robbery as a co-conspirator.
    (C)  Mitch is guilty of bank robbery as a principal in the second degree.
    (D)  Mitch is not subject to accomplice liability.

**Answer:**

(D) In order to be guilty as an accomplice, generally two requirements must be met: (1) the individual must have **the intent to promote or facilitate commission of the crime** and (2) **he must "aid," "abet," or give encouragement** in the commission or attempted commission of the crime. There is a split of authority as to whether some lesser mental state will suffice for accomplice liability, such as **mere knowledge** that one is aiding a crime. The majority view, however, is that accomplice must intend that his acts have the effect of assisting or encouraging another. Here, the facts state that Mitch "feigned agreement." If Mitch only pretended to agree without actually intending to aid and abet the gang members, then no accomplice liability will be imposed.

b. **Accomplice distinguished.** Whereas modern law has abolished the distinction between parties, one who is *an accessory after the fact is not an accomplice,* nor is he punished to the same extent as prescribed for the parties to the felony.

c. **Misdemeanor required.** At common law, an accessory after the fact could only exist as to a misdemeanor.

### V.  CRIMES AGAINST THE PERSON

#### A.  MURDER

1. **Common Law Definition.** At common law, murder was defined as the unlawful killing of a human being with malice aforethought.

2. **Actus Reus Requirement**. The actus reus may be a voluntary act, an involuntary act (where the defendant is aware of his loss of control, such as an epileptic driving a car), or an omission to act where there is a legal duty to act.

3. **Person Requirement.** The act must actually and proximately cause the death of *another living person.* The common law requirement for a living person was one "born alive" (though a state may extend criminal liability to include a fetus after the first trimester).

4. **Actor Requirement.** The death must be caused by someone other than the victim.

   a. **Suicide.** Suicide is not homicide, because the death must be caused by another.

   b. **Aiding in suicide.** To persuade or aid another to commit suicide is a sufficient basis for murder in some jurisdictions.

5. **Causation Requirement.** The defendant's conduct must be both the actual cause and a legal cause of the victim's death.

   a. **Cause-in-fact requirement.** For common law murder, we apply the "but for" test. In other words, to convict the defendant of murder, the factfinder must find that the victim's death would not have occurred but for the defendant's actions.

   b. **Proximate cause requirement.** Where the victim's death was a "natural and probable" consequence of the defendant's conduct, the defendant may be guilty of murder even where he did not foresee the exact chain of events that resulted in the victim's death.

(1) Note that, where an intervening act occurs that is outside the universe of foreseeable events caused by the defendant's acts, such an intervening act will cut off the chain of causation and will cause the defendant to be acquitted of murder.

c. **Timing requirement.** At common law, the victim's death had to occur within one year and one day of the defendant's actions. Any deaths occurring after that time could not subject a defendant to criminal liability for murder.

d. **Simultaneous acts.** Where two or more persons act simultaneously but independently and together cause the victim's death, each may be guilty of murder.

e. **Pre-existing condition.** Where a victim has an unusual condition that contributes to his death, a defendant can still be found guilty of murder. The defendant is said to "take the victim as he finds him." Therefore, such a condition will not negate the causation requirement.

6. **Mercy Killing.** Hastening the process of dying (such as "mercy killing") is murder.

7. **Justification or Excuse.** Where a homicide is justified or excused, there is no murder.

8. **Mens Rea Requirement.** The mens rea for murder, comprising the malice afterthought requirement, falls into four distinct categories:

   a. *intent to kill;*

   b. *intent to cause serious bodily harm;*

   c. *depraved-heart murder; and*

   d. *felony-murder.*

9. **Intent to Kill Murder**

   a. **Definition.** Conduct where the defendant consciously desires to kill another person or makes the resulting death inevitable (absent justification, excuse, or mitigation to voluntary manslaughter), constitutes an intent to kill.

   b. **Deadly weapons doctrine.** Under the "deadly weapons doctrine," an inference of intent to kill is raised through the intentional use of any instrument which, judging from its manner of use, is calculated to produce death or serious bodily injury.

   c. **Specific-intent crime.** Intent to kill murder is a specific-intent crime.

10. **Intent to Cause Serious Bodily Harm or Injury Murder**

   a. **Definition.** An unintentional killing proximately resulting from an act intended to cause great bodily injury satisfies the malice element for general-intent murder absent justification, excuse, or mitigation.

**Question:**

Belle and Ramirez were unemployed basket weavers who had recently been terminated from their jobs. As they were commiserating their misfortune, Belle thought of a great "get rich quick" scheme to defraud his insurance company. Belle told Ramirez that he was insured under a State Farm policy covering personal injuries. He suggested that Ramirez shoot him in the arm and fake a robbery attempt so that he could file a phony insurance claim to recover damages for his injury. In this jurisdiction it is a felony to file a false insurance claim.

As part of their scheme, Ramirez went to Belle's home one evening with a loaded pistol. They were standing together in the kitchen discussing how to best implement their plan. Finally, Belle told Ramirez to shoot him in the arm and then flee from the residence. After being shot, Belle planned to call 911 and have an ambulance transport him to the hospital where he would be treated for his wound. Following Belle's instruction, Ramirez proceeded to shoot Belle in the arm. Thereupon, Belle telephoned 911 to report the shooting and requested an ambulance immediately be sent to his home.

Believing that Belle only suffered a superficial arm wound, Ramirez drove home after the shooting. The bullet, however, severed an artery and Belle began to bleed quite profusely. Before the ambulance arrived, Belle lost consciousness from the loss of blood and passed out on the kitchen floor. When the paramedics arrived at Belle's home, they were unable to revive him and he was pronounced dead at the scene.

Which of the following is the most serious crime for which Ramirez should be found guilty?

(A) Felony-murder
(B) Intent to inflict serious bodily injury murder
(C) Assault with a deadly weapon
(D) Involuntary manslaughter

**Answer:**

(B) This is a truly "classic" Multistate question dealing with murder. There are four types of murder: (1) intentional killing with premeditation or deliberation; (2) intent to inflict serious bodily injury; (3) felony-murder; and (4) depraved-heart (or reckless killing) murder. On last summer's MBE Exam a similar type of **intent to inflict serious bodily injury murder** was tested. Note that Ramirez intended to inflict serious bodily injury when he deliberately shot Belle in the arm. Choice (A) is wrong because in order to convict a person of felony-murder, the underlying felony must be **malum in se** or an inherently dangerous felony. Defrauding an insurance company is **malum prohibitum** and does **not** involve a danger to life.

11. **Depraved-Heart Murder**

   a. **Definition.** Depraved-heart murder is **an unintentional killing resulting from conduct involving a wanton indifference to human life and a conscious disregard of an unreasonable risk of death or serious bodily injury,** absent any defense negating defendant's awareness of the risk.

   b. **Standard.** Unlike involuntary manslaughter, **depraved-heart murder involves extremely negligent conduct** (or recklessness) that is of a higher degree than gross or criminal negligence (which provides the standard for involuntary manslaughter).

   **Question:**

   One afternoon Ralph was driving his car on Wilshire Blvd. in downtown Los Angeles. Already late for a business appointment, he was becoming very upset because of the heavy traffic. Suddenly, he decided to drive his car along the sidewalk to avoid the traffic jam. While he was speeding down the sidewalk, pedestrians were hastily scurrying to avoid his auto. His car struck Amy, killing her.

   Which of the following is the best theory regarding Ralph's criminal liability?

   (A) Felony-murder, because he was committing an assault with a deadly weapon.
   (B) Transferred intent, because one is presumed to intend the natural and probable consequences of his (or her) acts.
   (C) Intentional killing, because Ralph's conduct was a substantial factor in causing Amy's death.
   (D) Commission of an act highly dangerous to life without an intent to kill with disregard for the consequences.

   **Answer:**

   (D) According to LaFave, "extremely negligent conduct, which creates what a reasonable man would realize to be not only an unjustifiable but also a very high degree of risk of death or serious bodily injury to another or to others—though unaccompanied by any intent to kill or do serious bodily injury—and which actually causes the death of another" constitutes "depraved-heart" murder. See **Criminal Law,** p. 541.

12. **Felony-Murder**

   a. **Definition.** Felony-murder is *an unintentional killing proximately caused during the commission or attempted commission of a serious or inherently dangerous felony.*

   b. **Limitations.** Several limitations have been placed on the scope of the felony-murder rule.

   (1) **Independence.** The underlying felony must be independent of the act causing the death. Therefore, where the underlying felony is murder, manslaughter, or aggravated assault, the defendant cannot be guilty of felony-murder.

   (2) **Inherently dangerous felony.** The felony must be an inherently dangerous one, such as *burglary, arson, robbery, rape, or kidnapping.*

   **MBE Exam Tip:** You can remember the underlying felonies for felony-murder with the pneumonic BARRK:

   Burglary
   Arson
   Rape
   Robbery
   Kidnapping

   (3) **Foreseeability.** The resulting death must be a foreseeable outgrowth of the defendant's actions. Note that most courts have generally been very liberal at applying the foreseeability requirement. Therefore, most deaths are considered foreseeable for purposes of felony-murder.

   (4) **Timing.** The resulting death must occur during the commission, or perpetration, of the felony.

   (a) **Post-felony killings.** If a killing occurs while the defendant is fleeing from the scene of the felony, he may still be guilty of felony-murder. However, if he has reached a place of temporary safety, the felony is deemed to have "terminated," and the defendant can no longer be found guilty of felony-murder.

   (5) **Defenses.** Any defense to the underlying felony negates the felony-murder.

   (6) *Redline* **limitation.** Under the *Redline* limitation, *a co-felon is not guilty of felony murder where the killing constitutes a justifiable or excusable homicide* (such would be the case where the police or the victim shoot one of the co-felons, but not where the killing is done by one of the felons).

13. **Statutory Modifications—Murder by Degrees**

   a. **Statutory definition—first degree murder.** Under modern statutes, first degree murder includes intent to kill murder committed with premeditation and deliberation, felony-murder, and, in some jurisdictions, murder accomplished by lying in wait, poison, or torture.

    (1) **Note:** If the murderer does any reflection or premeditation (even if the reflection is cursory and brief), he may be guilty of first degree murder.

b. **Statutory definition—second degree murder.** All other murder is second degree murder.

c. **Statutory classifications—felony-murder.** In most jurisdictions, a murder committed during the commission of an arson, mayhem, kidnapping, rape, robbery, or burglary will be classified as first degree murder. Killings occurring during the commission or attempted commission of other felonies will be second degree murders.

d. **Effect of voluntary intoxication.** A defense such as voluntary intoxication can reduce first degree intent to kill murder (specific-intent) to second degree murder by negating premeditation and deliberation, but cannot be used to negate a general criminal intent to reduce murder to manslaughter.

**Question:**

    In most states, the division of homicide into degrees is distinguished according to which of the following:

    (A)  the causal relationship between defendant's act and the resulting death
    (B)  the attendant circumstances surrounding the death
    (C)  the nature of the act causing the death
    (D)  the defendant's state of mind at the time the killing was committed

**Answer:**

(D) In most states murder is divided into two degrees for the purpose of awarding a more severe penalty for some murders than for others. Most commonly, *first degree murder encompasses intent-to-kill murder accompanied by premeditation and deliberation, and murder in the commission of four or five named felonies* (generally including burglary, arson, rape, robbery and kidnapping). In most states, murder not falling within the first degree murder category (e.g., intent-to-kill without premeditation and deliberation; intent to do serious bodily harm; and felony-murder where the felony is not one of the four or five named felonies) is second degree murder. According to LaFave, to be guilty of first degree murder the *defendant must not only intend to kill but in addition he must premeditate the killing and deliberate about it.* As a result, choice (D) is the correct answer. See LaFave, p. 563.

## B. VOLUNTARY MANSLAUGHTER

1. **Definition.** Voluntary manslaughter is ***an intentional killing mitigated by adequate provocation*** or other circumstances negating malice aforethought. Voluntary manslaughter is commonly called a "heat of passion" killing.

   a. **Adequate provocation**

      (1) **Definition.** Adequate provocation, measured objectively, must be such that a reasonable person would lose self-control.

      (2) **Connection between provocation and killing.** A causal connection must exist between the provocation and the killing.

      (3) **Timing.** The time period between the heat-of-passion and the fatal act must not be long enough that a reasonable person would have cooled off.

      (4) **Examples of adequate provocation.** Courts will commonly find that a defendant was adequately provoked where he killed after he was the victim of a serious battery or a threat of a deadly force or where he found his spouse engaged in sexual conduct with another person.

      (5) **Examples of inadequate provocation.** Where a defendant kills after an exchange of "mere words," courts generally will not find adequate provocation.

   **Question:**

   Caveman Calhoun was a famous professional wrestler who stood 6 feet 6 inches and weighed 350 pounds. Caveman was married to Zoe Zeal, who was a vivacious former actress. Caveman was insanely jealous and often told Zoe that he would kill her if he ever found out that she was unfaithful. Unknown to Caveman, Zoe was having an affair with Allen Marcus.

   Caveman and Zoe lived in Kansas City. One day Caveman told Zoe that he was flying to Chicago for a wrestling match and would return the following morning. After Caveman left the house, Zoe telephoned Marcus and told him to come over because Caveman was out of town. While Caveman was at the airport about to board his flight to Chicago, he learned that a blizzard had hit Chicago causing cancellation of his wrestling match.

   By this time, Marcus and Zoe were passionately making love and were unaware that anything was amiss. Caveman drove back home from the airport and unsuspectingly entered his house. He walked to the bedroom and upon opening the door saw Zoe and Marcus in bed together. Visibly upset, Caveman told Marcus, "Put your pants on and get the hell out of here." As Marcus was reaching for his pants, he pulled out a gun fearing that Caveman was about to attack him. When Caveman saw the gun, he jumped on Marcus and wrapped his monstrous arms around Marcus' neck. He angrily twisted his victim's neck, breaking it and killing Marcus.

Caveman is guilty for which, if any, of the following crimes?

(A) Murder
(B) Voluntary manslaughter
(C) Involuntary manslaughter
(D) None of the above

**Answer:**

(D) This rather simple Criminal Law question provides two very important "tips" for MBE success. First, *reading comprehension* is equally as important as your knowledge of the law. Second, you must always be on the lookout for "red herring" answer choices and Pavlov dog responses. In this question, for example, the facts clearly indicate that Marcus was the aggressor. When Caveman caught Marcus in bed with his wife, Caveman calmly remarked, "put your pants on and get the hell out of here." *Caveman did not threaten Marcus with bodily harm or injury.* It was only after Marcus brandished his weapon that Caveman acted in self-defense and killed him. This type of question frequently appears on the Multistate because many students will skim the facts and go for the Pavlovian answer (B) since they have been trained for that response anytime they see an apparent "heat of passion" killing.

b. **Other mitigating circumstances**

(1) **Homicide justification.** Where certain defenses when properly raised would justify homicide, these same defenses, when improperly used due to lack of a required element, have been allowed to mitigate murder to voluntary manslaughter.

(2) **Imperfect self-defense.** Imperfect self-defense may mitigate where a defendant was either at fault in starting an altercation or unreasonably, but honestly, believed that harm was imminent or that deadly force was necessary. Mistaken justification has been applied to self-defense, defense of others, crime prevention, coercion, and necessity.

(3) **Diminished mental capacity.** A minority of states allow diminished mental capacity short of insanity to reduce murder to manslaughter.

## C. INVOLUNTARY MANSLAUGHTER

1. **Definition.** Involuntary manslaughter is an ***unintentional killing resulting without malice aforethought*** caused either by criminal negligence or during the commission or attempted commission of an unlawful act.

2. **Criminal Negligence Involuntary Manslaughter**

   Criminal negligence requires that the defendant's conduct creates a high degree of risk of death or serious injury beyond the tort standard of ordinary negligence.

   a. **Requirements.** Gross negligence or criminal negligent conduct is required, but the majority of jurisdictions do not require that the defendant be consciously aware of the risk created.

3. **"Unlawful Act" Involuntary Manslaughter**

   a. **Definition.** Unintentional killing occurring during the commission or attempted commission of a misdemeanor which is malum in se (wrong in itself, rather than because of legislative proscription—includes all felonies, breaches of the peace, and crimes that outrage public decency) ***or a felony which is not of the inherently dangerous type*** required for felony-murder, is classified as involuntary manslaughter under the so-called ***misdemeanor-manslaughter rule.***

   b. **Limitations.** Whereas limitations do exist regarding the nature of the unlawful act and causation between the act and the killing, the malum in se misdemeanor need not be independent from the cause of death, unlike in felony-murder.

   c. **Foreseeability or criminal negligence.** Death resulting from a malum prohibitum crime can only be sufficient for involuntary manslaughter when the killing is either a foreseeable consequence of the unlawful conduct or amounts to criminal negligence.

## D. ASSAULT AND BATTERY

1. **Misdemeanors at Common Law.** Assault and battery were common law misdemeanors.

   **Note:** At common law, because assault and battery were only considered misdemeanors, they could not be used as underlying felonies for purposes of felony-murder.

2. **Felonies Under Modern Statutes.** Modern statutes have created ***aggravated forms of assault and battery which are felonies.***

3. **Battery**

   a. **Definition.** Criminal battery is defined *as the unlawful application of force to the person of another which results in bodily harm or offensive touching.*

   b. **General-intent crime.** Criminal battery is a general-intent crime; a defendant may be guilty of battery where he (or she) acts *(1) recklessly, (2) negligently, or (3) with knowledge that his/her act (omission) will result in criminal liability.*

   c. **Act of applying force.** The defendant's act of applying force may be direct or indirect.

      (1) **Put in motion requirement.** Where the defendant puts a force in motion, the force need not be applied directly. For example, if John tells his attack bull to charge at a visitor, John may be guilty of battery even though he did not personally touch the visitor.

   d. **Mental state.** The required mental state may be intentional, the result of conduct amounting to criminal negligence (drunken driving), or conduct, absent intent or criminal negligence, which causes injury during the commission of a malum in se crime.

      (1) **Aggravated battery.** In most jurisdictions, certain circumstances cause a simple battery to be elevated to an aggravated battery. Most commonly, these circumstances include:

         (a) where the defendant causes the victim serious bodily injury;

         (b) the defendant uses a deadly weapon to commit the battery; or

         (c) the defendant batters a woman, child, or law enforcement officer.

   e. **Defenses**

      (1) **Consent.** Consent may be a valid defense where it is not coerced or obtained by fraud, but it is no defense to a breach of the peace.

      (2) **Self-defense.** Self-defense is a valid defense to a battery charge.

      (3) **Defense of others.** Like self-defense, defense of others is a defense to battery.

      (4) **Crime prevention.** Where the defendant commits an offensive touching using unlawful force to prevent someone from committing a crime, this will be a defense to battery.

| BATTERY DISTINCTION | |
|---|---|
| **CRIMINAL BATTERY** | **TORTIOUS BATTERY** |
| i.  General-intent crime. | i.  Intentional tort. |
| ii.  Unlawful application of force to the person of another, resulting from defendant's **(1) negligent, (2) reckless, (3) careless, or (4) intentional contact.** | ii.  Defendant must act ***intending to cause an offensive or harmful contact*** to the person of another and an offensive or harmful contact results. |
| iii.  Mens rea (or mental culpability) may encompass (1) negligence, (2) recklessness, (3) carelessness, or (4) intention. | iii.  Must consist of an intentional act (or where there is a "substantial certainty" that an unpermitted contact will result); it cannot result from defendant's negligent or reckless conduct. |
| iv.  Transferred intent doctrine applies. | iv.  Transferred intent doctrine applies. |
| v.  Defenses: Where one intentionally touches another in (1) self-defense or (2) defense of others or (3) to prevent the commission of a crime or (4) where the defendant has the victim's consent. | v.  Defenses: Where one intentionally touches another in (1) self-defense or (2) defense of others or (3) to prevent the commission of a crime or (4) where the defendant has the victim's consent. |

**Question:**

Jimmy and Chrissy were playing tennis at the Biscayne Racket Club. After their match, they entered the club's cocktail lounge to have a couple of drinks. They were sitting at the crowded bar when Jimmy pulled out his tennis racket and said, "Chrissy, your backhand shot is terrible. Let me show you how you should be swinging your backhand." While sitting at the bar, Jimmy began to swing his racket carelessly. As Jimmy was swinging his arm in a backhand motion, he accidentally hit Ivan in the mouth with the metal edge of the racket. Ivan, who was standing behind Jimmy while drinking a beer, suffered a deep gash on his lip that required 20 stitches.

For which, if any, of the following crimes should Jimmy be found guilty?

(A) Assault
(B) Battery
(C) Mayhem
(D) No crime, because he hit Ivan accidentally

**Question:**

Assume for the purposes of this question only that before Jimmy began to swing his racket at the bar, he had drunk three vodka martinis and was inebriated. If Jimmy is prosecuted for hitting Ivan, he should be found

(A) guilty, because Jimmy was acting recklessly
(B) guilty, because Jimmy's recklessness cannot be negated by intoxication

     (C)  not guilty, because Jimmy's intoxication deprived him of the capacity to commit a criminal offense

     (D)  not guilty, because Jimmy hit Ivan accidentally

**Answers:**

(B) Criminal battery, in brief, is simply defined as the ***unlawful application of force to the person of another.*** Students should be aware that a battery must result in either (1) bodily injury or (2) offensive touching to the victim. Clearly, "bodily injury" will include such obvious matters as wounds caused by bullets or knives, and broken limbs or bruises inflicted by sticks, stones, feet, or fists. But, in addition to these more obvious bodily injuries, LaFave notes that offensive touchings (as where a man puts his hands upon a girl's body or kisses a woman against her will, or where one person spits into another's face) will suffice for battery in most jurisdictions. See LaFave, p. 604. Moreover, students must be aware that battery is a "general-intent" crime, which means the defendant need not intend to commit the crime. Rather, "general-intent" is used to encompass all forms of the mental state (or mens rea) requirement. Thus, a defendant may be guilty of battery where he (or she) acts (1) recklessly, (2) negligently, or (3) with knowledge that his/her act (omission) will result in criminal liability. In the present case, Jimmy committed a criminal battery because he recklessly swung his tennis racket in the crowded lounge area. Even though he didn't specifically intend to hit Ivan, Jimmy's conduct created an unreasonable risk of harm to others.

(B) Another key Multistate area deals with intoxication. Note that intoxication (whether voluntary or involuntary) is a defense to a crime if it negates the existence of an element of the crime. For example, one who takes and carries away another person's property by stealth or at gunpoint is not guilty of larceny or of robbery if he (or she) is too intoxicated to be able to entertain the necessary intent to steal. Likewise, one cannot be guilty of burglary when, although he (or she) breaks and enters another's house, his (or her) intoxication deprives him (or her) of the capacity to intend to commit a felony therein. It is important to point out, however, that ***intoxication cannot negate a "general-intent" crime.*** Why? Because "general-intent" crimes (e.g., rape and battery) do not require a defendant to specifically intend to commit an unlawful act or produce a specified result that can be negated by intoxication. Thus, voluntary intoxication cannot, according to the weight of authority, be a defense to battery where defendant recklessly strikes the victim ***because recklessness cannot be negated by intoxication.***

4. **Assault**

   a. **Attempt-to-commit-a-battery assault**

    The majority of states define assault as an ***attempted battery.*** This type of assault requires ***an intent to commit a battery*** (i.e., an intent to cause physical injury to the victim). Thus in those jurisdictions where an assault is limited to an attempted battery, an intent merely to frighten, though accompanied by some fear-producing act like pointing an unloaded gun at the victim, will not suffice. And since an intent to injure is required for an attempted battery, recklessness or negligence which comes close to causing injury (such as driving a car recklessly which just misses striking victim) **will not do** for an assault.

    (1) **Present ability requirement.** In some states by statute or case law there is the additional requirement that the assaulter have a "present ability" to commit a battery.

        **EXAMPLE:** Simon approaches Ralph holding a large rock. Simon attempts to hit Ralph over the head with a rock. Ralph turns and sees Simon with the rock and becomes frightened. Simon was not aware that there was an invisible screen between him and Ralph. Because Simon cannot succeed in causing bodily harm to Ralph, Simon will probably be acquitted of assault. On the other hand, if Ralph was not aware of the screen, Simon may still be guilty of assault based on creation of imminent fear of harm.

  b. **Intentional-creation-of-imminent-fear-of-harm assault**

    In this type of assault, the defendant must act with threatening conduct (mere words are insufficient) intended to cause reasonable apprehension of imminent harm in the victim. A conditional threat is generally insufficient, unless accompanied by an overt act to accomplish the threat.

  c. **Aggravated assault.** A simple assault may rise to the level of an aggravated assault under certain circumstances. Most commonly, the circumstances include:

    (1) where the defendant commits an assault with a dangerous weapon; *or*

    (2) where the defendant acts with the intent to rape or murder the victim.

## E. MAYHEM

1. **Common Law Definition.** The felony of mayhem at common law required an intent to maim or do bodily injury by an act that either (1) dismembered the victim or (2) disabled his use of some bodily part that was useful in fighting.

2. **Modern Definition.** Modernly, statutes have expanded the scope of mayhem to include permanent disfigurement.

    **EXAMPLE:** In a recent California case, an elementary school child was convicted of mayhem where he spit a spitball at a fellow student, hitting the other child in the eye and disfiguring him.

3. **Aggravated battery.** In states that have abolished mayhem, it is treated as a form of aggravated battery.

## F. KIDNAPPING

### 1. Common Law Elements

At common law, kidnapping consisted of:

a. *an unlawful*

b. *restraint of a person's liberty*

c. *by force or show of force*

d. so as to send the victim into another country.

### 2. Statutory Variations

a. **Location.** Under modern statutory law, it usually suffices that the victim be *taken to another location* (as opposed to another country, as required at common law) or concealed.

b. **Aggravated kidnapping.** A number of states define certain types of kidnapping as being of the aggravated type and thus deserving higher punishment (e.g., where the kidnapper restrains a small child, is masked, holds the victim for ransom, or kidnaps for the purpose of committing a robbery or a sexual offense).

> **MBE Tip:** *The MBE follows the modern view (not the common law) that the victim be taken to a different location rather than another country.*

## G. RAPE

1. **Common Law Definition.** At common law, *rape was the act of unlawful sexual intercourse by a male person with a female person without her consent.* While penetration was required, emission was not.

a. **Married persons exempted.** At common law, a man could not rape his wife. This is no longer the law in any state, but you should note how the question on the MBE is phrased.

2. **Threats.** Note that intercourse accomplished by threats may also constitute rape.

3. **Consent.** In addition, if the victim is incapable of consenting, the intercourse is rape. In this regard, inability to consent may be caused by the effect of drugs or intoxicating substances or by unconsciousness.

a. **Statutory rape.** Where a female is under the statutorily prescribed age of consent (usually 16), an act of intercourse constitutes rape despite her consent. A defendant's mistake as to the age of the victim is generally ***no defense to statutory rape.***

## H. OTHER

1. **Bigamy.** Bigamy is the crime of marriage by one individual to more than one other person.

2. **Incest.** Incest is the crime of sexual relations between individuals who are closely related to one another. The degree of relationship varies by state.

## VI. CRIMES AGAINST PROPERTY

## A. THEFT OFFENSES

1. **Larceny**

   a. **Common law elements**

      At common law, larceny was defined as:

      (1) ***the trespassory taking ("caption");***

      (2) ***and carrying away ("asportation");***

      (3) ***of the tangible personal property;***

      (4) ***of another;***

      (5) ***with the intent to permanently deprive the owner thereof.***

   b. **Taking.** The taking (sometimes called the "caption") requires the assertion of dominion and control over the property by a defendant who does not have lawful possession.

   c. **Carrying away.** The carrying away (asportation) is complete upon even the ***slightest movement*** (e.g., six inches will suffice).

   **Question:**

   > Olga Oslo was an executive vice-president in the investment banking department of the Doylestown National Bank. One afternoon, Olga was having lunch with her boss, Amy Alcott, at the Riverhorse Restaurant when Amy excused herself to go to the bathroom. As Amy stood up to leave the table, her wallet fell out of her pocketbook onto the floor. Amy was unaware of what occurred and proceeded to the restroom. Olga, however, saw the wallet fall. Intending to steal it, Olga picked up the wallet and placed it in her pocket. Before Amy returned to the table, Olga had a

change of heart and decided to give the wallet back. Thereupon, Olga told Amy what had happened and handed her the wallet when she returned from the bathroom.

Olga is guilty of which, if any, crime?

(A)  No crime
(B)  Larceny
(C)  Embezzlement
(D)  False pretenses

**Answer:**

(B) Commission of the crime of larceny requires a taking (caption) and carrying away (asportation) of another's property. A taking occurs when the offender secures dominion over the property, while a carrying away requires some *slight movement* away of the property. Once Olga picked up the wallet (with the intent to steal) and placed it in her pocket (sufficient asportation), she committed the crime of larceny despite the fact she later returned the property. It should be noted that even though Olga later had a "change of heart" and returned the wallet to Amy, that would not constitute a valid defense. According to LaFave, one who takes another's property intending to deprive the owner permanently is nevertheless guilty of larceny, although he later decides to return it and does so. **Criminal Law**, p. 639.

d. **Property**

(1)  **Common law.** Common law larceny was limited to *tangible personal property.*

(2)  **Statutory requirements.** Modern statutes have expanded the kinds of property to include theft of services and other intangibles (such as gas and electrical power, and written instruments that represent property rights).

(3)  **Abandoned property.** Abandoned property is not the subject of larceny, although lost or mislaid property is.

(a)  **Lost or mislaid property.** In order to be guilty of larceny for lost or mislaid property, there are two requirements. The finder:

1.  must intend to steal it, and

2.  either know who the owner is or have reason to believe (from earmarkings on the property or from the circumstances of the finding) that he or she can find out the owner's identity.

e. **"Of another."** Because the property must be "of another," a good faith claim of right is a valid defense.

f. **Custody versus possession.** Larceny is a crime against possession when committed *by one who has mere custody.*

   (1) **Employees.** Generally, *employees are said to have custody over their employer's property;* however, the employee has possession (and is guilty of embezzlement) where:

      (a) a third party gives property directly to an employee for the benefit of its employer; *or*

      (b) where *the employee is in a high level position* (e.g., office manager, bank president, corporate official).

   (2) **Bailees.** A bailee generally has possession.

      (a) **"Breaking bulk" doctrine.** When a bailee opens closed containers and then misappropriates property, under the "breaking bulk" doctrine, "constructive possession" is said to exist in the bailor, and the bailee, thus having only custody of the property, is guilty of larceny.

g. **Intent to permanently deprive.** Where a defendant recklessly exposes property to loss or deals with property in a manner involving a substantial risk of loss, the intent to permanently deprive is satisfied.

**Question:**

Sharon Smith, a famous Hollywood actress, went to the trendy Escada department store in Beverly Hills to shop. Valentino, the owner of the store, spotted Sharon and rushed over to greet her. Sharon told Valentino she needed a dress to wear at the Academy Awards presentation.

Thinking about how valuable the publicity would be, Valentino offered to loan Sharon a new designer dress that just arrived from Paris. Valentino told Sharon the dress was designed by Fabienne, the most eminent fashion designer in Paris. Sharon accepted Valentino's offer and wore the dress to the Oscar presentation. She received innumerable compliments and was extensively photographed by the paparazzi in the Fabienne gown. Afterwards, Sharon decided to keep the dress and has refused to return it as originally agreed.

Sharon was arrested and charged with embezzlement of the dress. Which of the following would provide Sharon with the best argument that she should be found guilty of larceny not embezzlement?

(A)  Sharon was given possession of the dress, not merely custody.
(B)  Valentino was not the owner of the dress but received it on consignment from Fabienne.
(C)  When Valentino gave Sharon the dress, she initially intended to return it but changed her mind after attending the Academy Awards presentation.
(D)  When Valentino gave Sharon the dress, she initially intended to keep it; but after attending the Academy Awards presentation, she changed her mind and returned the dress to Valentino.

**Answer:**

(D) Once again, the best method for answering multiple-choice or Multistate questions is by process of elimination. Choice (A) is wrong because if Sharon was given lawful possession of the dress, then her crime would be embezzlement not larceny. On the other hand, if she had mere custody, Sharon would be guilty of larceny. Embezzlement, a statutory crime, is generally defined as (1) the fraudulent (2) conversion of (3) the property (4) of another (5) by one who is already in lawful possession. Most embezzlement statutes simply provide that one in lawful possession (or entrusted with) another's property who fraudulently converts it is guilty. Choice (B) is wrong because as long as Sharon was in lawful possession of the dress, it is immaterial whether Valentino was the owner or simply received it on consignment. Likewise, choice (C) is wrong because it is an example of embezzlement. Since Sharon was entrusted with the dress, she was in lawful possession. Thereafter, if she misappropriated it, the crime would be embezzlement, not larceny. On the other hand, choice (D) is correct because the crime of larceny (or more properly larceny by trick) would be complete at the moment Sharon received the dress with the intent to steal. It is no defense that she changed her mind later and decided to return the dress.

h. **Continuing trespass.** Under *the doctrine of "continuing trespass,"* one who takes another's property (without authorization) intending only to use it temporarily before restoring it unconditionally to its owner (i.e., one who normally is found not to have an intent to steal) may nevertheless be guilty of larceny *if she later changes her mind and decides not to return the property after all.*

   (1) **Rationale.** As a general rule, the initial taking must be "wrongful" (i.e., without the owner's authorization). Because the initial taking was wrongful, the trespass is said to continue until the time the intent to steal is formed.

   (2) **Possession rightfully obtained.** This doctrine does not apply where the initial possession was rightfully obtained.

i. **Timing requirement.** The taking and carrying away (asportation) must concur in time with the intent to permanently deprive (animus furandi).

2. **Robbery**

    a. **Definition.** Robbery was a common law felony consisting of all the elements of larceny, *plus two additional elements:*

        (1) the taking must be *from the person or presence of the victim,* and

        (2) the taking must be accomplished *by force, intimidation, threat, or violence.*

    b. **Person or presence requirement.** The taking must be from the person of the victim or in his "presence," meaning an area within his control.

    c. **Threat of violence.** The threat of violence must place the victim in actual fear at the time of the taking.

        (1) Note that, as long as the victim is placed in fear, the fear may be baseless. In other words, fear and intimidation based on lies qualify as threats for robbery.

    d. **Lesser-included offenses.** Larceny, assault, and battery are all a lesser-included offense to robbery.

    e. **Aggravated robbery.** Armed robbery, a form of aggravated robbery, carries a higher punishment than simple robbery.

    f. **Merger.** Larceny as well as assault and battery *merge* into robbery.

    **MBE Exam Tip:** As a result, a defendant *cannot be guilty of larceny and robbery* for the same criminal transaction.

    **EXAMPLE:** Sarah, an elderly woman, is walking down the street carrying her pocketbook and some grocery bags. A man bumps into her and then apologizes. Sarah continues home; upon arriving there, she finds that she has her grocery bags but does not have her pocketbook. If the man who bumped into her stole her pocketbook, he will be guilty of larceny but will not be guilty of robbery.

    **EXAMPLE:** Sarah, an elderly woman, is walking down the street carrying her pocketbook and some grocery bags. A man comes up behind her and says into her ear, "I have a gun in my pocket. If you do not give me your pocketbook, I will shoot you." Sarah, frightened, gives the man her pocketbook. The man is guilty of robbery.

    **EXAMPLE:** Sarah, an elderly woman, is walking down the street carrying her pocketbook and some grocery bags. A man comes up behind her and says into her ear, "I have a gun in my pocket. If you do not give me your pocketbook, I will shoot you." The man does not really have a gun in his pocket. Sarah, frightened, gives the man her pocketbook. The man is guilty of robbery.

**EXAMPLE:** Sarah, an elderly woman, is walking down the street carrying her pocketbook and some grocery bags. A man comes up behind her and holds a gun to her head, saying, "If you do not give me your pocketbook, I will shoot you." The gun, which looks realistic, is really a water pistol. Sarah, frightened, gives the man her pocketbook. The man is guilty of robbery.

**EXAMPLE:** Sarah, an elderly woman, is walking down the street carrying her pocketbook and some grocery bags. A man comes up and holds a gun to her ear, saying, "My boss is standing over there. He wants me to threaten you and take your pocketbook. If I don't, he will fire me. Will you help me out? Pretend that you are frightened and give me your pocketbook. If you don't, though, I still will not hurt you." Sarah, who is not frightened but feeling sorry for the man, gives the man her pocketbook. The man is not guilty of robbery.

3. **Embezzlement**

   a. **Definition.** Embezzlement is a statutory crime defined as:

      (1) *the fraudulent conversion or misappropriation*

      (2) *of the property of another*

      (3) *by one who is already in lawful possession.*

   b. **Larceny distinguished.** In distinction to larceny, embezzlement involves misappropriation *by a defendant who has lawful possession (as opposed to custody).*

   c. **Serious interference.** The conversion must amount to a serious interference with the owner's rights in such a way as to sell, damage, or withhold the property.

   d. **No requirement for personal gain.** No direct personal gain need result to the defendant.

   e. **Modern statutory requirements.** Embezzlement deals with tangible personal property, not services, although some modern statutes include real estate.

   f. **Negation of intent.** The specific fraudulent intent required may be negated by a claim of right or by an *intent to restore the exact property.*

| LARCENY | EMBEZZLEMENT |
|---|---|
| 1. Trespassory taking and carrying away the property of another. | 1. Property must be in the embezzler's lawful possession when he misappropriates it. |
| 2. Requires only a taking and an asportation. | 2. Requires a conversion (i.e., a serious act of interference with the owner's rights). |
| 3. Moving the property a short distance (i.e., the asportation) will do. | 3. The mere act of moving the property a short distance (the asportation for larceny) will not do. |
| 4. Requires an intent to steal (or, as stated in Latin, an animus furandi) which must concur with the larcenous conduct. | 4. Requires a specific-intent to defraud. |
| 5. Illustrative distinctions: | 5. Illustrative distinctions: |
| (a) An employer who hands his property to his servant (employee) retains possession of it, the servant having mere custody, so that the servant who misappropriates the property is guilty of larceny; | (a) A servant (employee) who receives his employer's property from a third person (to return to this employer) acquires possession, so that the servant who misappropriates the property is guilty of embezzlement; |
| (b) Generally minor employees (such as caretakers, janitors, nightwatchmen) are considered to have custody of their employers' property, and so they are guilty of larceny when they steal. | (b) Employees delegated with greater authority (such as office managers, corporate officials, public officials) are deemed to have possession, and so they are guilty of embezzlement when they fraudulently convert. |

4. **Obtaining Property by False Pretenses**

   a. **Definition.** The statutory crime of false pretenses consists of:

      (1) *a false representation of*

      (2) *a present or past material fact by the defendant*

      (3) *which causes the victim to pass title to his property*

      (4) *to the defendant*

      (5) *who knows his representation to be false*

      (6) *and intends thereby to defraud the victim.*

   b. **Material fact requirement.** The representation must relate to a material fact, not opinion ("puffing" is insufficient).

c. **Reliance on representation requirement.** The victim's reliance upon the representation must cause him to pass title.

d. **Distinguished from larceny by trick.** The distinguishing characteristic of false pretenses *is that title passes (thus giving ownership to the transferee)*, even though it is voidable due to defendant's fraud.

e. **Exchange of money—sale or trade.** Where money is delivered to the defendant in a sale or trade situation by the person defrauded, title generally passes and the crime is false pretenses.

f. **Exchange of money—gambling.** However, where money is exchanged by cheating at cards or betting, the defrauding party is receiving possession, not title, so the crime is larceny by trick.

g. **Modern scope.** The modern scope of false pretenses includes written instruments, stocks, bonds, notes, and deeds, as well as money and credit cards.

5. **Bad Checks.** All jurisdictions have enacted "bad check" legislation to deal with the situation of a no-account or insufficient funds check given with the intent to defraud. The giving of the check is an implied representation of sufficient funds, absent postdating or some other means of notification of inadequate credit by the drawer.

a. **Statutory requirements.** "Bad check" statutes generally do not require that any property be obtained from the victim as a result of issuing the bad check.

b. **Mental state requirement.** However, the requisite mental state of the drawer is often required to be that of knowledge of the insufficient funds and intent to defraud.

6. **Credit Card Fraud.** Obtaining property by means of a stolen or unauthorized credit card is also a statutory crime in most jurisdictions.

**Question:**

Bobby entered Macy's Department Store and took the elevator to the eighth floor toy department. He went there intending to purchase a new Monopoly game. Bobby, who only had $8.00 in his possession, saw that the Monopoly games were selling for $10.00. Realizing that he did not have enough money to pay for the Monopoly set, he ripped the $10.00 price tag off the box. While no one was looking, Bobby then took the $7.00 sticker from a Risk game and placed it on the Monopoly box. He then purchased the Monopoly game for $7.00 and walked out of the store.

With which one of the following crime(s) should Bobby be convicted?

(A) False pretenses
(B) Larceny
(C) Deceit
(D) Conversion

**Answer:**

(A) Choice (A) is correct because the crime of *false pretenses requires that the defendant by his lies obtain title* to the victim's property. Students should note that if one obtains possession without title by his lies, his crime is larceny by trick. At common law larceny consists of (1) trespassory (2) taking and (3) carrying away of the (4) personal property (5) of another (6) with intent to steal it. In this regard, students should be aware that larceny by trick is simply one way of committing the crime of larceny; it is not a crime separate from larceny.

7. **Larceny by Trick**

   a. **Definition.** Larceny by trick is a form of larceny whereby *the defendant obtains possession of the personal property of another by means of a representation or promise that he knows is false at the time he takes possession.*

   b. **Distinguished from false pretenses.** In larceny by trick, the defendant's fraud is used to cause the victim to convey *possession, not title*, as in false pretenses.

| False Pretenses | Larceny by Trick | Credit Card Fraud | Check Fraud |
|---|---|---|---|
| Defendant *obtains title* to personal property of another by means of a representation or promise that he knows is false at the time he takes title. | Defendant *obtains possession* of personal property of another by means of a representation or promise that he knows is false at the time he takes possession. | Defendant, intending to defraud the owner, obtains title to personal property through use of a stolen or unauthorized credit card. | Defendant, intending to defraud the owner, obtains title to personal property through use of stolen checks or one drawn on an account with insufficient funds. |

**Question:**

Driver drove his automobile into a Chevron service station. He told Attendant, "Fill it up with unleaded, please." Attendant went ahead and pumped 10 gallons of gas into Driver's tank. When Attendant approached Driver for payment, Driver shouted, "Thanks for the freebie, sucker," and drove off without paying.

Driver is guilty of

(A) larceny
(B) larceny by trick
(C) false pretenses
(D) embezzlement

**Answer:**

(B) Students should be aware that the distinction between obtaining possession and obtaining title—the principal dividing line between larceny by trick and the separate crime of false pretenses—is not always easy to draw. Remember that the crime of false pretenses requires that the defendant, by his lies, obtain *title* to the victim's property. If he obtains *possession* without title by means of his lies, his crime is larceny by trick. In *Hufstetler v. State*, 37 Ala. App. 71, 63 So.2d 730 (1953), defendant's conviction for larceny by trick was affirmed where he (Driver) suddenly drove off without paying for the gasoline. In this particular situation, the court held that the defendant got possession but not title because the fraud vitiated the (gas station) owner's consent.

8. **Extortion**

   a. **Common law definition.** Extortion was a common law misdemeanor involving the corrupt demand or receipt of an unlawful fee by a public official under color of his office.

   b. **Statutory definition.** Under modern statutory law, extortion is commonly called "blackmail." Blackmail is defined as obtaining the property of another ***by the use of threats of future harm to the victim or his property.***

   c. **Threat requirement.** The threat is the essence of extortion and includes threats to expose a person or his family to disgrace and threats to accuse the victim of a crime.

   d. **Completion of crime—timing.** Some statutes consider the crime complete upon the making of the threats with the specific-intent to obtain money or property, while other statutes require the threats to actually cause the victim to part with his property.

   e. **Robbery distinguished.** Unlike robbery, ***extortion does not require threats of immediate or imminent physical harm***, nor must the property be taken from the victim's person or presence.

   f. **Model penal code requirements.** The Model Penal Code expands the scope of liability for threats amounting to extortion.

   g. **Defenses.** Where such threats are honestly made as restitution for related past harm or compensation for lawful services, an affirmative defense may exist.

9. **Receiving Stolen Property**

   a. **Common law.** Receiving stolen property was a common law misdemeanor.

   b. **Statutory definition.** As a modern statutory crime, it is defined as:

      (1) ***the receiving of stolen property***

      (2) ***known to be stolen (actual or constructive notice)***

      (3) ***with the intent to permanently deprive the owner.***

c. **Control, not receipt, required.** The receiving of physical possession of the property, while the most common situation, is not required, as long as the defendant exercises ***control*** over the goods (such as arranging for a sale, having the thief place the goods in a designated place, or receiving the goods from another).

**MBE Exam Tip:** Because the property must actually be stolen, a frequent exam situation involves goods which have been recovered by the police for the true owner. Where the police take formerly stolen, but now recovered property to a "fence," the "fence" is ***not receiving stolen property***. Also, because the person receiving the property must ***subjectively*** know himself that the goods are stolen, through ***circumstantial evidence*** the student must sometimes infer that the property is stolen (as where goods are obtained through a secret transaction or for an inordinately low price). Thus, the property must be "stolen" at the time of the receipt, and the receiver must have knowledge that the property is stolen.

## B. CRIMES AGAINST THE HABITATION

### 1. Burglary

a. **Definition.** The common law crime of burglary consisted of:

(1) ***the breaking***

(2) ***and entering***

(3) ***of the dwelling house***

(4) ***of another***

(5) ***in the nighttime***

(6) ***with the intent to commit a felony or larceny therein.***

b. **Breaking requirement**

(1) **Actual breaking.** The breaking could be achieved by ***an actual breaking***, involving use of force, or the creation or enlarging of an opening (entering through an open door or a partially open window is insufficient).

(2) **Constructive breaking.** Breaking may also be achieved by ***a constructive breaking***, where entry is gained by fraud, misrepresentation of identity, or intimidation.

**EXAMPLE:** Defendant rings the front doorbell to victim's home. Victim, who is inside her home, walks to the door which is closed and asks, "Who's there?" Misrepresenting his identity, Defendant responds, "Domino's Pizza." Believing her son had ordered a pizza, victim opens the door. Defendant then punches victim, enters her home and steals her pocketbook.

c. **Entry requirement**

(1) **Open door.** Entry through an open door where the defendant later opens an inside closet door intending to steal is sufficient.

(2) **Insufficient entry.** Breaking into a trunk or safe, or breaking to exit, rather than to gain entry, is insufficient.

(3) **Entry of defendant's person.** Entry is achieved by placing any portion of the body inside the structure.

(4) **Insertion of a tool.** Insertion of a tool is sufficient for an entry if it is used to accomplish the felony, but insufficient if it is used merely to gain entry (inserting a tool merely to unlock the door, as opposed to shooting a bullet through a window intending to kill the victim).

(5) **Entry into surrounding area.** Entry into the curtilage, structure, or area immediately surrounding the dwelling is sufficient.

d. **Intent requirement.** At the time of entry, the defendant must have the intent to commit a felony or larceny therein.

e. **Statutory modifications.** Modern statutory modifications have changed several aspects of common law burglary: many jurisdictions have eliminated the breaking requirement and the nighttime requirement; expanded the dwelling house concept to include all enclosed structures, even vehicles; expanded burglary to include unlawful remaining in a structure; and expanded the intent to commit a larceny or felony to include misdemeanor theft.

**MBE Exam Tip:** On the Multistate Bar Examination (MBE), common law burglary should be followed unless a different statute is given in the facts.

**Question:**

Armando lived with his girlfriend, Angelina. They were not married but lived together for five years in a house that was owned by Angelina. One day Armando got angry at Angelina after learning that she was having an affair with another man. To get back at Angelina, Armando decided that he would set fire to her home. Late at night, using an electronic device, he opened the garage door and entered the structure. The garage was attached to the basement of Angelina's home.

Armando carried in a five gallon gasoline can and spilled the gasoline around the interior of the garage. Hearing suspicious noises, Angelina came into the garage. Before Armando could ignite the gasoline, he was stopped by Angelina who then called the police.

Armando was arrested and charged with burglary. He should be found

(A) guilty, because opening the garage door with the electronic device constituted a breaking and entering
(B) guilty, because he planned to commit arson on the structure
(C) not guilty, because there was no breaking into the dwelling "of another"
(D) not guilty, because he never actually set fire to the dwelling

**Answer:**

(C) Burglary, at common law, required the breaking and entering into ***"the dwelling of another."*** A person could not commit a burglary against his/her own dwelling. With respect to burglary, ***"it was the right of habitation and not the ownership of property that was being protected."*** See LaFave, **Criminal Law,** p. 797. As such, occupancy controlled the question of whether the dwelling was that of another. In this question, since Armando resided in the home, he would not be guilty of breaking into the dwelling "of another." Choice (C) is therefore correct.

2. **Arson**

   a. **Common law definition.** At common law, the crime of arson consisted of

      (1) *the malicious*

      (2) *burning*

      (3) *of the dwelling*

      (4) *of another.*

   b. **Malice defined.** Malice extended to either intentional or reckless burning. A mere negligent or accidental burning, however, would not suffice.

   c. **Burning defined.** With respect to the burning requirement, it was not necessary that the dwelling be substantially or totally damaged. Although *a mere blackening of the surface was not enough, there must have been some charring* (i.e., slight burning) of the premises.

   **Question:**

   Inca had been dating Eli for over a year. One day Inca was walking in Golden Gate Park when she noticed Eli sitting next to a woman on a park bench. Inca observed Eli kissing the woman and passionately embracing her. Despondent by her boyfriend's public display of infidelity, Inca aimlessly began wandering around the vicinity of the park. As she passed by the Blarney Stone Tavern, Inca decided to go in and have a drink.

After guzzling down a couple of beers, she started conversing with Raven, a customer seated next to her. The two women began commiserating about their relationships with unfaithful boyfriends. While they talked, Inca and Raven continued to drink beer with an occasional shot of Jose Cuervo tequila. They soon became intoxicated. As they discussed ways to get back at Eli, Raven suggested that they set fire to his home. With Inca in agreement, the two women staggered from the bar and went to Eli's home.

Under the cover of night, Inca and Raven picked up little twigs and tree branches and stacked them along the outside of Eli's home. Inca then lit them with her cigarette lighter. As the branches ignited in flames, Inca and Raven hurriedly ran away. Seeing smoke from his bedroom window, Eli ran outside and immediately extinguished the fire with a garden hose. The fire slightly charred a small section of the exterior of Eli's home but did not cause any significant damage.

If Inca is prosecuted for common law arson, she should be found

(A) guilty, unless her intoxication negated her criminal intent
(B) guilty, because voluntary intoxication is no defense since she knew she was setting fire to the dwelling house of another
(C) not guilty, if her malicious intent was formulated as a result of her intoxication
(D) not guilty, because the fire only slightly charred the exterior of the home

**Answer:**

(B) *Arson is defined as the malicious burning of the dwelling house of another*. By definition arson is a "general-intent" crime because it does not require a specific mental state of intent. As a general rule, voluntary intoxication is no defense for a "general-intent" crime. Therefore, choice (B) is correct.

1. Involuntary Manslaughter—Battery Which Results in an Unintended Death

2. Murder

3. Murder—"Depraved-Heart" Killing

4. Arson and Murder

5. Attempted Murder

6. Manslaughter

7. "Depraved-Heart" Murder

8. Involuntary Manslaughter

9. "Depraved-Heart" Murder

10. Murder

11. Felony-Murder Rule

12. "Depraved-Heart" Murder

**CASE PRECEDENT QUESTIONS**

13. Felony-Murder Rule—Explanation

14. Felony-Murder—Causal Connection (Accomplice Liability)

15. Arson—Defense of Duress

16. Homicide Statutory Definitions

17. Accomplice Liability

18. Violation of Statute

19. Felony-Murder Rule—Underlying Felony

20. "Depraved-Heart" Murder

21. Defense of Property—Deadly Force (Spring Gun)

22. Rape—Liability of Female Accomplice

23. Defense of Self-Defense—Duty to Retreat

24. Felony-Murder Rule

25. Self-Defense

26. Attempt—Specific-intent Crime

**CASE PRECEDENT QUESTIONS**

**CASE PRECEDENT QUESTIONS**

# CRIMINAL LAW

**Questions 1–3 each describe a criminal offense. In each case select the most serious offense for which the defendant could properly be convicted.**

    (A) Murder
    (B) Voluntary manslaughter
    (C) Involuntary manslaughter
    (D) Battery

1. Defendant had an argument with a neighbor. As they were quarreling, Defendant pulled out his pen-knife only intending to frighten the neighbor. Accidentally, Defendant slightly flicked neighbor's arm with the knife. Unknown to Defendant, his neighbor was a hemophiliac who then died from the knife infliction.

2. Defendant wished to see his high school basketball team win the state championship. During an important game, Defendant pulled out a gun and shot at the leg of a key player on the opposing team. Defendant only intended to inflict a slight wound, so that the opposing player would be unable to complete the game. When Defendant fired the shot, he unintentionally hit a player on his own high school team in the chest, killing him instantly.

3. Defendant hated his boss, who had recently demoted him to a less prestigious position. Late one afternoon, Defendant saw his boss walking down the hallway. Defendant pulled out a gun and fired four shots at his boss. Although none of the bullets directly hit his boss, one of the shots ricocheted against a wall and struck the boss in the head, killing him instantly.

**Question 4 is based on the following fact situation.**

Sean Stuckey owns and operates "Stuckey's," a convenience store and gas station on Route 66 outside Oklahoma City. Sean and his family reside above the convenience store in a second-floor apartment. One day Hal Oats, a truck driver, pulled into "Stuckey's" for gas.

After filling up the gas tank, Hal entered the convenience store for a bite to eat. He was scarfing down a bowl of chili when he noticed a cockroach in the food. Hal demanded a new serving of chili. When Sean refused, Hal stormed from the store in anger.

Hal jumped into his truck and decided to "get even" by causing some damage. He purposely drove into one of the gas tanks which ruptured the gas line. The collision caused a terrible explosion and the convenience store became engulfed in flames. Sean could not escape the blaze and burned to death.

4. At common law Hal should be found guilty of

    (A) arson only
    (B) murder only
    (C) arson and murder
    (D) arson, burglary and murder

**Question 5 is based on the following fact situation.**

Speedster was driving his car recklessly at a high rate of speed through a residential neighborhood. He was traveling at a speed of over 100 miles per hour when he noticed a scantily clad female jogger. Taking his eyes off the road, Speedster failed to see Lisa, six years of age, crossing at the intersection. She was struck by the vehicle and hurled 50 feet in the air. As a result of the collision, Lisa suffered severe internal injuries and fractured both legs and arms. She was hospitalized for 11 months and became permanently crippled.

5. If Speedster is charged with attempted murder, he should be found

(A) guilty, because a person is presumed to intend the natural and probable consequences of his or her acts
(B) guilty, because criminal liability is predicated upon defendant's willful and wanton disregard for the safety of others
(C) not guilty, because defendant did not intend to kill Lisa
(D) not guilty, if defendant offered to pay Lisa's medical expenses

## Question 6 is based on the following fact situation.

Fleming and Grayson were members of the Tau Kappa Epsilon fraternity at University of Southern California. During a fraternity party, Fleming pulled out a pistol, pointed it at Grayson, and said, "Beg for your life, sucker." Grayson, who knew that Fleming had a reputation as a practical joker, said, "Get lost, you jerk." Fleming then pulled the trigger and shot Grayson to death.

A statute in this jurisdiction provides: "Any intentional and premeditated killing with malice aforethought is murder in the 1st degree. Murder in the 2nd degree is any killing that occurs during the commission or attempted commission of a serious or inherently dangerous felony. Manslaughter includes all other types of unlawful homicide and unjustifiable killings."

Fleming was subsequently prosecuted for killing Grayson. At trial, Fleming testified that Millstone, a fellow fraternity member, gave him the pistol before the shooting and told him that it was unloaded. Fleming further testified that he believed Millstone and in jest pulled the trigger. To his surprise the gun discharged, killing Grayson.

6. If the jury believes Fleming, it should find him

(A) guilty of assault, but not murder or manslaughter
(B) guilty of manslaughter
(C) guilty of 2nd degree murder
(D) guilty of 1st degree murder

## Question 7 is based on the following fact situation.

One afternoon Ralph was driving his car on Wilshire Blvd. in downtown Los Angeles. Already late for a business appointment, he was becoming very upset because of the heavy traffic. Suddenly, he decided to drive his car along the sidewalk to avoid the traffic jam. While he was speeding down the sidewalk, pedestrians were hastily scurrying to avoid his auto. His car struck Amy, who had tripped trying to get out of his way, killing her.

7. Which of the following is the best theory regarding Ralph's criminal liability?

(A) Felony murder, because he was committing an assault with a deadly weapon.
(B) Transferred intent, because one is presumed to intend the natural and probable consequences of his (or her) acts.
(C) Intentional killing, because Ralph's conduct was a substantial factor in causing Amy's death.
(D) Commission of an act highly dangerous to life without an intent to kill with disregard for the consequences.

**Questions 8–12 are based on the four case summaries below. For each question, select the case that would be most applicable as a precedent.**

(A) Defendant is charged with first degree murder. Defendant admitted entering into a suicide pact with his ailing wife who was suffering from an incurable disease of multiple sclerosis. Pursuant to their agreement, Defendant shot and killed her. Losing his nerve, however, he failed to shoot himself. Defendant GUILTY.

(B) Defendant is charged with involuntary manslaughter. At trial, Defendant admitted firing a bullet into his neighbor's home believing no one to be inside. He testified that he fired the shot through his neighbor's living room window approximately two hours after seeing the entire family leave on a vacation trip. The shooting was in retaliation for not getting invited to his neighbor's annual Christmas party. Unknown to Defendant, Lois, neighbor's housesitter, was struck and killed by the bullet. Defendant GUILTY.

(C) Defendant is charged with second degree murder. At trial Defendant admitted driving his automobile at a speed of 60 miles per hour through a school zone with a posted speed limit of 15 miles per hour. Defendant testified that he was traveling through the school zone at 3:00 P.M. when he saw a group of children crossing the street about 100 feet in front of his vehicle. Although he did not intend to actually hit anyone, Defendant thought it would be amusing to speed up and see the children try to run away from his onrushing auto. Amy, a five-year-old student was struck and killed by Defendant's vehicle after she tripped and fell in the intersection. Defendant GUILTY.

(D) Defendant is charged with felony murder. Defendant was in the process of burglarizing a gas station at night when a policeman arrived at the scene. Defendant dropped his booty and sped off in a get away vehicle. As he was fleeing from the scene, Defendant happened to see Jones, an enemy, whom he shot and killed. Defendant NOT GUILTY.

8. Defendant had an argument with a neighbor. As they were quarreling, Defendant suddenly kicked his neighbor in the shin. Unknown to Defendant, his neighbor was a hemophiliac who bled to death.

9. Defendant was a member of Sigma Mu fraternity. As part of the fraternity's initiation ritual, each pledge was required to walk down a flight of stairs carrying a lighted kerosene lamp blindfolded. Davis, a pledge, was descending a stairway with a lighted lamp in his hand when Defendant threw a beer bottle at him. Although Defendant did not intend to harm Davis, the bottle hit the lamp which exploded, burning Davis to death.

10. Jones was arrested and charged with murdering Smith. Though Jones was innocent, he nevertheless was convicted because Defendant perjured himself at Jones's trial. Defendant, who despised Jones, perjured himself so that Jones would be convicted and sentenced to death. Defendant testified that he saw Jones kill Smith (which was a lie). This false testimony led to Jones's conviction and resulted in his death in the electric chair.

CRIMINAL LAW

11. Defendant was madly in love with his next-door neighbor, Nancy. One evening Defendant broke into Nancy's home intending to rape her. Unknown to Defendant, Nancy was away on a business trip. When Defendant entered the bedroom, he found Nancy's husband committing adultery with his wife. In a fit of rage, Defendant pulled out a knife and stabbed Nancy's husband to death.

12. Defendant was attending his company's Christmas party when he decided to play a practical joke. He pulled out a loaded pistol and fired a shot a few feet from where his secretary was standing. Defendant intended only to frighten his secretary. The bullet, however, ricocheted off the wall and struck the secretary in the back, killing her instantly.

**Question 13 is based on the following fact situation.**

13. Which one of the following situations would most likely result in a verdict of guilty of felony murder?

   (A) Ruly, an avid Kansas City Royals baseball fan, travelled all night to Royals Stadium to see a World Series game, planning to purchase tickets from a scalper at the stadium. However, Ruly arrived at the stadium after the game had started, and no tickets were available. He proceeded to sneak around the guard at the entrance gate and illegally entered the stadium. He watched the remainder of the game in the "standing room" section. Ruly became so enraged when the opposition took the lead in the ninth inning that he pulled out a gun from under his jacket and aimed it at the section of spectators in front of him. Before he could be subdued he had fired three shots, killing one person and severely injuring another.

   (B) Harold was in the public area of the Third Federal Bank, filling out a deposit slip, when Ron entered. Ron went to the teller's window and quietly slipped a note to the teller, demanding "everything in your cash drawer." Harold who was unaware of the robbery taking place, went to the adjoining teller's window and made his deposit. Upon obtaining his receipt, Harold suddenly collapsed and died of a heart attack. When Ron saw this, he panicked and left the bank before the teller could comply with his demand.

   (C) Moe and Jack planned to rob Pa's luncheonette during the noontime rush. At 12:30, as planned, Jack entered Pa's and pointed a gun at the cashier, who handed over $200. Jack left to meet Moe outside, as Moe was standing guard as a lookout. As soon as Jack ran out of the door, a police officer tried to grab him. Jack evaded the officer for a brief moment. Thinking that Moe had double-crossed him and informed the police of their plans, Jack fatally shot Moe.

   (D) Mitchell and Richard had been feuding for years. In order to "show him a thing or two," Mitchell decided to set fire to Richard's house. Before dawn one morning, Mitchell went to Richard's house and lit a match to gasoline he poured at Richard's front door. The house caught fire and quickly spread to Richard's bedroom, where Richard was able to leap out of the window without injury. Ray, a police officer who was driving by, saw Mitchell running away one block from Richard's house. Ray pulled his car up to Mitchell to determine if Mitchell was involved in setting the fire. Upon seeing the officer, Mitchell pulled out a revolver and shot him. Ray was pronounced dead in the emergency room of a nearby hospital.

## Question 14 is based on the following fact situation.

Late one night, Jimmie and Jessie broke into Gold's Jewelry Store. As they were looting the store, Mr. Gold, the owner who lived across the street, looked out his window and saw additional lights on in the store. Consequently, Mr. Gold hurriedly dressed and ran across the street to his store. Before he arrived, however, Jessie became scared and left the store through a back entrance. When Mr. Gold entered the store, Jimmie hid behind a display counter. As the owner walked towards the cash register, he discovered Jimmie in a crouched position. Startled, Jimmie pulled out a knife and stabbed Mr. Gold to death.

14. Can Jessie be found guilty, if he is subsequently arrested and charged with murder?

   (A) No, because the killing was unintentional.
   (B) No, because he had renounced his participation in the felony before the killing.
   (C) No, because Mr. Gold's death was not a foreseeable consequence of the burglary.
   (D) Yes, provided that he is also found guilty of burglary.

## Question 15 is based on the following fact situation.

After waiting in line for two hours to gain entry into Studio 69, a popular discotheque, Calvin was denied admission because his attire failed to conform to the club's dress code. When he was refused admittance, Calvin angrily shouted to the club's doorman, "You'll be sorry for this. After I'm through, Studio 69 will be reduced to rubble." Later that same evening, Calvin returned to the disco with two Molotov cocktails in his possession. He noticed Homer leaving the disco and followed him into a nearby parking lot. As Homer was about to enter his car, Calvin grabbed him, pointed a gun and said, "Follow me, you disco punk, or I'll blow your brains out." Calvin led Homer to the rear of the disco, handed him the Molotov cocktails, and directed him to throw the firebombs through an open window of the club. In fear of his life, Homer tossed the Molotov cocktails into the club, causing an inferno which killed twenty-five patrons.

15. If Homer is charged with felony murder for the death of the patrons, he will most likely be found

   (A) guilty, under the Felony Murder Rule
   (B) guilty, since duress is not a defense to murder
   (C) not guilty, since duress is a defense to arson
   (D) not guilty, since Homer was justified under the circumstances

CRIMINAL LAW

**Questions 16–18 are based on the following fact situation.**

In 1990, a nuclear accident occurred at the Yankee nuclear power plant that was located just outside the Gotham city limits. As a result of the accident, nuclear wastes were discharged into the Gotham River, causing widespread contamination of local oyster beds. This was particularly catastrophic in light of subsequent medical studies which revealed that thousands of persons who ate the contaminated oysters developed cancer, leukemia, and other fatal diseases.

For ten years, the Yankee nuclear facility was closed down. But in 2000 officials at the power plant announced plans to restart operations. Gotham residents and environmentalists were incensed by the news. One such opponent who was instrumental in organizing demonstrations against the reopening was Deb M. Straighter, a waitress at a Gotham sushi restaurant. Despite local opposition, the Nuclear Regulatory Commission (NRC) gave its approval and the Yankee nuclear plant reopened its facility. Deb, however, decided to continue her fight, and devised a plan to bring media attention to this problem.

She devised a scheme whereby she would contaminate oysters at her restaurant with small amounts of a poisonous substance called strychnine. Although she didn't want to seriously injure anyone, Deb believed that if some people got sick from eating the oysters they would attribute their illness to nuclear wastes from the power plant. To facilitate her plan, she enlisted the help of her boyfriend, Benny Peck. At first, Benny adamantly refused to go along with her scheme. But when Deb threatened to break off their relationship, Benny reluctantly agreed to assist her. Benny, a pre-med student at Gotham University, then sought the assistance of his friend, Phil Dispenser, a registered pharmacist. Benny falsely told Phil that he needed two ounces of strychnine for an experiment he was conducting with rats. Although a state statute made it a felony to sell strychnine without a prescription, Phil sold Benny the drug without a prescription. Benny then gave the strychnine to Deb who sprinkled it on some oysters at the restaurant where she worked. Mistakenly, she put too much of the poison on some of the oysters. A few of the customers who ate the oysters became sick and nauseous. One person suffered convulsions and died from the strychnine poisoning.

A statute in the jurisdiction provides: "Any intentional and premeditated killing or one occurring during the perpetration of a felony, is murder in the first degree. Murder in the second degree is murder with intent to cause serious bodily harm. Manslaughter is an unlawful killing due to recklessness." Assault with intent to kill or to cause serious physical injury is a felony in the jurisdiction. There are no separate felonies relating to adulterating food or poisoning.

16. The most serious crime for which Deb can properly be convicted is

(A) first degree murder, because her acts were intentional and premeditated
(B) first degree murder, because death occurred in the commission of a felony
(C) second degree murder, because of the intent to cause physical harm
(D) manslaughter, because her conduct was reckless

17. The most serious crime for which Benny can properly be convicted is

(A) first degree murder
(B) second degree murder
(C) manslaughter
(D) no crime

18. The most serious crime for which Phil can properly be convicted is

(A) first degree murder
(B) second degree murder
(C) manslaughter
(D) selling drugs without a prescription

## Question 19 is based on the following fact situation.

One evening Glover set fire to Horsey's occupied house. As a result of the blaze, Horsey's daughter was burned to death. Glover was charged with felony-murder on the first count and arson on the second count of the two count indictment. The jury found the defendant guilty on the first count, but returned an innocent verdict on the second count.

19. Glover's attorney's motion to set aside the guilty verdict on the felony-murder charge will most probably be

(A) granted, because the guilty verdict is plain error that adversely affects Glover's constitutional rights
(B) granted, because the verdicts are legally inconsistent and should lead to an acquittal of both charges
(C) denied, because the verdicts do not amount to a reversible error
(D) denied, because Glover's proper remedy is to seek an appellate review for a non-constitutional error

## Question 20 is based on the following fact situation.

Studious was a recent graduate of John Marshall Law School in Chicago. The night before his Illinois bar examination, Studious' next-door neighbor Noisy, was having a party. The music from Noisy's home was so loud that Studious couldn't fall asleep. Studious called Noisy and told her, "I'm taking my bar examination tomorrow morning. The noise from your party is keeping me awake. Would you please quiet things down?" Noisy responded, "Are you crazy, you killjoy? Do you think I'm gonna cut short my party for some jerk who wants to be a lawyer?" Noisy then abruptly hung up. Angered, Studious went into his closet and got a gun. He went outside and fired a bullet through Noisy's living room window. Not intending to shoot anyone, Studious fired his gun at such an angle that the bullet would hit the ceiling. He merely wanted to cause some damage to Noisy's home to relieve his angry rage. The bullet, however, ricocheted off the ceiling and struck Partygoer in the back, killing her. The Illinois Criminal Code makes it a misdemeanor to discharge a firearm in public.

20. Studious will most likely be found guilty for which of the following crimes?

    (A) Murder
    (B) Involuntary manslaughter
    (C) Voluntary manslaughter
    (D) Discharge of a firearm in public

## Question 21 is based on the following fact situation.

Mike Malibu owned a beautiful beach house in Newport overlooking the Hyannis Bay. Although Malibu and his family lived in the beach house during the summer months, the house was left unoccupied for the remainder of the year. In order to protect the beach house from vandalism during the time that it was vacant, Malibu installed an automatic spring-gun device. The spring-gun was connected to the front door and calculated to automatically fire at chest level when the door was opened. No warnings were placed on the premises.

Beachcomber, a local derelict, knowing that Malibu's beach house was unoccupied, decided to burglarize the home one evening. When Beachcomber forced open the front door and was about to enter the premises, the spring-gun automatically discharged (bullet), killing Beachcomber instantly.

21. If Malibu is subsequently prosecuted and charged with Beachcomber's death, the most serious crime for which Malibu will be found guilty is

    (A) voluntary manslaughter
    (B) involuntary manslaughter
    (C) murder
    (D) assault with a deadly weapon

## Question 22 is based on the following fact situation.

Ricky, a New York City policeman, was relaxing in his living room when his wife entered and asked what he'd like for dinner. Ricky replied, "Ethel, next door." Startled, Lucy asked Ricky what he meant by that remark. Ricky then said, "Look, I've had the 'hots' for Ethel for a long time. I've got this burning desire to go next door and rape her." As Ricky was about to walk out the door, he turned to Lucy and said, "You want to come along and watch?" Lucy shook her head as if to say okay and followed him next door.

Moments later, Ricky rang the doorbell and Ethel came to the door. After entering her home, Ricky grabbed Ethel's arm and began to rip off her clothes. Terribly frightened, Ethel pleaded with Ricky to stop. As he continued to assault her, Ethel then turned to Lucy and said, "Please tell him to get off me." Lucy, who despised Ethel, simply stood by and told Ricky, "Do it, honey . . . do it." Ricky raped Ethel repeatedly and afterwards threatened to kill her if she told anyone.

22. On a charge of raping Ethel, Lucy should be found

    (A) not guilty, because it is legally impossible for a woman to commit rape
    (B) not guilty, because Ethel's mere presence and oral encouragement, whether or not she had the requisite intent, will not make her guilty as an accomplice
    (C) guilty, because, with the intent to have Ethel raped, she shouted encouragement to Ricky
    (D) guilty, because she aided and abetted Ricky through her mere presence plus her intent to see Ethel raped

**Question 23 is based on the following fact situations.**

23. In which of the following situations would Andy be **not** guilty of homicide?

(A) Andy came into the G&B bar looking for a fight. He walked up to Barry, tapped him on the shoulder and said, "You bother me. Get out of here." Barry ignored him, and Andy proceeded to punch Barry in the face and stab him in the arm with a knife. Barry thereupon took out a knife that had been concealed in his pocket and stabbed Andy in the right arm. Andy, fearful that Barry would stab him in the heart, took out a gun and shot Barry to death.

(B) Andy was home in bed with a fever one Saturday night, and all the lights in his house were off. Maurice, who was scouting the neighborhood that night for a house to burglarize, broke into Andy's house through the basement window and went upstairs to the bedrooms to look for jewelry. Andy, who was not aware that someone else was in the house, was startled when he saw Maurice walk past his room towards the stairs leading to the outside doorway. Andy pulled out a pistol from under his pillow when he saw Maurice and shot him to death.

(C) Andy started a joke about Barry's brother. When word got to Barry about Andy's joke, Barry became incensed. He rushed to Andy's home, broke open the door, and found Andy preparing dinner in the kitchen. He immediately said, "Andy, I'm going to kill you." Andy knew that Barry had been convicted of attempted murder several years ago, and he cringed when Barry took out a gun and pointed it at him. Andy could have easily darted for the open front door and evaded Barry, but instead he suddenly pulled a knife from the kitchen wall, lunged at Barry and stabbed him to death. Unknown to Andy, Barry's gun was not loaded.

(D) Andy was a reporter for a Massachusetts newspaper and was sent on assignment to New York to cover the story of a mining disaster. He was sitting in his hotel room one evening trying to get a message to his editor when Maurice knocked at the door. Andy opened the door and Maurice announced a robbery. Andy took a lamp from the night table and threw it at Maurice. Maurice was momentarily stunned, and Andy then pulled a gun out of his own suitcase and shot Maurice to death.

## Question 24 is based on the following fact situation.

Wilder, an indigent, was walking through Central Park when he decided to rob someone. He hid behind a tree, lying in wait for a victim to approach. Shortly thereafter, Jody, a 16-year-old girl, was strolling in the park when Wilder suddenly jumped from his hiding place and accosted her. Although Wilder intended only to rob his victim, he punched her in the mouth and she fell to the ground. Wilder then grabbed her pocketbook and fled. Unknown to Wilder, Jody suffered a fractured skull when her head struck the pavement. She subsequently died from her head injuries.

24. Which of the following is the most serious crime for which Wilder can be found guilty?

    (A) Murder
    (B) Felony-murder
    (C) Involuntary manslaughter
    (D) Voluntary manslaughter

## Question 25 is based on the following fact situation.

A Missoula state statute provides: "Whensoever a person knows or should know that he (or she) is being arrested by a police officer, it is the duty of such person to refrain from using force or any weapon in resisting arrest." Violation of the Missoula statute is made punishable by fine and/or imprisonment.

At 10:30 A.M. on March 10, 1984, there was a bank robbery at the Missoula Savings Fund branch office. That afternoon around 1:00, police officer Kern arrested Henderson whom he suspected was involved in the crime. These above facts are uncontradicted. However, Kern and Henderson have given different accounts concerning what happened next.

According to Kern's version, after Henderson was apprehended the suspect resisted arrest and hit the officer in the mouth with his fist. Kern, who was momentarily stunned, pulled out his nightstick and struck Henderson over the head with it. On the other hand, Henderson claimed that after he was arrested by Kern, he told the officer, "You look like a horse's ass and smell even worse." Whereupon, Kern began hitting him with his nightstick. To avoid being hit again, Henderson hit Kern with his fist, knocking the officer down. Henderson was charged with assault.

25. Henderson should be found

    (A) not guilty, only if the arrest was unlawful without probable cause and the jury believes Henderson's account
    (B) not guilty, even if the arrest was lawful provided that the jury believes Henderson's account
    (C) guilty, provided the arrest was lawful regardless of which account the jury believes
    (D) guilty, even if the arrest was unlawful regardless of which account the jury believes

## Question 26 is based on the following fact situation.

Hink, a freshman at University of Michigan, was a member of Phi Alpha Delta fraternity. On Saturday night, Hink and his girlfriend, Lee, were attending a toga party at the fraternity house. While the party was in progress, a few brothers from Alpha Beta, a rival fraternity, vandalized some of the cars parked outside the Phi Alpha Delta fraternity house. They broke the headlights and stole the battery from Hink's car.

When the party ended, Hink and Lee left the fraternity house and got into his car. Hink, who was about to drive Lee home, was unaware what had happened. He tried to start the car but it wouldn't turn on. Two police officers, who were parked outside the fraternity house, watched Hink as he tried to start the car. They then approached Hink and charged him with attempting to violate a local Ann Arbor city ordinance making it a misdemeanor to drive at night without headlights.

26. Hink's best defense to the charge is

   (A) factual impossibility
   (B) mistake of fact
   (C) entrapment
   (D) no requisite intent

## Question 27 is based on the following fact situation.

Howie and Hymie Heir were young playboys who were always short of cash. They were the only living relatives of their wealthy uncle, Murray T. Kay who had been confined to a wheelchair with a serious heart ailment. As a result of some slow horses and fast women, Howie and Hymie found themselves in debt to the local syndicate. The syndicate threatened to kill Howie and Hymie unless they paid up within a month. They asked their uncle for some money but he refused. Whereupon Howie and Hymie decided to "accelerate" his inevitable death.

They beseeched Molly Maid, who was Uncle Murray's housekeeper and companion, to poison him. Molly, who had a crush on Howie, agreed but on the condition that they would pay her $10,000 from their inheritance. After Howie and Hymie agreed to her demand, Molly decided to place some cyanide in Uncle Murray's tea one morning. As Molly was preparing the tea, Uncle Murray was visited by his personal physician, Dr. Doom. When Molly was ready to serve the tea, Uncle Murray asked her to fix some tea for Dr. Doom also. Molly did so and then carefully set the tea on the table so that Uncle Murray's cup was facing him. However, when Dr. Doom reached over to get some sugar, he inadvertently took Uncle Murray's cup with the cyanide and drank it. Seconds later, Dr. Doom died from the poison.

27. Which of the following crimes are Howie and Hymie guilty of?

   (A) Conspiracy to commit murder of Uncle Murray only
   (B) Conspiracy to commit murder of Uncle Murray and Dr. Doom
   (C) Conspiracy to commit murder of Uncle Murray and murder of Dr. Doom
   (D) Solicitation, conspiracy to commit murder of Uncle Murray, and murder of Dr. Doom

## Question 28 is based on the following fact situation.

28. Under which of the following situations would Defendant most likely be found guilty of murder?

(A) Defendant conspired with Al and Bob to rob Bloomie's Department Store. On the day of the robbery, the three participants drove to Bloomie's in a stolen Ford van. In accordance with their plan, Defendant was to wait in the getaway van while Bob and Al conducted their heist. While Bob and Al were inside the department store, Defendant decided to renounce his involvement/participation in the scheme and hurriedly drove away in the van. In his haste Defendant failed to see Pedestrian jaywalking across the street and struck and killed Pedestrian.

(B) Defendant, accompanied by his girlfriend, Bubbles, was attending his law school graduation party. Both Defendant and Bubbles became highly intoxicated during the party celebration. As Defendant and Bubbles were leaving the party, Defendant handed Bubbles the keys to his automobile and directed her to drive home. While driving, Bubbles suddenly swerved the car across the median strip into the path of an oncoming car, fatally injuring the driver of the other vehicle.

(C) Defendant, whose driver's license had been revoked one week previously, was driving on an infrequently traveled country road one night. Knowing that his car brakes were defective, Defendant was traveling at 35 m.p.h. in a zone in which the speed limit was 25 m.p.h. when victim suddenly darted in front of his car. In an effort to avoid striking victim, Defendant applied his brakes to no avail. The car struck victim, resulting in victim's instantaneous death.

(D) One afternoon Defendant was delivering pornographic materials to various adult bookstores in the community. In this jurisdiction, the delivery of pornographic materials constituted a misdemeanor. As Defendant was enroute to Peeping Tom's Adult Book Store for his final delivery of the day, he inadvertently struck a blind man who was crossing an intersection. Six months later, the blind man died as a result of injuries sustained in the accident.

## Question 29 is based on the following fact situation.

Bennie Hana and Ginnie May, his 13-year-old niece, had just left the Grand Opera House late one evening and were walking toward a dimly lit parking lot to get to Bennie's car. Just as they reached the car, Barney Belch, who was visibly intoxicated, emerged from behind a trash can and approached them. Barney knocked Bennie to the ground and hit him over the head with the trash can, causing Bennie to become unconscious. Barney then forced Ginnie into the car, and raped her.

29. Barney is charged with assault with intent to commit rape, based on his attack on Ginnie. Barney's best defense would be which of the following statements?

(A) Although Ginnie May was only 13 years old, she appeared to be 16 years old to a reasonable man.

(B) Barney did not intend to rape Ginnie.

(C) Barney's intoxication at the time negated the required general-intent.

(D) It is impossible to prove that Barney was the perpetrator, because the parking lot was dimly lit.

## Question 30 is based on the following fact situation.

In which of the following situations is Defendant's conduct most likely to make him criminally responsible for Victim's death?

(A) Defendant shot Victim in the head. Victim was then taken to a hospital for treatment of the wound. An earthquake later struck the city, causing the hospital to collapse. Victim was crushed to death in the rubble.

(B) Defendant and Victim lived in the same apartment building. Defendant knew that Victim was having a love affair with Gilda, a married woman. One day Defendant learned that Victim was to be murdered by Gilda's husband. Although Defendant had ample time to warn Victim, he failed to do so. That night Victim was stabbed to death by Gilda's jealous husband.

(C) Victim, a gambler, was heavily in debt to the mob. Defendant, who was a mob enforcer, threatened to kill Victim if he didn't pay up. Frightened, Victim boarded the next airplane flight out of town. The airplane crashed, and Victim was killed in the wreckage.

(D) Defendant and Victim were driving to work together when Defendant, without provocation, stabbed Victim in the arm. Defendant then pushed him out of the car. Victim fell along the side of the street and fractured his ankle. Unable to move from the roadway, Victim was fatally crushed a half hour later by a car driven by a drunken driver.

## Question 31 is based on the following fact situation.

Barrow, Stern, and Larkin were roommates at Fremont College in Boston. During their Thanksgiving vacation, Barrow and Stern drove to New York City to visit relatives. While in New York, Stern was injured in an automobile accident. As a consequence, she couldn't return to Boston with Barrow. The day that Barrow was to drive back to college Stern asked her if she would deliver a package to Larkin. Barrow agreed and Stern gave her a small package which Barrow placed in her glove compartment.

While driving through Connecticut, Barrow was stopped for speeding. When the state trooper asked Barrow for her license and registration, she reached into the glove compartment. As she did, the package which Stern had given her fell onto the floor. When it hit the floor, the box broke open and a plastic envelope containing a white substance slid out. Seeing that the substance appeared to be cocaine, the state trooper arrested Barrow for possession of illegal narcotics under a state statute making it a felony to "wilfully possess" a controlled dangerous substance. The package did, in fact, contain cocaine.

31. If Barrow is later brought to trial for this charge, her best defense is that

(A) Barrow didn't know what was in the package
(B) Stern didn't tell her she was carrying illegal narcotics
(C) the package didn't belong to her
(D) the cocaine was illegally seized

# CRIMINAL LAW

## Question 32 is based on the following fact situation.

Liz, a junior at Lake Tahoe University, was studying late one night in her dormitory room. The dormitory in which she resided was a coed residence hall. At about 11:30 P.M., Liz left her room and entered the Girl's Lavatory on her floor. As Liz was washing her face and hands, Roger, the resident manager of the dorm, entered the bathroom. While Liz was leaning over the sink, Roger said, "Hey baby, I've had my eye on you for a long time. Let's go back to my dorm room and go to bed together." Frightened, Liz ran to an open window in the bathroom, and jumped onto the fire escape. As she exited down the fire escape, Liz accidentally fell, bruising her legs.

32. Which of the following crime(s), if any, would Roger most likely be convicted of?

   (A) assault
   (B) battery
   (C) assault with intent to commit rape
   (D) no crime

## Question 33 is based on the following fact situation.

Kyle was charged with attempted rape of Meredith. The crime allegedly occurred at a party at Kyle's home. During the party, Kyle invited Meredith into his bedroom to show her some of his etchings. When she entered his bedroom, Kyle ripped off her blouse and threw Meredith onto his bed. He then jumped on Meredith and tried to pull off her skirt. When Meredith began to scream, some of the guests rushed into the bedroom and pulled Kyle off the victim. At trial, Kyle testified that he wanted to have sexual intercourse with Meredith but he believed that she was consenting. Kyle further testified that he had consumed a pint of whiskey earlier in the evening and was intoxicated at the time the incident occurred.

33. If the jury believes that Meredith did not consent but also believes that Kyle in his intoxicated state honestly believed that she was consenting, the defendant should be found

   (A) guilty, because consent is determined by the objective manifestations of the victim and not the subjective beliefs of the defendant
   (B) guilty, because voluntary intoxication is no defense
   (C) not guilty, because he honestly believed that she was consenting
   (D) not guilty, unless his belief that she was consenting was unreasonable

## Question 34 is based on the following fact situation.

Kareem, Russell, and Elgin went to Wilt's house. Kareem intended to take a John Coltrane jazz album that he believed was his and Wilt was keeping unlawfully. Russell believed that the John Coltrane album was Kareem's and intended to help Kareem take it. When Elgin learned that Kareem and Russell were going to break into Wilt's home, he decided to accompany them. He planned to find some items inside which might be worth taking.

Arriving at Wilt's home, Kareem opened the front door which was closed but unlocked. Upon entering, Elgin went to Wilt's upstairs bedroom and found a Rolex watch which he took. In the meantime, Kareem and Russell went to the living room and began rummaging through Wilt's record collection. Kareem found the John Coltrane album which he seized. The three men then left Wilt's home.

In this jurisdiction, burglary is defined as the breaking and entering of any structure with the intent to commit a felony or larceny therein.

34. Which, if any, individuals should be found guilty of conspiracy?

    (A) Kareem, Russell, and Elgin
    (B) Kareem and Russell
    (C) Russell and Elgin
    (D) None

## Question 35 is based on the following fact situation.

Mallory and Tinker agreed to burglarize Rosario's home. While they were planning out the burglary, Mallory informed Tinker that Rosario's home had a sophisticated alarm system that needed to be disarmed. Tinker told Mallory that he knew Blick, an alarm specialist, who could help disarm the security system.

Tinker then approached Blick and asked if he would assist them in disarming Rosario's alarm system. Blick said that he didn't want to participate in the crime but told Tinker how he could disarm the system himself. Mallory and Tinker thereafter went to Rosario's home to commit the burglary.

When they arrived at Rosario's home, they saw a vicious guard dog patrolling the fenced-in area of the home. Deciding it would be too risky to confront the dog, Mallory and Tinker abandoned their planned burglary.

35. Which of the following is the most accurate statement regarding the criminal liability of Tinker, Mallory, and Blick?

    (A) Tinker and Mallory are guilty of conspiracy.
    (B) Tinker, Mallory, and Blick are guilty of conspiracy.
    (C) Tinker and Mallory are guilty of conspiracy and Tinker, Mallory, and Blick are guilty of attempted burglary.
    (D) Tinker, Mallory, and Blick are guilty of both conspiracy and attempted burglary.

## Question 36 is based on the following fact situation.

Nickerson went to Chin's Convenience Store intending to rob it. Nickerson had a gun inside his coat pocket. When Nickerson entered the store, Chin, the proprietor, saw that he had his hand in his coat pocket. Although Chin did not actually see the gun, he noticed a bulge in Nickerson's coat pocket.

Paranoid because of a rash of recent robberies, Chin said, "Please don't hurt me . . . . I'll do anything you want." Chin then fainted and fell to the floor. Nickerson walked behind the counter and opened the cash register. He took $50 from the register and left the store.

36. If Nickerson is charged with robbery, he should be found

    (A) guilty, because Chin was placed in fear
    (B) guilty, because Nickerson entered the store with a gun in his possession
    (C) not guilty, because Nickerson did not make any threat of force
    (D) not guilty, because Nickerson did not take any money from the victim's person

**Question 37 is based on the following fact situation.**

Keefe Keefauver, aged 70, was a wealthy retiree who had amassed a fortune after selling his pharmaceutical company. Keefe and his wife, Kay, lived in an exquisitely decorated penthouse apartment overlooking Central Park in mid-town Manhattan. One night Keefe and Kay were returning home from dinner when they were accosted by Lex Lugar outside their apartment building. Lugar brandished a gun and told Keefe and Kay to take him to their apartment. Upon entering, Lex blindfolded Keefe and Kay and tied them up with duct tape to chairs in the living room. Lex then stole Keefe's wallet and assorted jewelry from the bedroom. After Lex exited the apartment, Keefe and Kay tried desperately to free themselves from their constraints. As Keefe was struggling, he suffered a heart attack and died.

37. Lex should be found guilty of

(A) burglary
(B) robbery and burglary
(C) robbery and murder
(D) burglary, robbery, and murder

**Question 38 is based on the following fact situation.**

This jurisdiction makes suicide a crime. Jilly, a day trader, is despondent over a failed marriage and catastrophic financial losses during the recent 2,000 point drop in the Nasdaq stock exchange. Jilly went up to the roof of her fourth story apartment building and decided to jump off. She landed on top of two pedestrians, Alex and Jean Pietro, who cushioned her fall and saved her life. Unfortunately, Alex and Jean Pietro were seriously injured when Jilly crashed on top of them.

38. Jilly is guilty of

(A) battery
(B) attempted murder
(C) attempted manslaughter
(D) reckless endangerment

**Question 39 is based on the following fact situation.**

Driver drove his automobile into a Chevron service station. He told Attendant, "Fill it up with unleaded, please." Attendant went ahead and pumped 10 gallons of gas into Driver's tank. When Attendant approached Driver for payment, Driver shouted, "Thanks for the freebie, sucker," and drove off without paying.

39. Driver is guilty of

(A) larceny
(B) larceny by trick
(C) false pretenses
(D) embezzlement

**Question 40 is based on the following fact situation.**

Peters stole a diamond necklace that he gave his girlfriend, Lucinda, as a birthday present. At the time Peters gave the necklace to Lucinda she did not know that it was stolen. Three weeks later, while Peters and Lucinda were passionately making love, she whispered in his ear, "Gee, darling, I really love the diamond necklace you gave me.... It must have cost a fortune." Peters responded, "Honey, the necklace didn't cost me anything.... I stole it." Startled by Peters's confession, Lucinda broke down and started crying. Moments later, however, after regaining her composure, Lucinda decided to keep the necklace.

40. Lucinda is guilty of

(A) receiving stolen property
(B) larceny
(C) larceny by trick
(D) no crime

## Question 41 is based on the following fact situation.

Olga Oslo was an executive vice-president in the investment banking department of the Doylestown National Bank. One afternoon, Olga was having lunch with her boss, Amy Alcott, at the Riverhorse Restaurant when Amy excused herself to go to the bathroom. As Amy stood up to leave the table, her wallet fell out of her pocketbook onto the floor. Amy was unaware of what occurred and proceeded to the restroom. Olga, however, saw the wallet fall. Intending to steal it, Olga picked up the wallet and placed it in her pocket. Before Amy returned to the table, Olga had a change of heart and decided to give the wallet hack. Thereupon, Olga told Amy what had happened and handed her the wallet when she returned from the bathroom.

41. Olga is guilty of which, if any, crime?

(A) No crime
(B) Larceny
(C) Embezzlement
(D) False pretenses

## Question 42 is based on the following fact situation.

Bobby entered Macy's Department Store and took the elevator to the eighth floor toy department. He went there intending to purchase a new Monopoly game. Bobby, who only had $8.00 in his possession, saw that the Monopoly games were selling for $10.00. Realizing that he did not have enough money to pay for the Monopoly set, he ripped the $10.00 price tag off the box. While no one was looking, Bobby then took the $7.00 sticker from a Risk game and placed it on the Monopoly box. He then purchased the Monopoly game for $7.00 and walked out of the store.

42. With which one of the following crime(s) should Bobby be convicted?

(A) False pretenses
(B) Larceny
(C) Deceit
(D) Conversion

## Question 43 is based on the following fact situation.

Owens took his car to an auto mechanic to have the oil changed. When he returned to pick up his car later in the day, the mechanic told him the charge was $125. Owens objected and said the charge was excessively high. The mechanic indicated that the amount was reasonable and showed Owens a price listing substantiating the charge. As the two men were arguing, the mechanic excused himself to answer the telephone in the rear of his shop. While the mechanic was on the phone, Owens got into his car and drove off without paying the servicing charges.

43. If Owens is subsequently charged with larceny, he should be found

   (A) not guilty, because the car was his own property
   (B) not guilty, if the jury finds the servicing charge to be excessively high
   (C) guilty, if the jurisdiction has a statute making theft of services a crime
   (D) guilty, because he took the car without the mechanic's consent

## Question 44 is based on the following fact situation.

44. In most states the division of homicide into degrees is distinguished according to which of the following:

   (A) the causal relationship between defendant's act and the resulting death
   (B) the attendant circumstances surrounding the death
   (C) the nature of the act causing the death
   (D) the defendant's state of mind at the time the killing was committed

## Question 45 is based on the following fact situation.

Charles Blackhead, a law professor at Southwestern Law School, was hired to teach a bar review preparatory course for Bar Review of America (hereafter referred to as BRA). Blackhead, who specialized in Criminal Law, taught the BRA review course at the Los Angeles, San Francisco, and San Diego locations. After conducting the BRA review sessions, Blackhead submitted an expense voucher to Richard Kingviser, BRA's director. His expense voucher included a $225 travel expenditure to Santa Barbara where Blackhead had attended a symposium on Legal Jurisprudence.

Blackhead also submitted the $225 travel expenditure to Michael Speck, the Dean of Southwestern Law School, who had previously approved Blackhead's appearance at the symposium. Kingviser paid Blackhead for the Santa Barbara expenditure but indicated that the expense item was improperly billed to BRA.

45. Blackhead was indicted for false pretenses. In defense Blackhead contends that the double billing was the result of a bookkeeping error. Blackhead's defense should be

   (A) valid, if his mistake was reasonable
   (B) valid, if he didn't know that the billing to BRA included the Santa Barbara expenditure
   (C) invalid, if his bookkeeping error was unreasonable
   (D) invalid, because white collar crime imposes absolute criminal liability

## Questions 46–48 are based on the following fact situation.

Louie and Sam were told by their pal Clu that Manning Wholesalers were now utilizing the old River Warehouse as a storage area for their stock of new appliances. Late one night Louie and Sam broke into the warehouse, and proceeded to load the large crates of appliances onto their truck. As they were leaving, Sam inadvertently threw his cigarette butt into a refuse pile of old cardboard boxes and papers. Soon afterwards, the refuse ignited into a small fire. Although Sam had time to douse the fire without any danger to himself, he did not do so. Instead, he fled and climbed into the truck with Louie. Meanwhile, the fire quickly spread, engulfing the entire warehouse in flames.

46. At common law, Louie and Sam would be found guilty of:

    (A) burglary and arson
    (B) larceny and arson
    (C) larceny only
    (D) burglary, larceny, and arson

47. If Clu were later charged as a co-conspirator, in all likelihood he would be held responsible as:

    (A) an accessory before the fact
    (B) a principal in the second degree
    (C) an accomplice
    (D) none of these

48. Under present statutory law, Louie and Sam should be convicted of which of the following crimes?

    (A) Arson, burglary, and larceny
    (B) Arson and burglary
    (C) Larceny and burglary
    (D) Arson, robbery, and burglary

## Questions 49–50 are based on the following fact situation.

The state of Monrovia has a statute defining burglary as "the breaking and entering without privilege of any building or occupied structure with the intent to commit a felony therein." Late one night Farr broke into a warehouse which was located in Monroe, the largest city in Monrovia. He carried with him an incendiary device with which he intended to commit arson. After breaking a window and gaining entry into the building, Farr was immediately arrested by Murray, the night security guard. Murray did not see the incendiary device that was tucked under Farr's coat.

When Farr was apprehended by Murray, he offered the security guard $500 if he would let him go. Murray agreed. Farr then handed him the money and was about to leave the warehouse when Murray said to him, "By the way, if you give me another $250 I'll let you enter the building tomorrow night and do whatever you want." Farr responded affirmatively and gave Murray the additional $250. Farr told Murray he'd see him tomorrow night and then left. At no time did Murray see the incendiary device.

49. If Farr is later arrested, he should be found guilty for which of the following crimes under modern law?

    (A) Burglary only
    (B) Burglary and attempted arson
    (C) Burglary, attempted arson, and conspiracy to commit burglary
    (D) Burglary and conspiracy to commit burglary

50. If Murray is later arrested, he should be found guilty for which, if any, of the following crimes?

    (A) Conspiracy to commit burglary
    (B) Accessory before the fact to burglary
    (C) Accessory after the fact to burglary
    (D) None of the above

## Questions 51–53 are based on the following fact situation.

On Tuesday, March 22, Tom took his car to be repaired at the B&G Auto Center requesting that the car's shocks be replaced. John, the general manager, agreed to have the repairs completed by March 25. The repairs were completed by the garage mechanics, who then parked the car. Tom returned on the appointed day to pick up the car, and found it parked out front of the garage. Not intending to pay for the repairs, Tom entered the car with his spare key and drove off.

51. Under modern statutes, Tom should be found:

    (A) not guilty of larceny
    (B) guilty of larceny
    (C) guilty of fraudulent conversion
    (D) guilty of theft by deception

52. Suppose that Tom directs his employee to pick up the car at the Auto Center and gives him a $200 check to pay for the repair services. The employee proceeds as directed, but as he is returning to Tom's place of business, he decides to steal the car, driving instead to Stu's garage. Which of the following statements best describes the criminal liability of Tom's employee?

    (A) Unauthorized use of an automobile, by taking Tom's car without his permission
    (B) Fraudulent conversion, in fraudulently converting Tom's property to his own use
    (C) Larceny by bailee, in permanently depriving owner of his personal property
    (D) Embezzlement, in misappropriating Tom's property during the employer-employee relationship

53. In accordance with Question 52, assume that the employee takes Tom's car to Stu's garage and tells Stu that he had "stolen" it and needs cash to skip town. Stu, in turn, contacts one of his "regular customers" telling him that he has a hot new 1986 Mark IV available for immediate sale. If Stu were later prosecuted for (I) larceny, (II) embezzlement, (III) conspiracy, and (IV) receiving stolen property, he should be found guilty of:

    (A) I and III
    (B) II and III
    (C) I, II, and III
    (D) III and IV

**Questions 54–55 are based on the following fact situation.**

Jimmy and Chrissy were playing tennis at the Biscayne Racket Club. After their match, they entered the club's cocktail lounge to have a couple of drinks. They were sitting at the crowded bar when Jimmy pulled out his tennis racket and said, "Chrissy, your backhand shot is terrible. Let me show you how you should be swinging your backhand." While sitting at the bar, Jimmy began to swing his racket carelessly. As Jimmy was swinging his arm in a backhand motion, he accidentally hit Ivan in the mouth with the metal edge of the racket. Ivan, who was standing behind Jimmy while drinking a beer, suffered a deep gash on his lip which required 20 stitches.

54. For which, if any, of the following crimes should Jimmy be found guilty?

    (A) Assault
    (B) Battery
    (C) Mayhem
    (D) No crime, because he hit Ivan accidentally

55. Assume for the purposes of this question only that before Jimmy began to swing his racket at the bar, he had drunk three vodka martinis and was inebriated. If Jimmy is prosecuted for hitting Ivan, he should be found

    (A) guilty, because Jimmy was acting recklessly
    (B) guilty, because Jimmy's recklessness cannot be negated by intoxication
    (C) not guilty, because Jimmy's intoxication deprived him of the capacity to commit a criminal offense
    (D) not guilty, because Jimmy hit Ivan accidentally

## Question 56 is based on the following fact situation.

Samantha believed that her cousin Sabrina was a sorceress who practiced witchcraft. One afternoon Sabrina told Samantha that because she hated her, she was going to invoke "evil spirits" to have Samantha killed. Believing that her cousin's malediction would surely result in her death, Samantha stabbed Sabrina to death. Samantha was arrested and prosecuted for murder. At trial, Samantha testified that she believed that her life was in danger and she acted in self-defense.

56. If the jury determines that Samantha honestly believed that she was acting in self-defense, she should be found

   (A) guilty, because Samantha's belief that her life was in danger was unreasonable
   (B) guilty, because Samantha's life was not actually in danger
   (C) not guilty, because Samantha's belief that her life was endangered was sufficient to excuse her use of force in self-defense
   (D) not guilty, because a reasonable belief to use force to defend oneself is not required in the face of an imminent threat of death

## Questions 57–59 are based on the following fact situation.

Ma and Pa Kettle owned and operated Kettle's Grocery Store. The grocery store was situated in the first floor of the building in which Ma and Pa occupied a second floor apartment. Late one evening Zeke and Grover were walking past Kettle's Grocery Store, when Grover turned to Zeke and said, "Hey man, I've heard that Pa Kettle has a lot of dough stashed in a cigar box in the store." Zeke replied, "Well, turkey, what are we waiting for?"

The two men then furtively walked to the rear of the building. They then proceeded to open the gate to the fenced-in backyard. Once inside the backyard, Zeke and Grover attempted to pry open the back window of the grocery store. Awakened by the yelping of his watchdog, Pa went out onto his second floor back porch and saw the two men below. Pa yelled out, "What are you guys doing down there?" Startled, the two men turned to run when Zeke noticed a large package lying outside the rear door to the store. Zeke picked up the package which contained baked bread that had been delivered earlier in the evening, and the two men then ran off.

Seeing the men running away with his bread delivery, Pa hastily descended the rear stairway, tripped, and fell down the flight of stairs breaking his neck, which resulted in his immediate death.

57. Which of the following crime(s) will Zeke and Grover most likely be convicted of?

   (A) Larceny
   (B) Burglary
   (C) Larceny and attempted burglary
   (D) Conspiracy to commit larceny and burglary

58. If Zeke and Grover are subsequently indicted for Pa Kettle's death, they will most likely be found

   (A) guilty of felony murder
   (B) guilty of involuntary manslaughter
   (C) guilty of voluntary manslaughter
   (D) not guilty, since it was unforeseeable that a death would occur under the circumstances

59. Assume for the purposes of this question only that after Pa Kettle was awakened by his dog, he picked up his loaded shotgun, and proceeded onto his back porch. Seeing the men below, Pa shouted, "Who are you? What's going on down there?" Zeke, pointing his finger at Pa then yelled, "Don't make another move or you're a dead man." Honestly believing that Zeke was aiming a gun at him and about to shoot, Pa fired his shotgun, fatally wounding Zeke. If Grover is subsequently charged with Zeke's death under the Model Penal Code, he should be found

(A) guilty of felony murder
(B) guilty of voluntary manslaughter
(C) guilty, since a felon may be convicted of the murder of a co-felon
(D) not guilty, since Pa was justified in killing Zeke

## Question 60 is based on the following fact situation.

60. Under which one of the following situations would defendant(s) most likely be found guilty of larceny?

(A) Smith took his watch to Jeweler Goldman for repairs. Goldman inspected the watch and informed Smith that the watch needed a minor mechanism adjustment which he would perform that afternoon. Smith gave the watch to Goldman and told him that he would return the following day to pick it up. As Goldman was repairing the watch, he discovered that it was an extremely valuable antique. He then substituted the watch for a less expensive facsimile which Smith picked up the next day.

(B) As Staush and Sid were walking down Main Street, they noticed Slick park his metallic gold Corvette and enter Barney's Pool Hall. When they approached the car, Staush observed that Slick had left the keys in the ignition. Knowing that Slick would be hustling pool all evening, they hopped into the Corvette and drove off, intending to return the car later that evening.

(C) During a Saturday night "craps" game in the back room of Harry's Bar, Roller lost $150 to Duce. Roller left the bar after losing his money, and returned an hour later with a gun in his possession. Honestly believing that the $150 still belonged to him, Roller confronted Duce in the back room and demanded the return of his money. Frightened, Duce handed the money back to Roller.

(D) One afternoon Blackie noticed JohnJohn riding his ten-speed Peugeot bike in Central Park. Blackie, who always wanted to own a European racing bike, saw his opportunity when JohnJohn left his bike unattended to participate in a touch football game. Blackie jumped on the bike and quickly rode away. Later that evening Blackie called JohnJohn and demanded $200 for the return of the bike. JohnJohn agreed to Blackie's demand. The following day, JohnJohn paid Blackie the money and Blackie, in turn, returned the bike to JohnJohn.

## Question 61 is based on the following fact situation.

The state of Columbia has the following statute in effect:

> "No person shall sell, barter, furnish or give to a minor under sixteen years of age an air gun, rifle, shotgun, pistol, or other firearm; or being the owner or having charge or control thereof, knowingly permit it to be used by a minor under such age. Whoever violates this statute shall be fined not more than $1,500 (One Thousand Five Hundred Dollars), or imprisoned not more than 45 days, or both."

Mrs. King, the mother of Arnold, purchased a Daisy BB gun, an air rifle, which she gave to her son. Mrs. King, a policewoman, who was familiar with firearms, trained Arnold in the systematic practice of care in the use of the air rifle. One afternoon, Arnold, who was 15 years of age, was playing with his friends, Brent and Coleman. The three boys took turns firing the air rifle, which discharged small pellets, at various targets in Arnold's backyard. As Coleman was using the BB gun he fired a shot over Brent's head, intending to frighten him. The pellet missed Brent, but struck Fanny, the King's next-door neighbor, in the eye, severely injuring her.

61. Mrs. King is subsequently charged with violating the Columbia statute. As her defense, Mrs. King claims that she erroneously believed the statute prohibited firearms to be given or sold to minors under 15 years of age. If Mrs. King's mistaken belief is honestly held to have been made, it should

(A) result in her acquittal, because she didn't have the necessary mental state required for the crime
(B) result in her acquittal, if Coleman is 16 years of age or older
(C) not prevent her conviction, because mistake of law is no defense
(D) not prevent her conviction, because mistake of fact is no defense

## Question 62 is based on the following fact situation.

One morning in the laundromat, Duneberry approached Kirksey and said, "If you don't pay me $500.00 by July 2nd, I'll beat you to a pulp." A week later on July 2, Duneberry met Kirksey at a local bar, and demanded the money. Kirksey handed Duneberry the $500.00. After receiving the money, Duneberry then punched Kirksey in the stomach and hurriedly left the bar.

62. Under modern statutory law, Duneberry will most likely be found guilty of which of the following crimes?

(A) Extortion and battery
(B) Extortion and robbery
(C) Assault and battery
(D) Assault and robbery

# CRIMINAL LAW

## Question 63 is based on the following fact situation.

Marcia was walking past Goldblatt's Jewelry Store when she noticed a sign in the window which read:

> "Special Sale . . . Today Only! All Southwest Indian Jewelry (including Zuni, Navaho, and Apache rings, bracelets, and necklaces) . . . 50% Discount"

Upon reading the sale notice, Marcia entered the Jewelry store. She asked Mr. Goldblatt, the store's owner, if he had any Zuni bracelets with turquoise and mother-of-pearl inlay. Mr. Goldblatt answered affirmatively and showed Marcia two display trays of Zuni bracelets. As Marcia was looking at a few of the pieces, the telephone in the store began to ring. Mr. Goldblatt excused himself and walked to the rear of the store where he answered the telephone call. While Mr. Goldblatt was speaking on the phone, Marcia placed one of the bracelets in her pocketbook and walked a few feet toward the front door of the store. She was about to leave the store, without paying for the bracelet, when she suddenly noticed Clark, who was one of Mr. Goldblatt's employees. Thinking that Clark had seen her place the bracelet in her pocketbook, Marcia walked back to the counter and returned the bracelet to the display tray. In fact, neither Clark nor Mr. Goldblatt had seen Marcia take the bracelet.

63. If Marcia is subsequently prosecuted for larceny of the bracelet, she will most likely be found

(A) guilty, even though she returned the bracelet to the display tray
(B) guilty, only if Mr. Goldblatt or Clark had actually seen her place the bracelet in her pocketbook
(C) not guilty, because she returned the bracelet to the display tray
(D) not guilty, because she didn't leave the store with the bracelet in her possession

**Question 64 is based on the following fact situation.**

64. In which of the following situations would defendant most likely be found NOT GUILTY of robbery?

(A) On a dark alley in Center City, Defendant approached Lee and said, "Give me the gold ring on your finger or I'll shoot you with this gun." Lee gave him the ring. However, the ring really belonged to Herman, as Lee was just borrowing it for the evening to impress his girlfriend. In addition, the gun which defendant had in his possession was really a water pistol.

(B) Defendant broke into Gloria's house and took her stereo system. After he had placed the system in his car and was about to leave, Gloria came home and saw him. She raced to the car and started to hit Defendant through the open window in an attempt to get her stereo back. Defendant punched her in the nose and drove away with the system.

(C) Defendant was walking behind Mary in a shopping mall when he suddenly reached for her gold chain, pulled it from her neck and ran away into the crowds. Mary suffered a slight cut on her neck where the chain broke.

(D) Defendant picked the lock on Jerry's apartment door. The noise startled Jerry, who had been sleeping. Defendant overpowered Jerry, tied him up, and forced him to tell Defendant where he kept cash. Jerry told Defendant to look in the kitchen cabinet, which he did. Defendant found $120 in cash, took the money, and left the apartment.

**Question 65 is based on the following fact situation.**

Butler shot and killed Hadley at close range with a .22 caliber revolver. After the shooting death, Butler was arrested and charged with first degree murder. In this jurisdiction, first degree murder is defined as "knowingly or willfully causing the death of another human being."

65. Which of the following situations, if believed by the jury, would most likely result in Butler's acquittal of the first degree murder charge?

(A) Hadley, who was Butler's brother, suffered from an incurable case of cancer and asked Butler to kill him to put an end to his pain and suffering.

(B) Butler's killing was not done with premeditation or deliberation.

(C) Butler intended to kill himself, but the bullet grazed his head and struck and killed Hadley.

(D) Butler intended to kill Orlando, but Hadley unknowingly stepped in front of the intended victim and was struck and killed by the bullet.

**Questions 66–67 are based on the following fact situation.**

The Commonwealth of Mariposa has a statute prohibiting the sale of condoms and other contraceptive devices to any person under the age of 17. Violation of the statute is a misdemeanor punishable by a fine of not less than $500 or more than $5,000. The Mariposa courts have interpreted this statute as a public welfare offense requiring no particular mental state for its violation. As such, this is a strict liability crime whereby culpability is imposed on a defendant for doing the proscribed act.

Al Key, a recovering alcoholic, worked as a cashier at Thrifty Drug Store. Late on Saturday night while Al was working alone, he got the urge to have a drink. He opened a bottle of rum which the store sold and soon began drinking. A short time later, Al became inebriated and passed out. Not long thereafter, Nell Young, a 15-year-old, entered the store to purchase a package of condoms. He took a box of Trojans off the shelf and went to the cashier counter to pay for them. Seeing Al lying on the floor unconscious Neil left $3.95 (the exact price for the condoms) on the counter top and left the store.

66. If Al is prosecuted for violating the Mariposa statute, he should be found

(A) guilty, because since the offense does not require any mental state, Al's intoxication cannot be considered as a defense
(B) guilty, because Al's intoxication was voluntary
(C) not guilty, because A was unconscious
(D) not guilty, because Al's employer is vicariously liable for the violation that occurred

67. If Neil is prosecuted for violating the Mariposa statute, he should be found

(A) guilty, because he purchased the condoms while under the statutory age
(B) guilty, because the statute imposes absolute criminal liability
(C) not guilty, provided that he was unaware that the statute prohibited the sale of condoms to a person in his age group
(D) not guilty, provided that the legislative intent was not to make the purchase of condoms a criminal offense

## Question 68 is based on the following fact situation.

Late one night, Emmette, who had a long history of drug-related arrests, was attending a party at Calvin's house. During the party, Emmette approached Calvin and said, "I got some 'crank' and 'crack' to sell, you interested?" Calvin knew that "crank" was a street name for the narcotic methamphetamine, and "crack" was cocaine in its crystallized rock form. Calvin replied, "How much you charging?" Emmette said, "I'll sell you the 'crank' for $75 a gram and the 'crack' for $100 a gram." Calvin told Emmette that he wanted one gram of each. Emmette then went out to his car and brought back the drugs which he sold to Calvin. Immediately thereafter, Calvin, who was an undercover narcotics agent, arrested Emmette and charged him with conspiracy to sell narcotics and sale of narcotics. He was convicted of both crimes and given consecutive seven year sentences.

68. On appeal, Emmette's best argument is which of the following?

(A) There was no true agreement between him and Calvin and, hence, no conspiracy.
(B) There was no true agreement between him and Calvin and, hence, no sale.
(C) He cannot be convicted of both sale and conspiracy since each crime requires an agreement and, hence, each offense is essentially the same crime.
(D) He cannot be convicted of both sale and conspiracy because both crimes arose from the same criminal transaction, and, hence, imposition of consecutive sentences for each crime violates double jeopardy.

## Question 69 is based on the following fact situation.

Caveman Calhoun was a famous professional wrestler who stood 6 feet 6 inches and weighed 350 pounds. Caveman was married to Zoe Zeal, who was a vivacious former actress. Caveman was insanely jealous and often told Zoe that he would kill her if he ever found out that she was unfaithful. Unknown to Caveman, Zoe was having an affair with Allen Marcus.

Caveman and Zoe lived in Kansas City. One day Caveman told Zoe that he was flying to Chicago for a wrestling match and would return the following morning. After Caveman left the house, Zoe telephoned Marcus and told him to come over because Caveman was out of town. While Caveman was at the airport about to board his flight to Chicago, he learned that a blizzard had hit Chicago, causing cancellation of his wrestling match.

By this time, Marcus and Zoe were passionately making love and were unaware that anything was amiss. Caveman drove back home from the airport and unsuspectingly entered his house. He walked to the bedroom and upon opening the door saw Zoe and Marcus in bed together. Visibly upset, Caveman told Marcus, "Put your pants on and get the hell out of here." As Marcus was reaching for his pants, he pulled out a gun fearing that Caveman was about to attack him. When Caveman saw the gun, he jumped on Marcus and wrapped his monstrous arms around Marcus's neck. He angrily twisted his victim's neck, breaking it and killing Marcus.

69. Caveman is guilty for which, if any, of the following crimes?

(A) Murder
(B) Voluntary manslaughter
(C) Involuntary manslaughter
(D) None of the above

## Questions 70–71 are based on the following fact situation.

While on a camping trip, Foster became intoxicated and decided to take a walk late at night. He was so drunk he could not find his way back to the campsite. He did, however, come across a secluded mountain cabin, in which he decided to take shelter for the night. Since the door to the cabin was locked, he broke a window and entered the structure. Once inside, he fell asleep on the sofa. When he awoke the next morning he was hungry. Foster then found some food in the refrigerator which he cooked and ate. After fixing his breakfast, he inadvertently forgot to turn off the stove.

Before leaving the cabin, Foster looked around to see if there was anything worth stealing. He opened the door of the bedroom and found a gold watch on the nightstand. He placed the watch in his pocket and left the cabin.

70. If Foster is arrested and charged with burglary, under the common law, his best defense(s) would be that

I. He was drunk when he broke into the cabin.
II. The crime was not completed until the morning hours.
III. He had no intent to commit a felony at the time of the breaking and entering.
IV. The cabin was empty when he entered it.

(A) I and II
(B) III and IV
(C) I and III
(D) II and III

71. Assume for the purposes of this question only that a gas leak occurred, causing the stove (which Foster left on) to start a fire. If Foster is charged with arson, under common law he will be found

    (A) guilty, since the fire resulted from the commission of a felony
    (B) guilty, if Foster was criminally negligent
    (C) not guilty, since Foster did not commit a felony
    (D) not guilty, since arson requires the presence of malice

## Question 72 is based on the following fact situation.

Fanny Feingold, an elderly 89-year-old woman, lived in Miami Beach. Fanny, whose only source of income was her $428 monthly social security check, lived in a dilapidated rooming house located next to Wolfie's Liquor Store. Each month, Fanny would cash her social security check at the liquor store. Wolfie, the proprietor, knew Fanny very well. She had been a frequent customer for over 20 years. After operating the liquor store since 1954, Wolfie decided to sell the business to Juan. Unaware that Juan was the new owner, Fanny entered the store and tried to cash her social security check one morning. Juan told Fanny that he was sorry but it was his policy not to cash any more social security checks. Terribly upset, Fanny reached into her pocketbook and said, "Listen, buddy, I've got a bomb in here, and, if you don't give me the money, I'm going to blow this joint to smithereens." Actually, Fanny did not have a bomb in her possession. Juan, who was not deceived by her threat, felt sorry for Fanny and gave her $428 in cash. Fanny, who walked with the assistance of a cane, took the money and limped out the store. After she left, Juan noticed that Fanny had not endorsed the check.

72. Fanny has committed which, if any, of the following crimes?

    (A) No crime
    (B) Robbery
    (C) Attempted robbery
    (D) Theft by false pretenses

## Questions 73–75 are based on the following fact situation.

Will Mington was holding his sixth annual Halloween party at his home, in the city of Widener. His parties attracted a wide variety of diverse individuals. On the night in question, Dunebar and his pal Russ were loafing at the Village Pub, when a number of the invited guests came in to purchase spirits for Will's party. Dunebar and Russ decided to "crash." They hurried to Dunebar's house, threw on white sheets and arrived at Will's house around midnight when the party was in full swing. They came in the front door, which was unlocked and easily mingled with the costumed partygoers.

During the merriment, Dunebar and Ross wandered through the house and came upon Miss Maudine, Will's national champion Old English Sheepdog and her five-week-old puppies in a third floor bedroom. Dunebar and Russ had read about Miss Maudine's champion puppies in the *Widener Bugle*. They each picked up two of the pups with the idea of holding them for ransom.

As they were descending the stairs with the pups hidden under their sheets, Will heard the puppies yelping. Will, in his Detective Marlowe costume, confronted them and asked to see what was under their sheets. Dunebar then grabbed one of the pups by the throat, held it in front of Will, and said, "If you don't get out of the way, I'm gonna choke this pup to death." Rick Rookie, an off-duty policeman who was attending the party, overheard Dunebar's threat, drew his service revolver and exclaimed,

"Don't move or I'll shoot!" Dunebar, thinking the gun to be a toy pistol, rushed for the front door. Rick fired at the fleeing Dunebar, fatally wounding him.

73. At common law, if Russ is subsequently charged with burglary, he will probably be found

   (A) guilty, since he and Dunebar "crashed" the party
   (B) guilty, since he intended to hold the puppies for ransom
   (C) not guilty, since he and Dunebar "crashed" the party only to have a good time
   (D) not guilty, since the front door was unlocked

74. Russ should be charged with which of the following crimes?

   (A) larceny and conspiracy
   (B) larceny, conspiracy, and kidnapping
   (C) larceny, conspiracy, and attempted extortion
   (D) robbery, conspiracy, and attempted extortion

75. On these facts, if Rick Rookie is charged with Dunebar's murder, he should be found

   (A) guilty
   (B) not guilty, since the killing constituted justifiable homicide
   (C) not guilty, since the killing constituted excusable homicide
   (D) not guilty, since Rookie warned Dunebar before he fired his gun

## Question 76 is based on the following fact situation.

Anita had been spreading rumors around town that Leslie was a lesbian. After Carol informed Leslie about these rumors, Leslie was furious and decided that she would teach Anita to keep her mouth shut. Late that night Leslie went over to Anita's house with the intent to punch Anita in the mouth. When Leslie arrived at Anita's home, she peered into the bedroom window and saw Anita asleep in the bed. Leslie proceeded to pry open the bedroom window and climbed inside. Leslie then grabbed Anita, who had awakened and shouted, "This will teach you not to spread nasty rumors about me," after which Leslie punched Anita in the face and hurriedly fled from the home. The force of the blow fractured Anita's jaw and caused her to bleed profusely. Unable to procure any medical assistance, Anita died shortly thereafter from loss of blood.

76. If Leslie *is* subsequently prosecuted for burglary, at common law she will most likely be found

   (A) guilty, since she broke into Anita's home at night with the intent to commit a felony therein
   (B) guilty, since Anita died as a result of the blow inflicted by Leslie
   (C) not guilty, since Leslie did not intend to kill Anita
   (D) not guilty, since Leslie did not intend to commit a felony at the time of the breaking and entry

## Question 77 is based on the following fact situation.

77. In which situation below would the actions of Defendant(s) constitute a burglary at Common Law?

(A) Defendant, seeking shelter from a severe snowstorm, broke into Jones's house. When he awoke the next morning, Defendant noticed a transistor radio which he had put into his pocket before fleeing Jones's house.

(B) Defendant was walking past Smith's home at approximately 9:00 P.M. when he saw Smith sitting in a chair near the window. Angered at Smith for "stealing" his former girlfriend's affections, Defendant picked up a large brick which was lying nearby on the ground, and hurled it through the window, intending to kill Smith.

(C) Late one afternoon, Defendants were walking down Spruce Street when they noticed an open window in Dr. Malloy's office. Defendants crawled through the window, broke open his medicine cabinet, and stole hypodermic needles and a jar of amphetamines.

(D) Late one evening as Roger was registering at the Ben Franklin Hotel, Defendants noticed that he was carrying a large "wad" of money in his wallet. After Roger had retired to his room and was asleep, Defendants broke into his room at 7:00 A.M., took his wallet out of his pants pocket, and fled.

## Question 78 is based on the following fact situation.

Swenson Swine was a flamboyant gigolo who preyed upon wealthy women. One day Swenson had the good fortune of being introduced to Babs Button, an heiress to a $900,000,000 family inheritance. Babs was enamored by Swenson's charm and accepted his dinner invitation at L'Heritage, the city's most expensive restaurant. Hoping to impress Babs, Swenson went so far as to lease a Rolls Royce Corniche for the evening. He picked Babs up in his rented Rolls and drove to L'Heritage, where they had a delightful dinner. After a dessert featuring cherries jubilee, Swenson was handed the check which totaled $749.87. Realizing he didn't have enough money to pay the bill, Swenson excused himself and went to the men's room. While he pondered his predicament, Swenson decided to set fire to the wastepaper in a trash container. He hoped that the fire would serve as a diversion so he could run out of the restaurant without paying. He set fire to the wastepaper and then went back to his table. As he anxiously waited, Allen Smithee, the maitre d', grabbed Swenson and told him that he had seen what occurred in the bathroom. Allen, who had been seated in a bathroom stall, saw Swenson set the fire through a crack in the door. Allen extinguished the fire which had charred a portion of the ceiling. He then detained Swenson until the police arrived. This jurisdiction defines arson as the malicious burning of any structure.

78. If charged with arson, Swenson should be found

   (A) guilty, if the jury determines that he was reckless as to the restaurant being damaged by fire
   (B) guilty, because he set the fire for the purpose of committing an unlawful act, i.e., larceny by trick for non-payment of the dinner
   (C) not guilty of arson or attempted arson, unless the jury finds that he intended to burn the restaurant
   (D) not guilty of arson but guilty of attempted arson

## Question 79 is based on the following fact situation.

Frankie Flame was charged with felony murder as a result of his setting fire to Abby Cadabra's house. Abby was upstairs sleeping when the fire was set, and he died in his bedroom during the fire.

79. If Frankie can prove the facts to support his defense, which of the following assertions would *least likely* remove liability for felony murder?

   (A) Frankie did not intend to kill Abby.
   (B) Frankie was insane when he set the fire.
   (C) Frankie was coerced by another to set the fire.
   (D) Abby died of a heart attack before the fire spread to his bedroom.

## Question 80 is based on the following fact situation.

Husband and Wife were chronic alcoholics. One afternoon Husband drank a fifth of Jack Daniels bourbon and was stone-drunk when Wife returned home from work. When Wife saw Husband's condition, she got very angry because they had planned to go out to dinner and celebrate their 10th wedding anniversary. While Husband was passed out on the living room couch, Wife decided to fix herself a martini, a cocktail consisting of gin and a twist of lemon. After drinking two martinis, Wife became extremely inebriated. A short while later, Wife began preparing a third martini and tried to slice a lemon for the drink. As she did so, the knife slipped and she severely cut her hand. With blood gushing from the wound, Wife called Husband to help her. He momentarily awoke, stood up but fell back on the couch. He failed to render any assistance, and Wife bled to death.

80. If Husband is subsequently charged with manslaughter, he will be found

   (A) guilty, because he owed Wife a duty to assist her
   (B) guilty, because criminal negligent conduct cannot be negated by voluntary intoxication
   (C) not guilty, because Wife caused her own injury
   (D) not guilty, if he was physically unable to assist her

## Question 81 is based on the following fact situation.

The Ames Penal Code provides:

"Section 21. An assault is an unlawful attempt, with or without present ability, to commit a battery on the person of another. It is a misdemeanor punishable by imprisonment of up to 6 months."

Harry Sapiens was a lawyer who worked in the law firm of Scylla and Charybdis, located in Amityville, Ames. Harry, who had a reputation of being a prankster, decided to play a practical joke on Seymour Scylla, the senior partner of the law firm. Harry donned a cowboy mask and entered Mr. Scylla's office. As Mr. Scylla was talking on the phone with his back to the door, Harry pulled out a toy cap gun and said, "This is a stickup. Give me your wallet or I shoot." When Mr. Scylla turned around to face Harry, he pulled the trigger of the gun. This caused the toy pistol to make a loud noise, but Mr. Scylla was not struck by anything.

Although Mr. Scylla was not frightened, he fired Harry because of the incident citing unprofessional conduct. Harry was subsequently charged with criminal assault under the above mentioned penal code statute. At trial, Harry testified that he was only playing a practical joke on Mr. Scylla and was trying to scare him as a harmless prank.

81. If the jury believes Harry, they should find him

   (A) guilty, because he intended to frighten Mr. Scylla
   (B) guilty, because the statute does not require the present ability to commit a battery
   (C) not guilty, because Harry did not intend to cause physical injury to Mr. Scylla
   (D) not guilty, because the facts state that Mr. Scylla was not frightened

## Questions 82–83 are based on the following fact situation.

Hayden, a first year student at Georgia Law School, worked as a part-time law clerk at the prestigious firm of Foote, Ball, & White. He was permitted to borrow law books and legal treatises to take home for his own personal use. One afternoon Hayden was preparing a brief in the firm's law library when he noticed a book entitled *Promiscuity in Law School* lying on the conference table. Making sure no one was watching him, he took the book and placed it in his attache case. He planned to take the book home that night with the intention of not returning it.

A short while later, Hayden was about to leave the law office when he was stopped by Chandler, an associate in the firm, who asked him to open his attache case. Chandler explained that some files from the law office had been stolen. As a result, he was conducting a "spot check" of employees to determine who was responsible for the thefts. Startled, Hayden refused to permit Chandler to look in his attache case. Hayden said that he had just purchased a new issue of "Hustler" magazine and he was embarrassed to have Chandler see it. Having his suspicions aroused, Chandler raised his clenched fist and exclaimed, "Bullshit! If you don't hand over that (bleep) attache case, I'm going to bust you in the mouth." Hayden, who unknown to Chandler, suffered from a serious heart condition, had a seizure and died as a result of fright produced by the threatened attack.

82. Which of the following is the most serious crime of which Chandler should be found guilty?

   (A) Assault
   (B) Voluntary manslaughter
   (C) Involuntary manslaughter
   (D) Murder

83. Assume for the purposes of this question only that Hayden did *not* die as a result of fright produced by the threatened attack. If Hayden is subsequently charged with larceny of the book, which of the following claims, if true, would LEAST aid him in his defense?

(A) Since the law firm had failed to give him his salary for two weeks, he took the book as security for the debt.
(B) He intended to return the book after reading it.
(C) Chandler had given him possession of the book.
(D) Chandler had given him custody of the book.

**Questions 84–85 are based on the following fact situation.**

Kimberly Lacy was a young aspiring actress who had recently redomiciled in California after graduating high school in Alpine, Texas. One afternoon, she received a telephone call from her agent, Marvin Masterson, who invited her to dinner to discuss a new film contract. Kimberly agreed to meet Masterson at her favorite Beverly Hills sushi (Japanese raw fish) restaurant "Tokyo" later that evening.

When Kimberly arrived, she parked her car, a 1967 Chevrolet Impala convertible, at the Rodeo Parking Co. lot across the street from "Tokyo." The parking attendant directed Kimberly to leave her keys in the car and he handed her a receipt stub as she left. At "Tokyo," Kimberly and Marvin discussed her new movie role while enjoying their favorite dishes of halibut sashimi, quail eggs with uni (sea urchin), and salmon skin handrolls. After Kimberly agreed to accept her new acting role, Marvin accompanied Kimberly to the Rodeo Parking Co. lot.

Kimberly handed her receipt to the attendant who informed her that the parking charge would be $14. Visibly irate, she told the attendant that $14 was much too high for a two-hour parking fee. At which point, the parking attendant told Kimberly that unless she paid the $14, he could not return her car. She adamantly refused to pay the $14, and Marvin drove Kimberly home in his car.

When they arrived at her home, Marvin suggested that they could return to the parking lot after it had closed and regain possession of the car with a spare set of keys. Kimberly agreed that Marvin's suggestion was a great idea, and they returned to the parking lot later that same evening after it had closed. With her spare set of keys, Kimberly entered the car and then drove it home.

84. If Kimberly is subsequently charged under a relevant state statute with larceny, she will most likely be found

(A) guilty, because she failed to pay the $14 before regaining possession of her car
(B) guilty, since she was under a binding contractual obligation to pay the parking fee
(C) not guilty, because the $14 charge was excessively high
(D) not guilty, because Kimberly cannot be charged with larceny of her own motor vehicle

85. If Marvin is subsequently prosecuted, he could most appropriately be found

(A) guilty of larceny, but not conspiracy to commit larceny
(B) guilty of conspiracy to commit larceny, but not larceny
(C) guilty of both larceny and conspiracy to commit larceny
(D) not guilty of either larceny or conspiracy to commit larceny

## Question 86 is based on the following fact situation.

Morris was at a bar drinking beer when he started conversing with Jill who was seated at the next bar stool. During the course of their conversation, Jill told Morris that she was just laid off her job and desperately needed money to pay her rent. Morris, a practical joker, pointed to a nearby coat rack and said, "Hey, see that fur coat there. Why don't you take it?" Morris then told Jill that he would cause a disturbance to distract attention while she ran out the bar with the coat. Believing that it was a good idea, Jill agreed to take part in the scheme.

Thereupon, Morris lit a matchbook and threw it on top of the bar. He then yelled, "Fire…the bar's on fire, help!" When everyone turned to look at Morris, Jill ran to the back of the bar, took the fur coat, and scurried outside unnoticed. Just as Jill left the bar and was running down the sidewalk, she was apprehended and arrested by a police officer. Later, Morris confessed that the fur coat that Jill took really belonged to him.

86. With respect to Morris and Jill's criminal liability, which of the following is most correct?

   (A) Morris and Jill are guilty of conspiracy and larceny.
   (B) Morris and Jill are guilty of larceny.
   (C) Jill is guilty of larceny.
   (D) Morris and Jill are not guilty of either conspiracy or larceny.

## Question 87 is based on the following fact situation.

Jay Johnstone, a baseball card dealer, lived in Vancouver. He agreed to sell an extremely rare card of Babe Ruth from a 1933 Goudy collection to Richie Hebner for $8,000. Hebner lived in Portland which was located 70 miles from Vancouver. As part of their agreement, Dee Liver, a courier, was hired to pick up the card from Johnstone and transport it to Hebner. He was then to get the purchase money from Hebner and bring it back to Johnstone.

But rather than entrusting the genuine Ruth card to Liver, Johnstone gave him a counterfeit replica that was valueless. After picking up the envelope containing the facsimile, Liver left Johnstone's home and embarked on his trip to Portland. The Vancouver police, however, received a tip concerning the scheme and intercepted Liver's car before he left the city limits. Thereafter, Johnstone was arrested and charged with attempting to obtain property by false pretenses.

87. If, in a common law jurisdiction, Johnstone contends that the scheme had not progressed far enough to constitute an attempt, it will

   (A) be to his advantage to claim that Liver was his accomplice and was participating in the scheme to receive a share of the proceeds
   (B) be to his advantage to claim that Liver knew nothing of the scheme but was simply an innocent courier hired by Johnstone to make the delivery
   (C) be to his advantage to claim that Liver knew nothing of the scheme but was simply an innocent courier hired by Hebner to make the delivery
   (D) make no difference whether Liver was Johnstone's accomplice or was an innocent agent

## Questions 88–89 are based on the following fact situation.

After Wife found out about Husband's infidelity, she decided to have him killed. Wife approached Cain to solicit his assistance in carrying out the planned murder. Although Wife believed that Cain was a "hit man" for the Mafia, he in fact was an FBI agent investigating organized crime.

Wife told Cain she would pay him $10,000 if he accepted the job and then pay him an additional $10,000 after the killing was completed. Upon hearing Wife's proposal, Cain manifested his complete concurrence in the scheme and expressed his willingness to participate. However, Cain secretly intended not to go through with the plan and he merely feigned agreement because he wished to trap Wife. Wife told Cain she would deliver the first payment the next day. But before making the initial payment, Wife learned that Cain was really an FBI agent. Fearful that she might be prosecuted for planning Husband's murder, Wife contacted the police and renunciated her participation in the criminal endeavor.

88.  At common law, Wife will most likely be found

(A) guilty of solicitation
(B) guilty of conspiracy to commit murder
(C) guilty of solicitation and conspiracy to commit murder
(D) not guilty of either solicitation or conspiracy to commit murder because under the circumstances she manifested a complete renunciation of her criminal intent

89.  Assume for the purposes of this question only that after Wife approached Cain to murder Husband, Cain refused any involvement in the contemplated crime. Wife became angry at Cain and she hired Abel to beat him up. Before the planned attack, Wife discovered that Cain was an FBI agent. Afraid she might be prosecuted for a federal offense, Wife reported the planned attack (on Cain) to federal authorities. If Wife is subsequently charged with the statutory offense of conspiring to commit an assault on a federal officer, Wife will probably be

(A) convicted, because Wife's knowledge that Cain was an FBI agent is not a material element of the crime
(B) convicted, because withdrawal is never recognized as an affirmative defense to conspiracy
(C) acquitted, because Wife was unaware that Cain was an FBI agent
(D) acquitted, because Wife's abandonment of the plan aborted the conspiratorial objective

## Question 90 is based on the following fact situation.

Wilson, an employee of Royal's Electronic Discount Outlet, stole a Texas Instrument programming computer from the store's warehouse. Wilson then sold the computer, which retailed for $1,650, to Brett for $325. When Brett received the computer, it was still in its original Texas Instrument carton.

90. Brett is subsequently prosecuted for receiving stolen property. At trial, Brett claims that he didn't know the computer was stolen. The defendant will likely be

   (A) acquitted, if the jury determines that Brett's belief that the computer was not stolen was reasonable
   (B) acquitted, if the jury determines that Brett's belief that the computer was not stolen was honest, even though unreasonable
   (C) convicted, because the purchaser of stolen property at a price well below its market value raises a presumption of guilt
   (D) convicted, if the jury determines that Brett did not believe the computer was stolen because such a belief would have been unreasonable

## Question 91 is based on the following fact situation.

Defendant entered the Brandywine Tavern and ordered a beer. Bartender politely told Defendant he would have to wait until two other patrons were served. Defendant became irate and pulled out a small penknife. Although Defendant intended only to frighten Bartender, he accidentally nicked Bartender's arm with the penknife. Bartender's arm became infected and he died from gangrene two months later.

91. The most serious crime which Defendant can be convicted of is

   (A) battery
   (B) involuntary manslaughter
   (C) assault with a deadly weapon
   (D) murder

## Question 92 is based on the following fact situation.

92. Under which of the following situations would defendant *not* be guilty of the attempted crime at common law?

   (A) Fence received an anonymous call from undercover detectives who informed him that they wanted to dispose of several pieces of diamond jewelry, which were reportedly stolen from the DuPee family collection. Unbeknownst to Fence, the police had recovered the stolen jewelry the previous day. When Fence "purchased" the goods, he was immediately arrested and charged with attempt to receive stolen property.
   (B) Shuffles was dancing with his girlfriend Sheila at a local disco when Sheila collapsed in his arms. Shuffles then carried Sheila to his car and engaged in sexual intercourse with her. Although Shuffles believed that Sheila was intoxicated, she had, in fact, actually died of a heart attack while dancing. Shuffles is charged with attempted rape.
   (C) After a preliminary examination, Doc informed Audrey that she was two months pregnant. Although Doc knew that abortions were illegal in this jurisdiction, he agreed to perform an abortion on Audrey anyway. During the operation, it was discovered that Audrey was not even pregnant. Doc is charged with attempt to perform an illegal abortion.

(D) Reefer called Joey to obtain some marijuana. Although Joey did not have any marijuana in his possession, he told Reefer that he had some dynamite "Panama Red" for sale. Believing that Joey had some high quality "grass," Reefer purchased an ounce of the substance, which he did not know was actually oregano. While Reefer was smoking a "joint" of the innocuous weed on the street corner, Cop arrested him and charged him with attempted illegal use of a narcotic substance.

## Question 93 is based on the following fact situation.

93. Under which of the following situations would criminal liability LEAST likely be imposed on Defendant-accomplice?

(A) Defendant is an operator of a telephone answering service with positive knowledge that one of his clients was using his service to facilitate the illegal distribution of cocaine.

(B) Defendant is a service station attendant who knew that the buyer of gasoline was using his product to make Molotov cocktails for terroristic use.

(C) The Defendant is a hotel registration clerk who knew that one of his "regular" guests was using her room for purposes of prostitution.

(D) Defendant is owner of a car which he permits Drunk, whom he knows to be intoxicated, to drive. As a consequence, Drunk is involved in an accident which causes Victim's death.

## Question 94 is based on the following fact situation.

Elvis and his girlfriend Priscilla broke into Bobby's house late at night with intent to steal his stereo system. Although they believed that Bobby was away on a business trip, actually he was sleeping in an upstairs bedroom. While they were inside the house, Priscilla announced that she had changed her mind and urged Elvis to leave.

Bobby, who was awakened by the noise downstairs, descended the staircase to investigate. Upon seeing Bobby, Priscilla again urged Elvis to flee. Instead Elvis attacked Bobby and tied him up with a rope. Thereupon, Elvis and Priscilla departed with Bobby's stereo equipment. After they left, Bobby choked to death from the ropes while trying to free himself.

Priscilla and Elvis were charged with murder but were acquitted. Thereafter, Priscilla was apprehended and prosecuted for felony murder.

94. Which of the following is Priscilla's best argument for acquittal?

(A) The acquittal of Priscilla and Elvis precludes any subsequent prosecution under the doctrine of res judicata.

(B) Bobby's suicidal effort to free himself was a supervening cause of death.

(C) Since Priscilla changed her mind, she cannot be found guilty of burglary.

(D) Priscilla withdrew from the commission of the underlying felony of burglary.

# CRIMINAL LAW

## Questions 95–96 are based on the following fact situation.

Quentin Waverly, a wealthy playboy, incurred heavy gambling losses to Bookie as a result of his "passion for the ponies." Short of cash, Quentin sought his Uncle Moneybags's help. When Uncle Moneybags refused to loan his irresponsible nephew any money, Quentin decided to "get even." One morning as Maid was preparing Uncle Moneybags's breakfast, Quentin stealthily entered the kitchen, and unnoticed, dropped arsenic poisoning into the teapot from which his Uncle was always served his tea. Quentin then hurriedly left the house and went to play golf. Shortly thereafter, Maid served Uncle Moneybags the poisoned tea, thus causing his unfortunate death.

95. Quentin's culpability for Uncle Money-bags's death would most probably be as a (an)

(A) accessory before the fact
(B) principal in the first degree
(C) principal in the second degree
(D) none of the above

96. If Maid is prosecuted for administering the arsenic poisoning, she will most likely be held responsible as a (an)

(A) principal in the first degree
(B) principal in the second degree
(C) accessory after the fact
(D) none of the above

## Question 97 is based on the following fact situation.

One evening, Steve received a telephone call from an unidentified source who informed him that his (Steve's) wife was having an affair with Reggie. As a result, Steve drove to Reggie's house with a loaded shotgun. Believing that Reggie was in an upstairs bedroom, Steve fired the shotgun through the dining room window. Although Steve did not intend to harm Reggie, he discharged the firearm in order "to teach the bastard a lesson." Unbeknownst to Steve, Reggie's wife, Lavender, was in the dining room and suffered a minor gunshot wound.

97. If Lavender recovers from her injuries, Steve should be found

(A) guilty of attempted murder of Lavender only
(B) guilty of attempted murder of Reggie only
(C) guilty of attempted murder of both Reggie and Lavender
(D) not guilty of attempted murder of either Reggie or Lavender

## Question 98 is based on the following fact situation.

Penny Sherwood worked as a patent attorney in the San Francisco law firm of Montana, Maldonano, and Mullins. Late one evening, she left the office and walked outside to her car. While in the parking lot, she noticed a gold Rolex watch lying on the ground. When Penny picked it up, she immediately identified the watch as belonging to Miller X. Mullins, the senior partner in her law firm. She took it home with her, intending to return it the next day. The following morning, however, Penny decided to keep Mullins's watch and did so.

98. In a common law jurisdiction, Penny has committed

(A) larceny only
(B) embezzlement only
(C) both larceny and embezzlement
(D) neither larceny nor embezzlement

## Questions 99–101 are based on the following fact situation.

It was raining hard in Fresno one evening as Harry, a cab driver, was looking for one last passenger. Sue flagged him down and directed him to take her to her home at 16 Parkside Lane. Harry recognized Sue as a former girlfriend, and Sue invited him into her house when they arrived.

Unknown to Harry, Sue was an undercover police officer who worked in the sex crimes unit. When they were inside Sue's house, Sue made sexual advances toward Harry, who responded by kissing her and holding her hand. Sue was about to kiss Harry again, when she got up to answer the phone in the kitchen.

While she was on the phone, Harry picked up Sue's solid gold ring that she had carelessly left on the living room table. Harry planned to take the ring to a jeweler the next week and return it to Sue with a diamond in it, in appreciation for her hospitality. He put it into his pocket and got ready to leave.

As he left her house, Harry reminded Sue that she had not yet paid her fare of $2.50. She handed Harry a $20.00 bill and said, "Harry, keep the change."

Before Harry reached the garage and returned the cab, he stopped into a bar. There he met a shady-looking character, Bob, who offered to sell him a two-month-old color TV for $50.00. Bob said that he would take only cash and that he also had some unboxed silverware and jewelry he could sell Harry from his van, which was parked outside. Bob said, "You better decide fast, because I've got to get out of town right away." Harry, who knew that the TV was worth $500.00, gave Bob $50.00 and Bob gave Harry the TV, which was not in a box. Bob did not tell Harry that he had just stolen the television from a house down the street.

99. If Harry is subsequently arrested and charged with attempted rape of Sue, he should be found:

(A) not guilty
(B) not guilty, solely because he was entrapped
(C) not guilty, if he raises the proper alibi defense
(D) not guilty, if he was predisposed to commit the crime

100. Based on the above facts, for which of the following crime(s) should Harry be convicted?

(A) Battery upon Sue and larceny of the ring
(B) Larceny of the ring
(C) Embezzlement of the ring
(D) Receiving stolen property

101. Assume that in his trial for attempted rape of Sue, Harry takes the witness stand and testifies that Sue gave him a ride that evening in her car and forced him to go to her house. Harry's testimony may be used in a subsequent trial as evidence that Harry committed the crime of

    (A) misprision of felony
    (B) misprision
    (C) perjury
    (D) compounding a felony

## Question 102 is based on the following fact situation.

Late one evening while Dr. and Mrs. Winston were away on vacation, several members of the Purple Gang, a right wing pro-gun organization, entered the Winstons' home through a broken basement window. The gang knew that Dr. Winston was a collector of antique weapons. After ransacking the house, they found Dr. Winston's prize collection of Revolutionary War guns. They then wrapped the guns in two of the Winstons' Oriental rugs and hurriedly left the house.

Upon returning from their vacation the Winstons notified the police of the theft. During the investigation, Richard Tracy, Chief of Detectives, received a "hot tip" that the guns could be found in an old abandoned warehouse on the riverfront. When the police entered the warehouse, they found Harvey Ringer, the famous "Catman" burglar, with the guns. Upon questioning, Harvey told the police that he had planned to dispose of the guns through Foxy Fields. With Dr. Winston's consent, the police authorized Harvey to deliver the guns to Foxy and sell them for $10,000. As soon as Foxy paid Harvey and took possession of the guns, the police arrested him.

102. With which of the following crimes should Harvey Ringer be convicted of?

    (A) Larceny
    (B) Possession of stolen property
    (C) Burglary and receiving stolen property
    (D) Burglary and possession of stolen goods

## Question 103 is based on the following fact situation.

Keefe Kenworth drove to Madison Square Garden to see the Westminister Dog Show. Keefe parked his car on the street two blocks from the Garden. While he was inside the arena watching the show, Grayson Gotti stole the car and drove it to Coney Island. Grayson planned to take the car to a deserted warehouse and strip the vehicle. While he was driving Keefe's car, the brakes suddenly failed and the auto veered out of control. The car jumped the sidewalk and crashed into a home owned by Eva Evert, causing extensive damage to the dwelling.

Grayson was arrested and charged with larceny and the separate crime of malicious destruction of property. At trial, the prosecution and the defense both stipulated that the malfunctioning of the car's brakes caused it to veer out of control and damage Eva's home.

103. Assume that Grayson is convicted of larceny for the theft of Keefe's car. With respect to the second charge of malicious destruction of property, he should be found

    (A) not guilty, because the malice requirement is not satisfied since the destruction resulted from the car's malfunctioning
    (B) not guilty, because malicious destruction of property is a lesser included offense of larceny
    (C) guilty, because malice can be inferred from Grayson's intent to steal
    (D) guilty, because malicious destruction of property is a general-intent crime

## Questions 104–106 are based on the following fact situation.

Zoe was caught in a thunderstorm while walking down Main Street in the city of Tampa. As Zoe was about to open an umbrella that she was carrying, Wesley, a stranger to Zoe, came up to her, snatched the umbrella out of Zoe's hand, and said, "You thief! That's my umbrella." Enraged by being accosted in such a manner, Zoe grabbed for the umbrella with one hand and pushed Wesley with the other. Wesley held on to the umbrella but fell over backwards onto the sidewalk, which was wet and slippery. As he fell over, the umbrella swung out and hit Xavier, another stranger, who had seen Wesley grab the umbrella and, thinking that Wesley was a thief, was coming to Zoe's aid. Xavier fell to the ground and was knocked unconscious when his head hit the sidewalk. When Zoe saw Wesley and Xavier hit the ground, she calmed down, she decided the umbrella was not worth all the commotion, and walked off.

A few moments later, Wesley got up in a daze and stepped into the gutter, where he was struck by a car driven by Dodge, who was passing another car on the right in violation of a regulation of the State Department of Motor Vehicles. Wesley died in the hospital two hours later.

Xavier regained consciousness and walked home, vowing never to act as a good samaritan again. The umbrella which Zoe had been carrying did in fact belong to Wesley, whose initials, "W.W." (for Wesley Walker), appeared on the shaft. Zoe had mistaken the umbrella for her own in a restaurant where she had lunch earlier in the day. She didn't realize her mistake until the next day when she returned to the restaurant and found her umbrella still lying there against the wall.

104. Which of the following is the most serious crime for which Zoe could be found guilty?

(A) Battery
(B) Larceny
(C) Involuntary manslaughter
(D) No crime

105. Which of the following is the most serious crime for which Dodge should be found guilty?

(A) Motor vehicle violation
(B) Involuntary manslaughter
(C) Voluntary manslaughter
(D) Murder

106. According to the "alter ego" rule, which of the following statements is correct with respect to the amount of force that Xavier was entitled to use in Zoe's defense?

   I. Xavier was justified in using reasonable force in Zoe's defense since he reasonably believed that she was in immediate danger of unlawful bodily harm from Wesley.
  II. Not knowing the true facts, Xavier was not justified in using force to protect Zoe because Wesley was privileged to recapture his umbrella.
 III. Since Xavier did not stand in any personal relationship with Zoe (e.g., husband, parent, relative, etc.) he was not justified in using force in her defense.

(A) I only
(B) II only
(C) III only
(D) Either II or III but not I

# CRIMINAL LAW

## Question 107 is based on the following fact situation.

The Commonwealth of Meridian has the following criminal statute in effect:

> "A person is not responsible for criminal conduct if at the time of such conduct, as a result of mental disease or defect, he lacks substantial capacity to appreciate the wrongfulness of his conduct, or to conform his conduct to the requirements of law."

One afternoon, Kermit was babysitting for his five-year-old nephew, Lonnie. As they were playing catch outside, Kermit threw the ball over Lonnie's head and it rolled into the street. Instinctively, Lonnie ran after the ball but tripped over the gutter and fell in the street. When he tripped, Lonnie severely sprained his ankle and couldn't stand up. Moments later, a large garbage truck was backing up and ran over Lonnie, killing him. Although Kermit saw Lonnie's predicament, he made no effort to rescue him.

Subsequently, Kermit was charged with involuntary manslaughter. At trial, Kermit testified that he was so shocked when he saw Lonnie fall near the garbage truck that he froze and was unable to move until it was too late. Following Kermit's testimony, an expert witness testified for the defense that reactions of the sort described by Kermit are not unusual when a truly shocking event occurs.

107. If the jury believes the testimony of Kermit and his expert witness, Kermit's best defense is which of the following?

   (A) Kermit was suffering from temporary insanity.
   (B) Kermit lacked the requisite mental state required for the commission of the crime.
   (C) Kermit's failure to act was not voluntary.
   (D) Kermit's criminal liability was superseded by that of the truck driver.

## Question 108 is based on the following fact situation.

The city of West Covina has enacted an anti-noise statute that "prohibits amplification devices operated in public places which emit loud and raucous noises." The municipality passed the law to protect the quiet and tranquility of its residents and to avoid distractions to traffic.

Tupac Tulane, a high school senior, was driving in his Jeep Cherokee listening to music from a CD player that was situated in the back of his vehicle. As Tupac drove past West Covina High School, he turned up the volume to its highest level. He was listening to a rap song from Notorious B.I.G. when a police car drove alongside. Hearing the "loud and raucous" music, the police officers arrested Tupac and charged him with violating the anti-noise statute.

Before Tupac was brought to trial, the state Supreme Court ruled the West Covina noise amplification statute unconstitutional as vague and overbroad. As a result, the charges against Tupac were dropped and his case was dismissed. Thereafter, the West Covina District Attorney's office decided to prosecute Tupac for violating a state attempt statute.

The attempt statute provided that legal impossibility was no defense. Thereupon, Tupac was charged with attempting to violate the anti-noise statute. At trial, Tupac took the stand to testify in his own behalf. He testified that when he was arrested, he had purposely turned up the sound of his CD device to its highest decibel level because "Give Me the Loot," his favorite song of Notorious B.I.G., was playing.

108. Will Tupac be found guilty of violating the attempt statute?

(A) Yes, because he possessed the requisite intent to turn up his CD player to a loud noise level.
(B) Yes, because dismissal of the initial charge was not a final judgment and, therefore, double jeopardy does not attach.
(C) No, because double jeopardy precludes prosecution for attempt after the initial prosecution was dismissed.
(D) No, because a defendant cannot be retried for attempted commission of a crime that has been ruled unconstitutional by a state Supreme Court.

**Question 109 is based on the following fact situation.**

Wilber deserted his wife Henrietta in August 1977. A month later, Henrietta was notified by World Airways of her husband's death in an airplane crash in the Pacific Ocean. All passengers aboard were reported lost at sea and presumably drowned. Henrietta, after making diligent inquiries in good faith, became convinced that her husband was dead. Three years later she married Sam. A few months after her re-marriage, the newspaper announced that Wilber had been found on a deserted Pacific island and was rescued. Henrietta was then prosecuted under the following state bigamy statute.

Sec. 571.2—Bigamy.

"Whoever, being married, shall marry any other person during the life of the former spouse shall be guilty of a felony: provided, that nothing in this Act shall extend to any person marrying a second time whose spouse shall have been continually absent from such person for a period of seven years last past, and shall not have been known by such person to be living within that time."

109. On the charge of bigamy, Henrietta should be found

(A) guilty
(B) not guilty, because of Henrietta's mistake of fact regarding her husband's death
(C) not guilty, because of Henrietta's mistake of law regarding her husband's death
(D) not guilty, because Henrietta did not have the requisite mens rea to be held criminally liable

# CRIMINAL LAW

## Questions 110–114 are based on the following fact situation.

Questions 110–114 each describe a criminal offense with regard to the following federal statute relating to the failure of federal prisoners to return to prison.

Sec. 1212—Failure to Return to Prison

(A) Any prisoner temporarily released who fails to return to his designated place of confinement at the prescribed time is guilty of a misdemeanor (punishable by one year in jail).

(B) Any prisoner temporarily released who willfully fails to return to his designated place of confinement at the prescribed time is guilty of a felony of the third degree (punishable by three years, imprisonment).

(C) Any prisoner temporarily released who willfully fails to return to his designated place of confinement at the prescribed time and remains out of federal custody for more than 14 days beyond the prescribed time of his return is guilty of a felony of the second degree (punishable by six years' imprisonment).

(D) Any prisoner temporarily released who willfully fails to return to his designated place of confinement beyond the prescribed time of his return and commits a serious felony while released is guilty of a felony of the first degree (punishable by 10 years' imprisonment).

110. On January 1, 1999, federal prisoner Dineen is temporarily released for mercy purposes and is told to report back to prison at 9:00 A.M. on January 4, 1999. Dineen attends the funeral of his wife. Because of his extreme grief, Dineen begins a drinking spree. He finally sobers up in his friend's apartment on January

17. Dineen glances at his digital watch that has not been properly set, and that incorrectly fixes the current date at January 15. Dineen decides not to return for another couple of days and resumes his drinking. He finally returns on January 19, believing that it is January 17.

111. On January 1, 1999, federal prisoner Howe is temporarily released for mercy purposes and is told to report back to prison at 1:00 P.M. on January 4, 1999. After visiting his wife who has just given birth to their second child, Howe stops at a tavern to have a drink to celebrate two hours before his prescribed time of return. A hold-up of the tavern occurs, and Howe is shot and rushed to a hospital. After being treated for his gunshot wounds, Howe is returned to prison three days later.

112. On January 1, 1999, federal prisoner Liddy is temporarily released and is told to report back to prison at noon on January 4, 1999, but due to a typographical error, his release form sets January 4, 2000, as his prescribed date of return. Following his release, Liddy visits an attorney friend who advises him that in his opinion Liddy has no legal obligation to return to prison until January 4, 2000. Liddy follows his attorney's advice, and does not return to prison on January 4, 1999. He remains out of prison until March 1, 1999, when he is captured by FBI agents and returned to prison.

113. On January 1, 1999, federal prisoner Squealy is temporarily released for mercy purposes and is told to report back to prison at 9:00 P.M. on January 4, 1999. After visiting his sick mother in the hospital, Squealy goes to see some of his old friends about nine hours before his prescribed time of return. Squealy is given a mescaline pill, a hallucinogen,

which causes him to lose track of time. His "trip" lasts until January 6, when he returns to prison.

114. On January 1, 1999, federal prisoner Veasey is released to attend the wedding of his daughter, and is told to report back to prison at noon January 4, 1999. On the morning of January 4, Veasey visits some of his former cohorts who try to persuade him to remain out of prison long enough to assist them in a bank robbery. When he refuses, he is told that he will never see his daughter alive again. Because of the threat, Veasey agrees to drive the getaway car. After Veasey drives his friends to the bank, he speeds away when they are inside and returns to prison at 2:00 P.M. on January 4, 1999.

**Question 115 is based on the following fact situation.**

115. Under which of the following situations would Defendant's intoxication NOT negate his criminal culpability?

(A) Defendant had consumed a fifth of Old Grand Dad bourbon. Later that same day, he approached Victim with a knife and told her to accompany him or he would stab her. He led Victim to his car and then ordered her to disrobe. As Victim was removing her panty hose, she suddenly kicked Defendant in the head (temporarily dazing him). Victim then safely ran from the car. Defendant is arrested and charged with the crime of assault with intent to commit rape.

(B) Defendant attended a wedding reception at the Brown Place Hotel where he drank ten vodka daiquiris (each drink containing one ounce of liquor). Following the reception, Defendant engaged in a violent argument with the hotel's parking lot attendant. Defendant took a tire iron from his car and threw it at the attendant. The tire iron missed the attendant and hit Victim as he was entering the hotel. Defendant is arrested and charged with assault with intent to commit battery.

(C) Defendant had been drinking liquor all evening at the Palomino Bar with three of his cohorts. An undercover detective overheard Defendant and his buddies plot to rob the bar after closing hours. When Defendant attempted to draw a pistol from his coat, he was quickly disarmed and placed under arrest by the detective. Defendant is charged with the crime of conspiracy to commit robbery.

(D) At his law school graduation party, Defendant drank two six packs of Pearl beer (each bottle containing 12 ounces). Around midnight, Defendant was approached by Jane who asked him to drive her home. Although Jane was only 15 years old, she had the appearance of a woman in her mid-to-late twenties. Defendant, who had his eye on Jane all night, quickly agreed and he showed her the way to his car. Once inside, Jane removed her clothes and dared Defendant to engage in sexual intercourse. Without hesitation, Defendant willingly obliged. The age of consent in this jurisdiction is 17 for females. Defendant is subsequently arrested and charged with statutory rape.

CRIMINAL LAW

## Question 116 is based on the following fact situation.

Hector had been drinking at the Rendez-Vous Tavern for three hours and was visibly intoxicated. Horace entered the bar and sat down next to Hector. After ordering a beer, Horace turned to Hector and said, "Hey buddy, you're sure an ugly looking dude." Hector ignored Horace's insult and turned to walk away. Horace then pushed Hector against the bar and said, "Your face makes me sick to my stomach." Hector then pulled out a razor and slashed Horace's throat, killing him.

116. If Hector is prosecuted for Horace's murder, he will most likely be found

   (A) guilty, since his intoxication was voluntary
   (B) guilty, since he was under a duty to retreat
   (C) not guilty, by reason of intoxication
   (D) not guilty, since there is no duty to retreat in a public place

## Question 117 is based on the following fact situation.

117. In which case would the Defendant's intoxication defense most likely negate his criminal intent?

   (A) Defendant is charged with raping Victim. At trial Defendant testifies that he was so inebriated that he was unable to understand that Victim did not consent to his conduct.
   (B) Victim was horseback riding when she was approached by Defendant, who rode up from behind and struck her horse with his riding whip, causing the horse to bolt and throw the Victim. On trial for battery, Defendant testified that he was so drunk that he was only "horsing" around and did not intend to injure Victim.
   (C) While intoxicated, Defendant wandered into Victim's barn, lit a match, and began looking for some whiskey which he thought was hidden there. Angered at not finding any liquor, Defendant threw the match into a bale of hay which quickly ignited, thus causing the destruction of Victim's barn. Defendant is charged with arson.
   (D) Defendant is charged with assault with intent to rape Victim. While on trial, Defendant testified that he was intoxicated to such an extent that he did not remember striking Victim.

## Question 118 is based on the following fact situation.

The state of Columbia enacted a statute making it illegal to knowingly sell, purchase or in any way distribute any form of contraceptives to a minor. Violation of the statute was a misdemeanor punishable by a $500 fine and up to 30 days in jail. After the statute's enactment, Mr. Sellers sold a can of "Whippit," a contraceptive foam, to Loretta who was 18 years of age. Before selling the product to Loretta, Sellers carefully examined the girl's driving license which indicated that she was in fact 18. Sellers nevertheless made the sale because he erroneously believed the age of majority to be 18. Sellers is subsequently charged with violation of the statute, and his mistake is honestly held to have been made.

118.  Such a mistake should

(A) not prevent his conviction, because mistake of the law is no defense
(B) not prevent his conviction, because the crime imposes absolute criminal liability
(C) result in his acquittal, because he took reasonable steps to ascertain Loretta's age
(D) result in his acquittal, because he did not possess the requisite mens rea

## Question 119 is based on the following fact situation.

Vic and Veasey, the Vasoline Brothers, broke into the home of Lester, President of Gold Nugget National Bank, and kidnapped Lester's wife, Lucy. Vic and Veasey took Lucy hostage, pointed a gun at her head, and demanded that she drive them to their hideout in her car. As Lucy was driving down Market Street, a lady pushing her baby in a stroller suddenly stopped in the middle of the intersection. In order to avoid hitting the lady and her child, Lucy

veered the car to the left, and intentionally struck bystander Young, instantly killing him.

119.  If Lucy is subsequently prosecuted for the murder of Young, she will most likely be found

(A) guilty, since she intentionally veered the car striking Young
(B) not guilty, by reason of necessity
(C) not guilty, by reason of duress
(D) not guilty, by reason of self-defense

## Question 120 is based on the following fact situation.

Believing that she was pregnant, Miss Dee Period, a young unmarried woman, came to the office of Dr. Abe Bortion, a licensed gynecologist, and wanted an abortion. Dr. Bortion examined her and determined that she was not pregnant, but decided that he would tell her she was, in order to earn his $500 fee. After receiving the $500, Dr. Bortion proceeded to have Miss Period admitted to Mount Sinai Hospital by falsely informing the hospital authorities that she had a benign tumor on her uterus which he was going to remove. He performed all the surgical procedures appropriate for an abortion under adequate hygienic conditions, but Miss Period began hemorrhaging and died.

120.  In a common law jurisdiction, for which crimes should Dr. Bortion be found guilty?

   I. Murder
  II. Manslaughter
 III. Battery
 IV. Larceny by trick
  V. False pretenses

(A) I and IV
(B) II and V
(C) III and IV
(D) I, III, and V

**Questions 121–125 are based on the four case summaries below. For each question, select the case that would be most applicable as a precedent.**

(A) *State v. Maloney.* Defendant is charged with the illegal sale and transfer of a firearm to Black, who had previously been convicted of bribery (a Class B felony). At trial, Maloney admitted selling the pistol to Black, but stated that he was unaware of the statute which prohibited sale of firearms to a convicted felon. Furthermore, defendant knew Black had been convicted of bribery which he mistakenly believed to be a misdemeanor. Defendant *NOT GUILTY.*

(B) *State v. Boozer.* Defendant is charged with the offense of selling intoxicating beverages to a minor in violation of the State Alcoholic Beverage Control Act. At trial Boozer admitted selling two bottles of "Mad Dog Rum" to Billy Smith, aged 15. Boozer testified that he believed Billy to be above the statutory drinking age of 18. In fact, Billy admitted telling Boozer that he was 18 years of age and from his physical appearance, Billy looked to be "of age." Defendant *GUILTY.*

(C) *State v. Dineen.* After dining one evening at the Red Coach Inn, Dineen accidentally removed another patron's raincoat from the coat rack in the inn's entrance hall. The owner of the raincoat saw Dineen leaving with "his raincoat," and notified the proprietor, who promptly called the police. Dineen was charged with larceny. Defendant *NOT GUILTY.*

(D) *State v. Redneck.* Redneck is charged with the statutory rape of Lucille, aged 16, in the State of Omega where the age of consent is 18. Defendant admitted that he and Lucille were attending a party on the evening in question and that she consented to having sexual intercourse with him. Redneck further testified that he mistakenly believed that the legal age of consent was 16. Defendant *GUILTY.*

121. Steve Fishco, proprietor of Hadfield's Seafood Wholesalers, received a telephone call from Shifty Morgan, who informed Steve that he had a "hot cargo" of Gulf Coast shrimp for "quick" sale. During their conversation, Steve asked Shifty if the shipment was in fact stolen. Shifty admitted that the shrimp were hijacked from a trailer truck soon after it left its Louisiana packing plant. Steve agreed to purchase the shrimp and arranged to meet Shifty later that evening. After purchasing the goods at the rendezvous, Steve returned to his warehouse and discovered that the goods were not shrimp but clams. Steve is charged with receiving stolen goods. At trial Steve's defense is that he honestly believed that the goods he purchased were shrimp.

122. John Lewis deserted his wife, Thelma, in August 1976. One month later, Thelma was notified by International Airways that her husband was a victim in an air crash in which all passengers were killed. Believing that her husband had perished in the plane crash, Thelma married Wade Roe a year later. Shortly after her remarriage, Thelma learned that John, her first husband, had survived the crash and wanted a reconciliation. Thelma is then prosecuted under the following bigamy statute: "Whoever, being married, shall marry any other person during the life of the former spouse, shall be guilty of a felony."

123. The State of Dover required the issuance of a permit by the Secretary of State before any "securities may be sold to the public." Richard Spack, the director of Fairlawns Development Co., desiring to sell certain real estate interests, sought the advice of the Secretary of State. The Secretary informed Spack that his company's property interests were not subject to the state's Securities Act. Spack then proceeded to offer his company's real estate interests for sale to a number of interested buyers. It is later determined that Spack's company's real estate interests were, in fact, "securities" within the statutory provisions of the Security Act. Spack is charged with violation of the "securities statute."

124. One morning, Maybelle read in the Homesville *Chronicle* that the local public library was presenting an Elvis Presley memorial exhibit. The display was to include books, pictures, magazine articles, and record albums of the deceased recording star. Maybelle, president of the Homesville Elvis Presley Fan Club, rushed to the library to view the memorabilia of her idol. While she was looking at the display, Maybelle noticed a couple of Elvis's early rare albums which she had been unable to obtain for her own private collection. Excitedly, Maybelle picked up the albums and quietly walked out of the library. Maybelle is subsequently charged with larceny. At trial Maybelle's defense was that she honestly was unaware that such a taking was proscribed by criminal statute.

125. During his Uncle Felix's long illness, Eddie Sloan rendered many daily services. In gratitude for Eddie's ministrations, Uncle Felix promised to give Eddie his old 1957 Thunderbird after he had recovered. The following day, Uncle Felix died and the administrator of his estate took possession of Uncle Felix's property including the T-Bird. Believing the car to be rightfully his, Eddie entered Uncle Felix's garage one evening, and using his spare set of keys, drove away in the T-Bird. Eddie is charged with larceny.

**Question 126 is based on the following fact situation.**

During a drunken quarrel between Drew and Dixie Moore, Drew pointed his pistol at Dixie and said, "If I didn't love you, I'd kill you." Drew thought the pistol to be unloaded but, in fact, earlier that day his son had loaded the gun. As a joke, he fired the gun at Dixie, wounding her in the shoulder.

Patrolman Andy Adams, in his apartment across the hall, heard the shot coming from the Moores' apartment. Entering their apartment through the unlocked door, Andy saw Drew bandaging his wife's wound. When neither Drew nor Dixie would explain what had happened, Andy shepherded them both to his car, drove Dixie to the Medical Center and took Drew to the local precinct, where he was booked for assault and battery.

At the hospital, Dr. Doolittle removed the bullet from Dixie's shoulder without her consent. Even though the embedded bullet would not cause her any harm, he still decided to remove it.

Calling the hospital, Andy asked Dr. Doolittle to bring the bullet down to the precinct. When Doolittle arrived, Andy found Drew asleep in his jail cell. Without waking Drew, Andy directed Doolittle to take a sample of Drew's blood for a blood alcohol test. Later, Doolittle reported that the test showed that Drew was intoxicated.

Returning to the Moores' apartment to find the gun, Andy noticed broken glass in a rear window. On the ground below, Andy found a .22 caliber pistol, which the police ballistics expert identified as the weapon which had fired the bullet that was retrieved from Dixie's shoulder.

126. Assume that the prosecution drops the assault charge against Drew. He is later charged with committing a battery upon Dixie. If Drew attempts to prove that he was so inebriated that he could not have formed a criminal intent, this would constitute a

(A) good defense, because the charge requires a specific-intent

(B) good defense, because at least a general criminal intent is required for every offense

(C) poor defense, because voluntary intoxication is not a valid defense to battery

(D) poor defense, because Drew was not aware that the gun was loaded

## Question 127 is based on the following fact situation.

Gilbert, an ex-con who had just been released from Attica Penitentiary, approached Emmanuel and Smith and asked if they wanted to take part in a bank robbery. Emmanuel and Smith both agreed. Gilbert went ahead and planned the robbery. As part of his scheme, Gilbert stole a 1985 Toyota van which he intended to use as the getaway vehicle.

According to Gilbert's plan, he would pick up Emmanuel and Smith in the Toyota on Friday morning and drive over to the Glendale branch of the Home Savings Bank where the robbery would occur. Gilbert instructed his cohorts that he would be the getaway driver and wait in the van while they entered the bank armed with shotguns. However, the day before the robbery was to take place, Gilbert was arrested on a parole violation for carrying a concealed weapon and held in police custody. Emmanuel and Smith, nevertheless, decided to carry out the robbery using the van that Gilbert had stolen. On Friday morning, Emmanuel and Smith drove to the bank. When they entered, Smith, who was an undercover police detective, arrested Emmanuel.

127. Gilbert should be found guilty for which of the following crimes?

(A) Automobile theft and solicitation

(B) Automobile theft and conspiracy

(C) Automobile theft and attempted robbery

(D) Automobile theft, conspiracy, and attempted robbery

## Question 128 is based on the following fact situation.

Roxanne Rockefeller, a wealthy socialite, often wore expensive jewelry while walking her dog in Central Park. Her friends warned her against wearing such valuable ornaments because they feared she would be an easy target for muggers. In order to persuade Roxanne not to wear her expensive jewelry in the park, her friend, Renee Richards, decided to play a practical joke on Roxanne. One morning, Renee dressed like a man and hid in an area of the park that she knew Roxanne customarily walked through. That morning while Roxanne was strolling through the park with her dog, Renee suddenly jumped out from behind the bush. Brandishing a toy pistol, she grabbed Roxanne's diamond necklace from her neck. Startled, Roxanne became hysterical and began to plead, "Please don't hurt me." Renee then removed her male garb, handed the necklace back to Roxanne and said, "I just wanted to frighten you to teach you a lesson."

128. If Renee is subsequently prosecuted, she should be found guilty of which, if any, of the following crimes?

   (A) Battery
   (B) Assault
   (C) Robbery
   (D) No crime

## Question 129 is based on the following fact situation.

Shortly after breaking up with Ellis, Veronica began dating Dent. Ellis, who still loved Veronica, hated Dent. During the July 4th weekend, Veronica and Dent arranged to go camping at the Cautauqua Indian Reservation. While they were on their camping trip, Ellis and his friend Hood decided to beat up Dent. They went to the campsite where Veronica and Dent were staying, but they couldn't find the couple who were hiking in the woods.

Subsequently, Ellis was arrested and charged with conspiracy to commit an assault on a federal reservation. At trial, Ellis testified he didn't know he was on a federal reservation. Moreover, he stated that if he had known, he never would have agreed to the crime.

129. If the jury believes Ellis, he should be found

   (A) guilty, because federal conspiracy laws require no mental retainment of jurisdictional elements
   (B) guilty, because federal conspiracy laws require only an intention to commit a prohibited act, but do not require a knowledge of the surrounding circumstances
   (C) not guilty, because he didn't have the specific-intent to commit the crime of assault on a federal reservation
   (D) not guilty, because he did not agree to commit a crime on a federal reservation

## Questions 130–131 are based on the following fact situation.

Bonnie and Teela decided to rob the First National Bank in Clovis. They agreed to use unloaded guns in the robbery. As planned, Teela entered the bank while Bonnie stationed herself outside as a lookout. Teela approached Akeem, the bank teller, pointed her unloaded pistol at him and said, "This is a stick-up . . . give me your money and no one will get hurt."

While Akeem was handing the money to Teela, Bonnie got scared and fled. Meanwhile, Ralph, a bank patron who was in line, saw Teela pointing the gun at Akeem and fainted. He fell backwards and cracked his head on the marble floor. This resulted in a fatal head injury. Moments later, Teela left the bank with the loot. Thereafter, Teela and Bonnie were arrested.

130. If Teela is prosecuted for felony murder and acquitted, the most likely reason will be because

    (A) Teela's gun was unloaded
    (B) There was not a sufficient connection between Ralph's death and the robbery
    (C) Teela didn't intend to harm anyone during the robbery
    (D) This jurisdiction has adopted the Redline limitation to the felony murder rule

131. Assume for the purposes of this question only that Bonnie is subsequently prosecuted for felony murder and acquitted. Her acquittal most likely resulted because

    (A) Bonnie abandoned her participation in the crime
    (B) Ralph's death was accidental
    (C) Teela, as co-conspirator, was acquitted
    (D) Ralph was not placed in apprehension of bodily harm

**Questions 132–133 are based on the following fact situation.**

After weeks of deliberation, Clyde decided to embark on his plan to rob the Lobo Bank in Silver City. As part of his scheme, Clyde enlisted his girlfriend, Bonnie, who agreed to drive the get away car. On the day of the robbery, Bonnie and Clyde drove to the Lobo Bank. After Bonnie parked outside, she saw a security guard in the bank and said, "I've changed my mind . . . I'm not going through with it." Clyde, who was in the passenger seat, responded, "O.K. you yellowbelly coward, take off if you want but just leave the keys in the car and keep the motor running." Bonnie did as she was asked and then fled the crime scene by foot.

A few minutes later, Clyde went into the bank, robbed it, and then ran back to the car. He drove off and was speeding away from the bank when he looked behind him to see if he was being followed. As he took his eye off the road, Clyde's vehicle struck Walker, a pedestrian, who was crossing the street, killing her. About an hour later, Clyde was slowly approaching his hideout in the outskirts of town when Cindy, a five-year-old child, suddenly darted in front of Clyde's car. He applied the brakes but couldn't stop in time. The car struck Cindy, fatally injuring her.

132. For Walker's death, Bonnie should be found guilty of which, if any, of the following crimes?

    (A) Murder
    (B) Involuntary manslaughter
    (C) Voluntary manslaughter
    (D) No crime

133. For Cindy's death, Clyde should be found guilty of which, if any, of the following crimes?

    (A) Murder
    (B) Involuntary manslaughter
    (C) Voluntary manslaughter
    (D) No crime

**Question 134 is based on the following fact situation.**

Knowing that Slocum was away on vacation, Tyson and Waxman decided to burglarize her home. Since they didn't have a car, Tyson and Waxman asked Blauser to drive them to Slocum's home. Tyson and Waxman did not tell Blauser what they intended to do there. Blauser drove them to Slocum's house. While Blauser waited in the car, Tyson and Waxman entered the home by using a master key to unlock the front door. They then stole several items of expensive jewelry from Slocum's bedroom.

Concealing the jewelry in their underpants, they left the house and reentered Blauser's car. Unaware of the theft, Blauser drove Tyson and Waxman back to their apartments. The next day Tyson and Waxman pawned the jewelry for $5,000. Two weeks later, Tyson saw Blauser and gave him $500 and told him for the first time about the burglary. Blauser kept the money and did not report the theft to the police.

134.   If Blauser is subsequently prosecuted, he should be found

(A) guilty of receiving stolen property but not guilty of burglary
(B) guilty of burglary but not guilty of receiving stolen property
(C) guilty of burglary and receiving of stolen property
(D) not guilty of either burglary or receiving of stolen property

## Question 135 is based on the following fact situation.

Jose and Carlos were walking down the street when they ran into Jesus. Jose turned to Carlos and said, "Hey, man, that sucker owes me $10." Jose then stopped Jesus and demanded the money. Jesus replied, "Listen, amigo, all I got is a subway token, but I promise to pay you next week." Jose suddenly said to Carlos, "Give me your gun, I'm going to blow this low life away." Carlos gave Jose his gun and Jose shot Jesus to death. As Jose and Carlos were about to leave, Carlos turned to Jose and said, "Let me have my gun back. I think the creep's still alive." Carlos then fired two more shots into Jesus' body. Unknown to Carlos, Jesus did in fact die from the first bullet wound.

135.   Which of the following is the most serious crime that Carlos can be convicted of?

(A) Attempted murder
(B) Murder
(C) Assault with a deadly weapon
(D) Concealment of a deadly weapon

## Questions 136–137 are based on the following fact situation.

Thad and Jeremie were dealers at Harrah's casino in Atlantic City. They had been employed by the hotel for four years. One day they were unexpectedly fired by the casino's new manager, Donovan. Apparently, the hotel management hired Donovan to get rid of some of the old-time employees and replace them with new personnel at a lower wage scale. Angered by their firing, Thad and Jeremie vowed to "get back" at the hotel.

As their revenge, they decided to plant a bomb in the hotel and demand $1,000,000. After receiving the money, they would then reveal the location of the bomb and provide details for defusing it. Thad and Jeremie both agreed that Harrah's should be given adequate warning so that nobody would be injured.

In accordance with their plan, Thad, who was an electronics expert, built the bomb by himself. He alone then drove to the hotel where he placed the bomb in a hallway closet. Shortly thereafter, Jeremie telephoned the hotel and made a demand for the money. He said a bomb was in the hotel and that it would explode in 24 hours unless the money was paid. The hotel treated Jeremie's demand as a crank call and refused to make any payment.

With their plans having gone awry, Thad and Jeremie agreed that Thad should return to the hotel and defuse the bomb. As Thad was driving back to the hotel, the bomb exploded, killing thirty people. A subsequent investigation revealed that a faulty wire caused the bomb to detonate prematurely. A New Jersey statute provides that detonating or attempting to detonate a bomb or explosive device in or near a building or dwelling is a felony.

136. If Thad and Jeremie are charged with violating the aforementioned New Jersey bombing statute, which of the following statements is correct?

   (A) Both are guilty, since each participated in the planning of the crime.
   (B) Thad is guilty since he built and transported the bomb, but Jeremie is not guilty because his telephone call was not a "substantial step" in the furtherance of the crime.
   (C) Neither is guilty, because the hotel's gross negligence in failing to heed the telephone warning constituted an independent intervening cause of the explosion.
   (D) Neither is guilty, because neither intended for anyone to be killed as the bomb exploded prematurely.

137. If Thad and Jeremie are charged with murder and conspiracy to commit murder, which of the following statements is correct?

   (A) Thad and Jeremie are both guilty of murder, but neither is guilty of conspiracy to commit murder.
   (B) Thad and Jeremie are both guilty of murder and conspiracy to commit murder.
   (C) Only Thad is guilty of murder, but Thad and Jeremie are both guilty of conspiracy to commit murder.
   (D) Thad and Jeremie are neither guilty of murder nor conspiracy to commit murder.

**Question 138 is based on the following fact situation.**

Regis and Jose, students at New Paltz State College, were spending a leisurely afternoon listening to music and smoking marijuana in Regis's dormitory room. They had just consumed a six pack of Amstel beer when Jose asked his pal if there was anything else to drink. Regis indicated there wasn't and suggested that Jose drive to the liquor store and buy another six pack of beer. Jose told Regis that his car wasn't working and asked Regis if he could borrow his. Regis assented and gave Jose the keys to his car. Regis knew that Jose was drunk and under the influence of marijuana when he loaned him his car.

Jose was driving to the liquor store at an excessive rate of speed. As he approached the intersection of Main and Spruce Streets, he was traveling at 70 m.p.h. (30 miles over the posted speed limit). When he came to the intersection the light turned red. Jose, who made no effort to stop in time, drove through the red light and collided with a car driven by Cook. Cook, who had entered the intersection on a green light, was killed in the accident.

138. In the event that Regis can be convicted of manslaughter and sentenced to prison, it will most likely be upon the basis of

   (A) responsibility for the accident as an accomplice
   (B) recklessness in lending his car to Jose
   (C) joint venture in lending his car to Jose for a common purpose
   (D) vicarious liability for the conduct of Jose

**Question 139 is based on the following fact situation.**

One afternoon, police officers observed Blanda, a 46-year-old man, and Brooke, a 14-year-old girl, smoking marijuana together. They arrested Blanda and charged him with the separate offenses of (1) possession of a controlled dangerous substance and (2) contributing to the delinquency of a minor. Brooke was also arrested and charged with being an accomplice to the crime of contributing to the delinquency of a minor.

139. At trial Brooke's best defense is that
   (A) smoking marijuana does not necessarily make her an accomplice to the crime
   (B) Blanda, the adult principal, must be convicted before any prosecution can be maintained against a minor
   (C) a minor cannot be prosecuted for an adult crime
   (D) since the statute was designed to protect minors, Brooke cannot be prosecuted as an accomplice

**Questions 140–143 are based on the four case summaries below. Read the summaries of the decisions in the four cases, (A)–(D), below. You should then decide which is most applicable as a precedent to each of the cases in the questions that follow. Note that each case may be the correct precedent for one question, more than one question, or none of the questions.**

(A) Peter and Paul decided to commit a holdup at the Greenwich Savings Bank. On October 31, they entered the bank with loaded pistols. Peter approached Mary, a bank teller, pulled out a gun, and said, "Hand over all your money or I'll blow your brains out." As Mary was giving Peter the money from her cash drawer, she secretly set off a silent alarm. Moments later the police arrived and exchanged shots with the bank robbers. During the shoot-out, Dooley, a police officer, accidentally shot and killed Travers, a bank patron. Peter and Paul were found guilty of felony murder.

(B) Loudon and Wainwright agreed to rob Muni's Liquor Store. After a long discussion, it was decided that they would use unloaded guns. Unbeknownst to Loudon, however, Wainwright decided to load his .38 caliber pistol. When the co-felons entered the liquor store brandishing guns, Hector, the proprietor, reached into his counter drawer and pulled out a .45 caliber pistol. Before Hector could fire his weapon, Wainwright shot and killed him. Loudon and Wainwright were found guilty of felony murder.

(C) Waylon and Willie agreed to commit a holdup at the Second City Bank, in which Jessi worked as a teller. They obtained her cooperation in the plan. The three of them agreed that Waylon and Willie would enter the bank and carry out the "holdup" at Jessi's window. She would give them the money, apparently under the threat of the holdup. On April 1, as planned, Waylon and Willie entered the bank with their guns drawn. Willie ordered everyone to stand still. Waylon went to Jessi's window and, pointing a gun at her, demanded money. As he did so, Cash, the bank security guard, pulled out a gun and shot Waylon, killing him instantly. Willie was found not guilty of felony murder.

(D) Porter and his wife, Dolly, attended a party one evening. During the party, Porter became extremely intoxicated. Afterwards, Porter insisted on driving home although Dolly admonished him to drive carefully. In this jurisdiction it is a felony to drive while intoxicated. As Porter was operating his vehicle within the posted speed limit, a truck traveling on the opposite side of the street crossed over the median strip and crashed head-on into Porter's auto, killing Dolly. It was later determined that the truck had a defective steering column which caused it to veer across the roadway. Porter was found not guilty of felony murder.

140. Carlos and Santana decided to burglarize a warehouse one night. They gained entry through a broken window. While ransacking a storage area, the two men were suddenly confronted by Brown, a security guard. Startled, Carlos picked up a wooden box lying nearby and threw it at the security guard. Brown then drew his pistol and fired a shot at Carlos. The bullet missed Carlos but hit Cooley, a police officer who had just arrived at the scene, killing him instantly.

141. Ozzie, a labor union leader, kept a loaded gun in a night table drawer in his bedroom. Although Ozzie was the registered owner of the firearm, his gun permit had expired. One afternoon his nine-year-old son, Ricky, was playing "Cops and Robbers" with his friend, Porky. During their game, Ricky went into his father's bedroom and took the gun out of the drawer. Thinking that the gun was unloaded, Ricky aimed the weapon at Porky and pulled the trigger. The gun discharged and a bullet struck Porky, fatally injuring him.

142. Brewster Bradley III was a wealthy industrialist. Late one evening Willis and Reed broke into Bradley's home and kidnapped his son, Bill. Thereafter, they threatened to kill the youngster unless a $1,000,000 ransom was paid. After receiving the ransom, the kidnappers told Brewster that his son could be found tied to a tree in the Adirondack Mountains. Bill died from exposure before being located by the rescue party.

143. Rod and Stewart entered into an agreement to rob the Hollywood Savings Bank. According to their plan, Rod would approach the teller's window and demand the money while Stewart would be posted at the door with a rifle, keeping guard. After entering the bank, Rod became angry at Stewart because he was picking his nose and not paying attention. Intending to scare Stewart, Rod fired a bullet over his cohort's head. The bullet, however, ricocheted off a wall and struck Stewart in the back, killing him instantly.

## Questions 144–145 are based on the following fact situation.

Belushi lived on the island of Nantucket. The island, which is located off the coast of Massachusetts, is accessible only by a regular ferry service. The last scheduled ferry leaves Nantucket at 9:10 P.M. and arrives at the mainland at 11:30 P.M. each evening.

On Halloween night many children came to Belushi's home "trick or treating." He gave each child a small bag containing an assortment of candy and lollipops. At about 8:30 P.M. Belushi again heard the doorbell ring and when he opened the door, he was confronted by three persons who were all wearing "Mr. T" masks and heavy chain necklaces. They pushed Belushi inside his house and threatened him with bodily harm if he didn't cooperate. After tying him up with their heavy chains, the trio then proceeded to ransack the victim's home.

As they were preparing to leave, one of the looters asked Belushi, "Do you have any drugs here?" He responded, "No, but my dealer's supposed to be bringing me some coke around 9:30 tonight." One of the masked intruders looked at a clock and said, "Hey, it's 9:00 P.M., we can't wait!" Another member of the group responded, "It's cool, we still got 10 minutes left." They then placed many of Belushi's valuables and other possessions into a large sack, and hurriedly left his house.

About one hour later, Belushi freed himself and telephoned the police. Belushi, who was familiar with the ferry schedule, told the police that he was certain that the trio were returning to the mainland on the last ferry because of their conversation. As a result, the Nantucket police department contacted the law enforcement officers on the mainland, who decided to go to the ferry station and await the arriving vessel.

Without attempting to get a warrant, the police stopped all the cars leaving the ferry. In one vehicle, the police noticed three women fidgeting rather nervously. Upon searching their auto, the police found Belushi's stolen property hidden under the front seat. The women, later identified as the Pointer sisters, were immediately placed under arrest.

144. At their trial for armed robbery, the Pointer sisters move to suppress the use of the property confiscated by the police as evidence. Their motion should be

(A) granted, because the police did not have a warrant to search their car
(B) granted, because the police did not have probable cause to suspect that their car contained evidence of the crime
(C) denied, because the police had probable cause to search their car and under the circumstances no warrant was required
(D) denied, because even though the detention was unlawful, the police had reasonable suspicion to believe that their car contained evidence of the crime since they observed the women fidgeting nervously

145. Assume for the purposes of this question that the Pointer sisters were the masked intruders who entered Belushi's home. So far as you can tell from these facts, what crimes can they be convicted of?

  I. Assault
 II. Battery
III. Larceny
IV. Robbery
 V. Burglary

(A) I, II, and IV, but not III and V
(B) III, IV, and V, but not I and II
(C) IV and V, but not I, II, and III
(D) IV, but not I, II, III, and V

**Question 146 is based on the following fact situation.**

Manning was angry at Thomas for marrying his old girlfriend. As Thomas was painting his house one afternoon, Manning fired a shot from his pistol at him. Although the shot missed Thomas, the bullet struck and killed Frances (Thomas's daughter). Manning is subsequently charged with the first degree murder of Frances. The relevant statutes in effect in this Jurisdiction are as follows:

Section 169: Murder in the first degree is the unlawful and intentional killing of a human being with malice aforethought.

Section 170: Malice is expressed when there is manifested a deliberate intention to take away the life of another.

146. Which of the following, if established, would provide Manning with his best defense?

(A) He intended to kill Thomas, not Frances.
(B) He only intended to wound Thomas.
(C) He was unaware of the elements of malice.
(D) The killing was the result of negligence in missing Thomas; therefore he can only be guilty of involuntary manslaughter.

### Question 147 is based on the following fact situation.

"Screwball" Palmer, a sophomore communications major, attended Princeton University. He was the star pitcher for the Princeton Tigers baseball team which won the NCAA (National Collegiate Athletic Association) baseball championship. His nickname was "Screwball" because he was a practical joker who liked to perform zany antics both on and off the baseball field.

Late at night after studying, he would often walk around the Princeton campus attired only in a London Fog raincoat and jockey undershorts. As he approached young women, he would "flash" them by opening his raincoat and exposing himself in his jockey shorts. Palmer believed that he was committing a crime by "flashing" himself in front of the unwary co-eds. In this jurisdiction it was a felony to "flash"

or expose oneself in the nude. But unknown to Palmer what he was doing was not a crime.

One night Palmer broke into the Eta Delta Pi sorority house intending to "flash" the sorority sisters. Clad only in his raincoat and jockey shorts, he entered the bedroom of Brooke, a physical education major, who was lying in bed studying for an anatomy exam. Brooke, who knew Palmer, said, "What are you doing here? Shouldn't you be studying for finals?" Palmer then took off his raincoat and responded, "Study this, baby!" "Screwball" then began to run through the sorority house in his jockey shorts. Shortly thereafter, the police arrived and placed Palmer under arrest.

147. If Palmer is prosecuted, he should be found guilty for which, if any, of the following crimes?

(A) Burglary only
(B) Attempted violation of the "flashing" statute
(C) Both burglary and attempted violation of the "flashing" statute
(D) Neither burglary nor attempted violation of the "flashing" statute

### Question 148 is based on the following fact situation.

Brian Bayer is the owner of Mercury Pharmaceutical Company. Mercury manufactures aspirin tablets which it sells in interstate commerce. Connie Consumer purchased a bottle of Mercury aspirin from Shore's Drug Store. Shortly after taking two of the aspirin tablets, Connie became extremely ill and began having convulsions. She was rushed to the hospital where it was determined that the Mercury aspirin tablets contained strychnine, a poisonous chemical alkaloid.

148. Bayer is subsequently charged with violating the Federal Pure Food and Drug Act which makes it a misdemeanor to transport impure drugs in interstate commerce. Bayer should be found

    (A) guilty, only if he had the authority and responsibility for packaging the aspirin tablets
    (B) guilty, only if he knew or should have known that the aspirin tablets were poisonous
    (C) guilty, only if he personally supervised the packaging of the aspirin tablets
    (D) not guilty, unless Bayer knew that other customers had purchased poisonous aspirin tablets in the past

**Question 149 is based on the following fact situation.**

149. In which of the following situations is Defendant most likely to be guilty of manslaughter?

    (A) Defendant was a guide on a nature walk in Yellowstone National Park. The group was traversing across a mountainous path when a coyote suddenly appeared. Defendant, who was carrying a loaded pistol, knew that mountain lions and coyotes habitated in the area. Defendant saw that the coyote was about to attack Marnie, who was one of the hikers. Although Defendant could have easily shot and killed the coyote, he did nothing. The wild animal then pounced on Marnie. As she was being devoured, Defendant and the other members of the group ran to safety.

    (B) Defendant, a registered nurse, asked her friend Wilma out to lunch. While eating, Wilma suddenly began choking on a chicken bone. Defendant,

who was trained in cardiopulmonary resuscitation (CPR), did nothing to help her friend. Wilma choked to death.

    (C) Defendant, a physician, was walking home from his office one afternoon when he saw a car hit a blind man who was trying to cross the street. The victim was knocked to the ground and seriously injured while the car sped away. Defendant, who could have saved the man's life if he had treated him, continued walking home without rendering assistance. The blind man died from loss of blood.

    (D) Defendant took his four-year-old daughter, Karen, out in the yard to play. As they were playing catch, the telephone began to ring. Defendant ran into the house to answer the phone. While he was inside, Karen's ball rolled into the street. As she went to retrieve it, Karen was struck and killed by a car.

**Question 150 is based on the following fact situation.**

Gaylord Getty was a wealthy businessman who wore expensive Armani suits and flashy jewelry. Gaylord liked to flaunt his wealth and often carried large sums of money. While he was on a business trip to Chicago, Gaylord stayed at the luxurious Ambassador Hotel, which was the ritziest and most fashionable hotel in the city. After having dinner with a few business associates, Gaylord returned to the hotel and decided to have an after-dinner drink at the hotel's legendary Polo Lounge.

Gaylord was at the bar sipping some cognac when Paris Prowse, a voluptuous model, approached and sat down next to Gaylord. Gaylord, who prided himself as a suave ladies' man, was attracted to Paris and immediately engaged her in conversation. After having a few drinks together, Gaylord invited Paris back to his room for a nightcap. Sensing that Gaylord was a high roller, Paris agreed to accompany Gaylord back to his hotel room. While they were lounging in his suite, Gaylord fixed Paris and himself another round of drinks.

A few minutes later Gaylord excused himself to go to the bathroom. While he was inside the bathroom, Paris took two Quaaludes, which are narcotic barbiturates, from her purse and placed them in Gaylord's drink. Paris realized that the Quaaludes were a strong sedative and hoped that they would cause Gaylord to pass out and become unconscious. She then planned to steal his wallet and jewelry. Upon returning from the bathroom, Gaylord proceeded to finish his drink as he desired to seduce Paris. Shortly thereafter, Gaylord passed out from the Quaaludes and fell asleep. While he was unconscious, Paris took a Rolex watch off his wrist and pulled the wallet out of his trousers. She took $300 in cash from the wallet. As she was ready to leave, Paris noticed that Gaylord had a diamond earring in his left earlobe. She then ripped out the earring from his ear and stole that as well. Gaylord suffered a cut in his earlobe when Paris snatched the earring.

The next morning Gaylord awoke and discovered that his Rolex, money and earring were missing.

150. Which of the following crimes will Paris be convicted of?

(A) Larceny
(B) Robbery
(C) Larceny and robbery
(D) Battery and larceny

## 1. (C)

Students must be aware that a battery which results in an unintended death equals involuntary manslaughter; therefore choice (C) is the correct answer. Remember the distinction between voluntary and involuntary manslaughter. The usual type of voluntary manslaughter involves the intentional killing of another under the influence of a reasonably induced emotional disturbance (otherwise known as in a "heat of passion") causing a temporary loss of normal self-control. Be aware that except for this reasonable emotional condition, the intentional killing would be murder. On the other hard, involuntary manslaughter is an unintended homicide (1) where there is an unlawful killing in the commission of an unlawful act not amounting to a felony or (2) in the commission of a lawful act without due caution or circumspection (known as "criminal-negligence" manslaughter). LaFave and Scott note that in this latter form of involuntary manslaughter, most jurisdictions require that the defendant's death-producing conduct involve a higher degree of negligence than ordinary (tort) negligence.

## 2. (A)

Although defendant may have intended only to cause serious bodily harm, his actions did in fact kill another human being. Such a killing is murder unless justified, excused, or mitigated. The fact that defendant shot the "wrong" basketball player would not change the outcome because he was aware (or should have been aware) that the shooting created a serious risk of death or grave bodily harm.

## 3. (A)

This is an example of a "depraved-heart" killing. Students should be aware of the following types of conduct that have been held to involve a "very high degree" of unjustifiable homicidal danger which will do for "depraved-heart" murder: (1) firing a bullet into a room occupied, as defendant knows, by several people; (2) shooting into a caboose of a passing train or into a moving automobile, necessarily occupied by human beings; (3) throwing a beer glass at one who is carrying a lighted

**Multistate Criminal Law Chart**

| DEGREES OF NEGLIGENCE SCALE OF 1–10 | |
| --- | --- |
| Reckless Conduct | 8–10 (VERY HIGH) |
| Gross or Criminal Negligence | 5–7 (HIGH) |
| Ordinary Tort Negligence | 1–4 (LOW) |

**DEPRAVED-HEART MURDER**

Unintentional killing resulting from defendant's **reckless** conduct which involves a very high degree of unjustifiable homicidal danger

**INVOLUNTARY MANSLAUGHTER**

Unintentional killing resulting from defendant's **gross or criminal negligent** conduct oil lamp; (4) playing a game of "Russian roulette" with another person; (5) shooting at a point near, but not aiming directly at, another person; (6) driving a car at very high speeds along a main street; (7) shaking an infant so long and so vigorously that it cannot breathe. See Scott and LaFave in their handbook on **Criminal Law,** pp. 540–545, for an excellent explanation of "depraved-heart" murder.

### 4. (C)

*Extremely negligent conduct, which creates not only an unjustifiable but also a very high degree risk of death or serious bodily injury* to another or to others (though unaccompanied by any intent to kill or do serious bodily injury), *and which actually causes the death of another constitutes "depraved-heart" murder.* By deliberately driving his truck over a gas tank, Oats's conduct created an unreasonable risk of causing death or serious bodily injury. Consequently, he will be guilty of "depraved-heart" murder for the death that resulted. In addition, he will be guilty of arson which is defined as the malicious burning of the dwelling house of another. Reckless conduct satisfies the malice requirement. Also, a place of business may be subject to arson (or burglary) if it is usually slept in by the proprietor. Since Stuckey and his family resided in the second-floor apartment of the convenience store, it will qualify as a dwelling house. Note that on a bar exam essay question, students should also discuss Oats's criminal liability under the felony-murder rule.

### 5. (C)

Students should be aware that Speedster is charged with *attempted murder.* LaFave and Scott in their **Handbook on Criminal Law** point out that the crime of attempt consists of (1) an intent to do an act or to bring about certain consequences which would in law amount to a crime; and (2) an act in furtherance of that intent which, as it is most commonly put, goes beyond mere preparation. As such, attempt is a specific-intent crime. Since the defendant in this example did not have the (specific) intent to kill Lisa, he would be found not guilty of the inchoate crime of *attempted* murder.

**Multistate Nuance Chart**

**CRIMINAL LAW**

### ATTEMPT—THE LIMITS OF LIABILITY

| | LEGAL IMPOSSIBILITY | FACTUAL IMPOSSIBILITY |
|---|---|---|
| Traditional View or Majority View | Valid Defense | No Defense |
| Modern View or Model Penal Code | No Defense (If defendant intended criminal act) | No Defense |

## 6. (B)

Practically every Multistate question will test a fine-line distinction or hornbook nuance. Typically, in this hypo most students will narrow the correct answer down to (A) assault or (B) manslaughter. Choices (C) and (D) are wrong because the killing was not premeditated or committed during the commission of a serious felony. Here, choice (B) "trumps" (A) because Grayson is guilty of manslaughter which in this jurisdiction includes "all other types of unlawful homicide." This definition thus encompasses misdemeanor-manslaughter which covers assault or battery causing death situations. At common law assault and battery were misdemeanors and anytime the crime of assault (or battery) causes an unintentional killing, the defendant is guilty of misdemeanor-manslaughter.

## 7. (D)

According to LaFave, "extremely negligent conduct, which creates what a reasonable man would realize to be not only an unjustifiable but also a very high degree of risk of death or serious bodily injury to another or to others—though unaccompanied by any intent to kill or do serious bodily injury—and which actually causes the death of another" constitutes "depraved-heart" murder. See **Criminal Law,** p. 541.

**Multistate Nuance Chart**

**CRIMINAL LAW**

| DEPRAVED-HEART MURDER | INVOLUNTARY MANSLAUGHTER |
|---|---|
| 1. unintentional killing that results from defendant's extremely negligent (or reckless) conduct | 1. unintentional killing resulting from defendant's gross or wanton negligence |
| 2. extremely negligent conduct which creates a *very high degree* of unjustifiable homicidal danger | 2. defendant's death-producing conduct must involve a higher degree of negligence than ordinary (tort) negligence |
| 3. defendant must subjectively be aware of the *great risk* which his conduct creates | 3. also covers "unlawful-act" (or misdemeanor) manslaughter |

**4. illustrative distinctions:**

| | |
|---|---|
| (a) firing a bullet into a room which defendant knows is occupied by several people; | (a) firing a bullet into the window of what appears to be an abandoned cabin; |
| (b) driving a car at a very high speed or recklessly along a main street; | (b) driving a car at a very high speed or recklessly along an infrequently traveled country road; |

(c) firing a bullet into a passenger train; | (c) firing a bullet into a freight train;

(d) throwing an object from the roof of a tall building onto the busy street below | (d) throwing an object from the roof of a house in a residential neighborhood

## 8. (B)

Most jurisdictions punish as involuntary manslaughter, death-causing conduct in the commission or attempted commission of an unlawful act (generally a misdemeanor), especially if that act is malum in se. LaFave notes that an intentional battery (a misdemeanor at common law) is an unlawful act and one which is assignable to the malum in se category of unlawful acts. Therefore, it is universally held, as a specific instance of unlawful-act manslaughter, that one is guilty of involuntary manslaughter who intentionally inflicts bodily harm upon another person, as by a moderate blow with his fist, thereby causing an unintended and unforeseeable death to the victim (who, unknown to this attacker, may have a weak heart or a thin skull or a blood deficiency). In the present case, since Defendant committed a battery upon neighbor by kicking him, he would be found guilty of involuntary manslaughter (where the battery resulted in the unintended death of the victim).

## 9. (C)

Defendants in case summary (C) and in this question should both be guilty of depraved-heart murder. It is generally held that extremely negligent conduct, which creates what a reasonable man would realize to be not only an unjustifiable but also a very high degree of risk of death or serious bodily injury to another or to others—though unaccompanied by any intent to kill or do serious bodily injury—and which actually causes the death of another, may constitute (depraved-heart) murder. Although neither Defendant (in case summary (C) or in question 9) intended to kill his victim, each would, nevertheless, be guilty for depraved-heart murder which resulted from their grossly negligent, or reckless, conduct.

## 10. (A)

Since Defendant in case summary (A) and Defendant in this question both intended to have their victims killed, they are guilty of first degree murder. While the method of producing an intentional death is usually some weapon in the hands of the murderer, sometimes more subtle means are used. LaFave states that words alone may be used to produce an intentional death, as where one perjures an innocent man into the electric chair. (Note that a few states so provide by statute, e.g., California, Colorado, and Nevada, but even without such a statute it should constitute murder as surely as if he had fired a gun into his victim.)

## 11. (D)

In both felony-murder situations, the death was *not causally connected to* the underlying felony. At common law, one whose conduct brought about an unintended death in the commission or attempted commission of a felony was guilty of (felony) murder. However, many jurisdictions have limited the rule by requiring that the death be *foreseeable* and *causally connected to* the felony. In both case summary (D) and in the present question, neither death was causally connected to the underlying felony. Rather each death occurred only as a consequence of some intervening act, and therefore neither (death) was a "foreseeable" consequence of the felony.

## 12. (C)

One who shoots at a point *near, although not aiming directly at,* another person is, nevertheless, guilty of "depraved-heart" murder for the killing.

## 13. (D)

Mitchell in choice (D) would most likely be found guilty of felony murder. At common law one whose conduct brought about an unintentional death in the commission of a felony was guilty of felony murder. Today the majority of American jurisdictions have limited the felony murder rule in regard to the causal connection between the felony and the resulting homicide. Scott and La-Fave in **Criminal Law,** p. 557, state that in most jurisdictions, even more than a "but–for" causal relationship is required, the usual rule being that the death must be the *foreseeable* and *natural* result of the felony. In short, whether there is a sufficient causal connection depends on whether the defendant's felony dictated his conduct which led to the homicide. Under the circumstances presented in choice (D), Mitchell was naturally fleeing from the scene of the arson (he set fire to Richard's house) when he shot Ray, the police officer. Thus the necessary causal connection exists, placing the homicide "in the commission of" the arson. Choice (A) is an example of "depraved-heart"–type murder. Choice (B) is incorrect since a causal connection did not exist between the bank robbery (the felony) and Harold's fatal heart attack. Note that Harold was not even aware of the bank robbery taking place. Choice (C) is also wrong, since Jack *intentionally* shot Moe, his co-felon, and would be found guilty of murder. No causal relationship existed between the robbery and the death of the co-felon.

## 14. (D)

Note that at the early common law, one whose conduct brought about an unintended death in the commission or attempt of a felony was guilty of murder. LaFave and Scott note that today, however, the law of felony-murder varies substantially throughout the country, largely as a result of efforts to limit the scope of the felony-murder rule. Generally, the homicide must have some *causal connection* with the felony in order to qualify for felony murder; more than a mere coincidence of time and place is necessary. In most jurisdictions even more than a but-for causal relationship is required, the usual rule being that the death must be the "foreseeable" or "natural result" of the felony. Aside from these matters, however, the term "in the commission of" implies a more or less close causal connection between the felony and the homicide. LaFave and Scott note, in this regard, that the defendant, having committed a robbery or burglary, is carrying away the booty at the time of the homicide is not so much relevant as to the matter of time as it is as a matter of causal relation. Thus, one who carries booty is often more in need of a homicide to effect an escape than one who does not. To illustrate, where a robber, carrying in his car the fruits of his robbery, is stopped by a policeman for speeding some time after and some distance away from the place of robbery and he shoots the policeman to death to prevent his discovery of the stolen goods, the *causal connection* between the robbery and the homicide is quite close. A similar shooting by a robber *without booty* would lack the causal connection necessary to place the homicide "in the commission of" the robbery. As such, whether there is a sufficient causal connection between the felony and the homicide depends on whether the defendant's felony dictated his conduct which led to the homicide. In the present example, it clearly did. Jimmie killed Mr. Gold obviously to prevent discovery of the looting of the jewelry store. With regard to the vicarious responsibility of Jessie (for Mr. Gold's death), it is often said that all parties are guilty for deviations from the common plan which are the foreseeable consequences of carrying out the plan (e.g., an accidental shooting during an armed robbery being a typical example of a foreseeable deviation from the plan to rob). Under the established rule, accomplice liability extends to acts of the principal in the first degree which were a "natural and probable consequence" of the criminal scheme the accomplice encouraged or aided. Choice (D) is therefore correct because the *causal connection* between the burglary and the homicide was sufficiently close. Note that choice (B) is wrong because a mere change of heart or flight from the crime scene will not effectuate withdrawal from the crime. Rather LaFave and Scott note it is necessary for the accomplice (1) to repudiate his prior aid or (2) do all that is possible to countermand his prior aid or counsel and (3) do so before the chain of events has become unstoppable.

**15. (C)**

It has been recognized that duress may be a valid defense to arson under the holding of *Ross v. State*, 82 N.E. 781 (1907). In addition, duress has been held a good defense to kidnapping and the lesser crimes of robbery and burglary. Keep in mind that even though duress is *not* a defense to murder, it may be a defense to felony-murder if it negates the underlying felony.

**16. (D)**

A key to choosing the correct answer in Criminal Law questions on the MBE is to follow the statutes given in the facts. In this case, first degree murder requires an ***intentional and premeditated*** killing or a killing caused during the commission of a felony. Second degree murder requires ***an intent to cause serious***

**bodily harm,** whereas manslaughter requires an unlawful killing due to **reck-lessness.** The main issue to be determined is Deb's mens rea. She did not intend to kill anyone with the strychnine, although her plan was premeditated. First degree murder requires *both* premeditation and intent. Likewise, the killing did not occur during the commission of a felony, since Deb's action did not consti-tute an assault. Assault is defined in the facts as a felony when it is committed with *intent to kill* or with *intent to cause serious physical injury.* Deb did not pos-sess either of these mental states, since the facts say that she "didn't want to seri-ously injure anyone." Therefore, no first degree murder conviction is proper and choices (A) and (B) are incorrect. Choice (C), second degree murder, is incor-rect for the same reason, namely that Deb did *not* intend to cause serious bodily harm. By process of elimination, choice (D), manslaughter, is correct because Deb's mental state was one of **recklessness.** Recklessness is generally defined as *a high degree of negligence*, (i.e., more than ordinary negligence) *measured by an objective reasonable person standard, which creates a high and unreasonable degree of risk.* LaFave and Scott, **Criminal Law,** p. 208.

## 17. (C)

Benny will be liable to the same extent as Deb, as a party to the crime. One is liable as an accomplice to the crime of another if he (1) *gives assistance or encourage-ment* or fails to perform a legal duty to prevent it, (2) *with the intent thereby to promote or facilitate commission of the crime.* LaFave and Scott, **Criminal Law,** p. 502. Benny "agreed to assist" Deb "to facilitate her plan." The criminal plan in this case was a commission of a *battery* by poisoning the oysters with strychnine. Since the scope of accomplice liability extends to "all natural and probable consequences" of the underlying offense, Benny will be responsible for the foreseeable death due to strychnine poisoning. As an accomplice, he may be convicted to the same extent as the principal, Deb, for manslaughter. Choice (C) is correct.

## 18. (D)

Phil, the pharmacist, gave the strychnine to Benny in violation of the state statute making it a felony to sell strychnine without a prescription. Phil may be convicted of selling drugs without a prescription. Choice (D) is correct. No accomplice theory of liability will arise under the facts because Phil had no *knowledge* of Deb's criminal intent when he sold the poison to Benny. Benny falsely told Phil he needed the strychnine for an experiment with rats. Choice (C) is therefore incorrect. Choice (B) is incorrect because Phil did not intend to commit any serious bodily harm.

## 19. (B)

Students should note that in order for one to be found guilty of murder under the felony-murder rule, he *must* also be found guilty of the underlying felony. Thus, as in the present example, if a defendant is found innocent of the underlying felony, he cannot be found guilty of felony-murder. Briefly, the felony-murder rule provides that one whose conduct brought about an unintended death in the commission or attempted commission of a felony was guilty of murder.

## 20. (A)

Studious is guilty of depraved-heart murder. LaFave instructs that the following types of conduct have been held to involve a "very high degree of unjustifiable homicidal danger" which will do for depraved-heart murder: (1) firing a bullet into a room occupied, as the defendant knows, by several people; (2) shooting into a moving automobile, necessarily occupied by human beings; (3) throwing a beer glass at one who is carrying a lighted oil lamp; (4) playing a game of "Russian roulette" with another person; and (5) shooting at a point near, but not aiming directly at, another person.

## 21. (C)

Just as one cannot use deadly force to protect his property from trespass or theft, so too he cannot use a deadly spring gun (or other mechanical device) as a protection against vandalism. Note that the Model Penal Code has adopted the view that use of a deadly mantrap is never justifiable. In *State v. Barr* 39 P. 1080 (1895), "spring gun, set to protect an empty cabin, killed the trespasser trying to enter; conviction of murder *held* affirmed."

## 22. (C)

Lucy is guilty of rape under accomplice liability. According to LaFave, one is liable as an accomplice to the crime of another if "he (a) gave assistance or encouragement or failed to perform a legal duty to prevent it (b) with the intent thereby to promote or facilitate commission of the crime." Note that choice (C) is more correct than alternate (D) because Lucy "aided" and "abetted" Ricky by shouting encouragement not by her mere presence. Choice (A) is wrong because even though a woman cannot technically rape another woman, a woman can be convicted on an accomplice liability theory. See LaFave, p. 502.

## 23. (C)

Alternative (C) is the best answer. Andy would have the strongest case successfully alleging the defense of self-defense. The facts in Choice (C) are sufficient to indicate that Andy has a reasonable belief that he was in immediate danger of deadly force or serious bodily harm. It is immaterial that Andy did not know that Barry's gun was not loaded. As a general rule, one who is not the aggressor in an encounter is justified in using a reasonable amount of force against his adversary when he *reasonably believes* (a) that he is in immediate danger of unlawful bodily harm from his adversary and (b) that the use of such force is necessary to avoid this danger. See Scott and LaFave, **Handbook on Criminal Law,** p. 391. In reference to our hypothetical, Andy not only had such reasonable belief to justify the use of deadly force but he also was not under a duty to retreat from his own home. It is important for students to be aware of the problems involving the "duty to retreat" when deadly force is used in self-defense. The majority of American jurisdictions hold that the defender (who was not the original aggressor) need *not* retreat, even though he may do so safely, before using deadly force upon an assailant whom he reasonably believes will kill him or do him serious bodily harm. However, even in the minority of jurisdictions that require retreat, the defender (1) need not retreat unless he knows he can do so in complete safety and (2) he need not retreat from his home or place of business.

## 24. (B)

As a general rule, one whose conduct brings about an unintended death in the commission or attempted commission of a felony is guilty of felony-murder. In many states, the felony-murder rule is limited in its application to *serious felonies* that must be dangerous to life. ***Examination Tip:*** These felonies can be remembered by the mnemonic BARRK: Burglary; Arson; Rape; Robbery; and Kidnapping. Since Jody's death occurred during the commission of a robbery, Wilder would be guilty of felony-murder. Choice (C) is wrong even though some students will find Wilder guilty of misdemeanor-manslaughter for punching Jody in the mouth (e.g., battery). Although death-causing conduct in the commission or attempted commission of an unlawful act (i.e., misdemeanor) is involuntary manslaughter, if the act occurs during the commission of a serious felony then the crime is felony-murder. Choice (D) is incorrect because voluntary manslaughter consists of an *intentional* killing committed under extenuating circumstances. Here, Jody's killing was *un*intentional, not intentional. Lastly, choice (A) is not the best answer because felony-murder is a specific type of murder.

## 25. (B)

One who is not the aggressor in an encounter is justified in using a reasonable amount of force against his adversary when he reasonably believes (a) that he is in immediate danger of unlawful bodily harm from his adversary and (b) that the use of such force is necessary to avoid this danger. Note that the Missoula statute denoted in the facts is simply a distractor or "red herring." Henderson is being charged with the crime of assault, not with violating the resisting arrest statute. As a result, self-defense may be a valid defense to assault. Therefore, choice (B) is correct.

## 26. (D)

First, it is necessary to keep in mind that Hink is being charged with the crime of attempt. Remember, attempt is a specific intent crime. If Hink did not intend to violate the ordinance, then he would not possess the requisite state of mind required for commission of the crime. That's why choice (D) would provide Hink with his best defense. Note that choice (A) is wrong because factual impossibility is no defense to a charge of attempt.

## 27. (C)

First, Howie and Hymie are guilty of conspiracy to murder Uncle Murray. They entered into an agreement to murder their uncle and had the specific-intent to carry out their criminal objective. On the other hand, Howie and Hymie are *not* guilty of conspiracy to murder Dr. Doom. There was neither an agreement nor intent to murder him. The defendants are also guilty of murder under an accomplice theory of liability. Obviously, they were responsible for encouraging Molly to kill Uncle Murray. Note that choice (D) is incorrect because solicitation is a lesser included crime of conspiracy and merges into it.

## 28. (A)

Under the theory of felony-murder, Defendant in situation (A) would be found guilty of murder for causing the death of Pedestrian (during the commission or attempted commission of the robbery/burglary at the department store). It should be pointed out that Defendant's "withdrawal" would be *in*effective, so as not to exonerate him of criminal responsibility for Pedestrian's death. Note that a withdrawal is effective only if communicated to his confederates made in time for his companions to effectively abandon the conspiracy. Thus, notice is insufficient unless it is given to all of the other conspirators.

## 29. (B)

This question illustrates a number of Multistate principles: *(1) answer the precise question asked, reading carefully; (2) select the BEST of the four answers; (3) if you cannot identify any answer as correct, at least eliminate the incorrect choices to increase your odds of choosing the best answer; and (4) in choosing an answer, note that a choice that is only possibly correct is preferred over one that is absolutely wrong.* There are three important elements to the question asked: (a) a defense (b) to the crime of assault with intent to commit rape (c) based on an attack on the companion of a rape victim. Choice (A) is incorrect because this selection suggests an unsuccessful mistake of fact defense to the charge of statutory rape. Alternative (C) is wrong because the crime involved in the question is a *specific*-intent crime, and intoxication may be a defense only to a specific (not general) intent crime. In other words, choice (C) is an incorrect statement of law. Statement (D) is incorrect as the mere fact that the lot was "dimly lit" will not preclude a guilty verdict. Consequently, alternative (B) applies certainly an arguable and conceivably correct interpretation of the crime of assault with intent to rape.

## 30. (D)

This question deals with defenses to murder. In order to impose criminal liability, the defendant's conduct must be the "proximate" cause of the crime. No variation between the result intended or hazarded and the result actually achieved may be so extraordinary that it would be unfair to hold the defendant responsible for the actual result. LaFave and Scott, **Criminal Law,** p. 246. Where an intervening cause in the form of an unforeseeable act of God follows a defendant's criminal act and thereby causes death, the defendant may be relieved of liability. In choice (A), the earthquake caused the hospital to collapse, crushing the victim to death. As a superseding cause, the earthquake will cut off the defendant's liability, so choice (A) is incorrect. Similarly, in choice (C) the defendant will not be liable for Victim's death due to lack of causation, so this answer choice is incorrect. Although the threat to kill Victim may have frightened him enough to board an airplane, the defendant's act in itself did not proximately cause Victim's death; the plane crash did. Choice (B) is incorrect because *omission to act is a basis to impose criminal responsibility only where there exists a legal duty to act*—generally established by contract, by statute, or by relationship. Defendant had no familial or business relationship with Victim such that a duty to warn existed. Therefore, he would not be responsible for Victim's subsequent death. Choice (D) is correct by process of elimination, because in this situation, Defendant pushed Victim directly out of the car after stabbing him in the arm, thereby causing the fractured ankle. Because of the immobility of the ankle, Victim was unable to move from the roadway. Being run over subsequently by a drunken driver was not only *a direct intervening cause* of defendant's initial conduct, but it was a *foreseeable* result. Therefore, the claim of causation will not be broken and defendant will be criminally responsible.

## 31. (A)

Many statutes defining conduct which is criminal employ words or phrases indicating some type of bad-mind requirement: "intentionally" or "with intent to . . . ," "knowingly" or "with knowledge that …"; "fraudulently" or "with intent to defraud"; "willfully" and so on. In our case, choice (A) is the best answer because if Barrow didn't know what was in the package, she wouldn't possess the required mental state for the statutory crime.

## 32. (D)

In a majority of jurisdictions assault includes both (1) attempted battery and (2) the doing of an act which places another person in reasonable apprehension of receiving a battery. In those jurisdictions where an assault is limited to an attempted battery, an intent to commit a battery (i.e., an intent to cause physical injury to the victim) is required. The second type of criminal assault requires some *overt act* by the defendant to arouse a reasonable apprehension of bodily harm. Thus, threatening words alone, without any overt act to carry out the threat, or indecent proposals by a man to a woman, not accompanied by any attempt to carry them out without her consent, will not suffice.

## 33. (C)

It should be noted that the crime of attempt consists of (1) an intent to do an act or to bring about certain consequences which would in law amount to a crime;

and (2) an act in furtherance of that intent which goes beyond mere preparation. Remember that intoxication is a defense to a crime if it negates a required element of that crime; and this is so whether the intoxication is voluntary or involuntary. Generally speaking, intoxication (when it negates an element of the crime) does so by negating some mental element (i.e., intent or knowledge) which the crime requires. Choice (C) is correct because *intoxication (whether voluntary or involuntary) negates the element of intent required for the crime of attempt* to commit rape. This is a *classic* Multistate example because the *test maker is aware that many students will incorrectly choose choice (B)*. Note that if Kyle were charged with the crime of rape, then choice (B) would be correct (because intoxication is not a valid defense for the "general-intent" crime of rape). In this example, however, *Kyle is not charged with the crime of rape, but rather he is being charged with the crime of attempt to commit rape* (which is a "specific-intent" crime). In sum, intoxication is a valid defense for "specific-intent" crimes (if it negates the mens rea) but not for "general-intent" crimes (which do not require a specific mens rea).

## 34. (D)

The next two questions deal with conspiracy. The traditional definition of conspiracy requires the following two elements: (1) an agreement between two or more persons (which constitutes the act) and (2) an intent to achieve a criminal or unlawful objective. To constitute conspiracy at common law, there must be a combination of two or more guilty persons. Based on these facts, the "plurality" requirement is not satisfied because Kareem is an innocent party who believed that he was the true owner of the John Coltrane album. In addition, Elgin never entered into an agreement with Russell or Kareem but rather intended individually to commit a theft inside Wilt's home.

## 35. (B)

This same issue was tested on the July, 2006, MBE and involves an interplay between conspiracy and attempt. Clearly, Tinker and Mallory have entered into an agreement to burglarize Rosario's home and are guilty of conspiracy. The more difficult question is whether Blick can become a party to the crime of conspiracy even in the absence of any agreement on his part. According to LaFave, it is possible for a person to become a member of a conspiracy where he knew of the conspiracy and intentionally gave aid to the conspiratorial objective even though he did not enter into the agreement himself. **Criminal Law**, p. 534. Consequently, Blick is guilty of conspiracy because he aided the conspiratorial objective by telling Mallory and Tinker how they could disarm Rosario's alarm with the knowledge that they were planning to perpetrate a burglary. The next issue is which, if any, defendants are guilty of attempt. At common law attempt requires an act that constitutes a "substantial step" in the commission or attempted commission of a crime. In this regard, Mallory and Tinker did not perform a "substantial step" merely by going to Rosario's home without any entry.

## 36. (C)

Robbery at common law consists of the same six elements as larceny, namely, (1) a trespassory (2) taking and (3) carrying away of the (4) personal property (5) of another (6) with intent to steal it plus the two added elements of (7) the taking must be accomplished by force, violence, or intimidation and (8) the taking must be from the victim's person or presence. With respect to element 7, robbery requires that the taking be done by means of violence or intimidation. The commonest sort of fear in robbery, of course, is the fear, engendered by the robber's threat of immediate bodily injury or death, as where the robber points a gun, loaded or unloaded, at the owner with a threat to shoot unless the latter hands over his property. In this question, Nickerson did not actually threaten Chin nor did he brandish his gun. Therefore, choice (C) is the best answer.

## 37. (D)

First, Lex is guilty of burglary which at common law was defined as the (1) breaking (2) and entering (3) the dwelling house (4) of another (5) at nighttime (6) with intent to commit a felony or larceny therein. In the present case, students must assume that Lex intended to commit a larceny or felony when he led the victims into the apartment at gunpoint. Second, Lex is guilty of robbery because there was a violent taking of the victims' personal property. Although robbery requires presence, "the robber takes property from the victim's presence if he locks or ties the victim up in one room of a building and then helps himself to valuables located in another room." LaFave, p. 780. Third, Lex is guilty of felony-murder because Keefe's death was proximately related to the robbery and burglary. Note that (C) is wrong because burglary and robbery are separate criminal offenses.

## 38. (A)

There are three distinct ways of committing *a (criminal) battery: (1) where the defendant acts (or omits to act) with the intent to injure; (2) where he or she acts with criminal negligence but has no intent to injure; and (3) where the defendant commits an unlawful act (that does not amount to criminal negligence) where bodily injury results*. Here, Jilly would be guilty of battery under the second or third category. Choice (B) is wrong because she did not have the specific-intent to kill either victim. Rather, she recklessly caused their injuries. Choice (C) is incorrect because attempted manslaughter is a legal anomaly inasmuch as it is impossible to specifically intend to commit an unintentional killing. Choice (D) is a very appealing "distractor" but it is not the best answer because reckless endangerment is defined as placing "another person in danger of death or serious bodily injury." Certainly, Jilly's conduct of attempting suicide may have endangered the victims' lives. But once physical contact occurred, she committed an unlawful battery. Usually reckless endangerment occurs when defendant points a firearm at or in the direction of another. If, however, the defendant discharges the gun and the bullet strikes the victim, then the crime is battery.

### 39. (B)

Students should be aware that the distinction between obtaining possession and obtaining title—the principal dividing line between larceny by trick and the separate crime of false pretenses—is not always easy to draw. Remember that the crime of false pretenses requires that the defendant, by his lies, obtain *title* to the victim's property. If he obtains *possession* without title by means of his lies, his crime is larceny by trick. In *Hufstetler v. State*, 37 Ala. App. 71, 63 So. 2d 730 (1953), defendant's conviction for larceny by trick was affirmed where he (driver) suddenly drove off without paying for the gasoline. In this particular situation, the court held that the defendant got possession but not title because the fraud vitiated the (gas station) owner's consent.

### 40. (D)

The crime of larceny requires the trespassory taking and carrying away of the personal property of another with the intent to permanently deprive the owner. The ***mental state*** of intent to steal must concur in time with the ***act*** of taking and carrying away. In this question, Peters, not Lucinda, performed the act of stealing the diamond necklace. Lucinda decided to keep it ***three weeks later***. Therefore, she cannot be guilty *of* common law larceny. At most, Lucinda is an accessory ***after*** the fact.

### 41. (B)

Commission of the crime of larceny requires a taking (caption) and carrying away (asportation) of another's property. A taking occurs when the offender secures dominion over the property, while a carrying away requires some ***slight movement*** away of the property. Once Olga picked up the wallet (with the intent to steal) and placed it in her pocket (sufficient asportation), she committed the crime of larceny despite the fact she later returned the property. It should be noted that even though Olga later had a "change of heart" and returned the wallet to Amy, that would not constitute a valid defense. According to LaFave, one who takes another's property intending to deprive the owner permanently is nevertheless guilty of larceny, although he later decides to return it and does so. **Criminal Law,** p. 639.

### 42. (A)

Choice (A) is correct because the crime of false pretenses requires that the defendant by his lies obtain *title* to the victim's property. Students should note that if one obtains *possession without title* by his lies, his crime is larceny. At common law larceny consists of (1) trespassory (2) taking and (3) carrying away of the (4) personal property (5) of another (6) with intent to steal it. In this regard, students should be aware that larceny by trick is simply one way of committing the crime of larceny; it is not a crime separate from larceny.

## 43. (C)

Students should note that at common law larceny was limited to the taking (and carrying away) of *tangible personal property*. Modern statutes in most jurisdictions have broadened the scope of larceny to include the *theft of labor or services* or the use of property. However, LaFave warns that in the absence of a specific statutory provision, it has been held *not* to be larceny to make use of the labor and services of another. Consequently, choice (C) is correct, and Owens is guilty of larceny *if the jurisdiction has a statute* making theft of services a crime.

## 44. (D)

In most states murder is divided into two degrees, for the purpose of awarding a more severe penalty for some murders than for others. Most commonly, first degree murder encompasses *intent-to-kill murder accompanied by premeditation and deliberation,* and *murder in the commission of four or five named felonies* (generally including arson, rape, burglary, and robbery). In most states murder not falling within the first degree murder category (e.g., intent-to-kill without premeditation and deliberation; intent to do serious bodily harm; depraved-heart murder; felony murder where the felony is not one of the four or five named felonies) is second degree murder. According to LaFave, to be guilty of first degree murder the *defendant must not only intend to kill but in addition he must premeditate the killing and deliberate about it.* As a result, choice (D) is the correct answer. See LaFave, p. 563.

## 45. (B)

The crime of false pretenses consists in most jurisdictions of the following five elements: (1) a false representation of a material present or past fact (2) which causes the victim (3) to pass title to (4) his property to the wrongdoer, (5) who (a) knows his representation to be false and (b) intends thereby to defraud the victim. In the present case, choice (B) is the best answer because defendant *must have an intent to defraud* in order to be guilty of false pretenses. If Blackhead did not know that the billing to BRA included the Santa Barbara expenditure, then he didn't intend to defraud BRA.

## 46. (C)

At common law the defendants could only be convicted of larceny, which is the taking and carrying away of the personal property of another by trespass with intent to permanently deprive that person of his interest in the property. The defendants could not be convicted of burglary or arson since, at common law, both offenses required commission in the dwelling house of another.

## 47. (D)

Since Clu only furnished factual information concerning the contents of the warehouse without knowledge or participation in the planned scheme to commit the burglary, he cannot be held as co-conspirator or accessory before the fact.

## 48. (A)

Choice (A) is correct because modern statutes have broadened the property, which, if burned and/or burglarized, to include buildings. Students should note although the defendants did not intend originally to set fire to the warehouse, an arson was, nevertheless, committed by their failure to douse the fire without endangering themselves. In addition, the defendants should also be convicted of larceny for the reasons given in explanatory answer 46.

## 49. (B)

In accordance with the Monrovia burglary statute, Farr is guilty of burglary because he (1) broke into and (2) entered (3) the warehouse (4) with the intent to commit a felony therein. In addition, the defendant should also be found guilty of attempted arson because (1) he intended to commit arson and (2) engaged in an act constituting a "substantial step" in the commission of the crime—which consisted of Farr's breaking into the building with an incendiary device in his possession. Note that the Model Penal Code sets forth several categories of conduct which are sufficient as a matter of law to be corroborative of the actor's criminal purpose. In this regard, **Model Penal Code** Section 5.01(2)(f) holds that it is a "substantial step" to be in "possession of materials to be employed in the commission of the crime, which are specially designed for such unlawful use or which serve no lawful purpose of the actor under the circumstances."

## 50. (C)

Here, Murray should be found guilty as an accessory *after* the fact to burglary. According to LaFave, there are three basic requirements which must be met to constitute one as an accessory after the fact: (1) a completed felony had theretofore been committed by another; (2) he (or she) knew of the commission of the felony by the other person; and (3) he (or she) gave aid to the felon personally for the purpose of hindering the felon's apprehension, conviction, or punishment.

## 51. (B)

B&G Auto Center by servicing Tom's car acquired a mechanic's lien which gave them a superior possessory interest in the vehicle. Thus, Tom's act of taking the car without paying for repair services constituted the crime of larceny. Note that an owner-title holder may commit larceny from another who has a superior possessory interest.

## 52. (D)

Employee will be guilty of embezzlement where the goods are lawfully delivered to him by a third person on behalf of the employer and the employee-servant fraudulently converts the goods to his own use. Larceny, on the other hand, requires a trespassory taking; the thief must take the property out of the victim's possession, which means that he cannot already have it in his possession.

## 53. (D)

Stu should be found guilty of (III) conspiracy (since he entered into an agreement with Tom's employee to illegally convert the car) and (IV) receiving stolen property (which consists of (1) receiving possession of (2) personal property (3) known to have been stolen (4) by another (5) with the intent to permanently deprive the owner of his property).

## 54. (B)

Criminal battery, in brief, is simply defined as the ***unlawful application of force to the person of another.*** Students should be aware that a battery must result in either (1) bodily injury or (2) offensive touching to the victim. Clearly, "bodily injury" will include such obvious matters as wounds caused by bullets or knives and broken limbs or bruises inflicted by sticks, stones, feet, or fists. But, in addition to these more obvious bodily injuries, LaFave notes that offensive touchings (as where a man puts his hands upon a girl's body or kisses a woman against her will, or where one person spits into another's face) will suffice for battery in most jurisdictions. See LaFave, p. 604. Moreover, students must be aware that battery is a "general-intent" crime, which means the defendant need not intend to commit the crime. Rather, "general-intent" is used to encompass all forms of the mental state (or mens rea) requirement. Thus, a defendant may be guilty of battery where he (or she) acts (1) recklessly, (2) negligently, or (3) with knowledge that his/her act (omission) will result in criminal liability. In the present case, Jimmy committed a criminal battery because he recklessly swung his tennis racket in the crowded lounge area. Even though he didn't specifically intend to hit Ivan, Jimmy's conduct created an unreasonable risk of harm to others.

## 55. (B)

Another *key* Multistate area deals with intoxication. Note that intoxication (whether voluntary or involuntary) is a defense to a crime if it negates the existence of an element of the crime. For example, one who takes and carries away another person's property by stealth or at gunpoint is not guilty of larceny or of robbery if he (or she) is too intoxicated to be able to entertain the necessary intent to steal. Likewise, one cannot be guilty of burglary when, although he (or she) breaks and enter's another's house, his (or her) intoxication deprives him (or her) of the capacity to intend to commit a felony therein. It is important to point out, however, that ***intoxication cannot negate a "general-intent" crime.*** Why? Because "general-intent" crimes (e.g., rape and battery) do not require a defendant to specifically intend to commit an unlawful act or produce a specified result that can be negated by intoxication. Thus, voluntary intoxication cannot, according to the weight of authority, be a defense to battery where defendant recklessly strikes the victim because *recklessness cannot be negated by intoxication.*

**56. (A)**

Another *important* Multistate testing area deals with self-defense. Generally speaking, one who is not the aggressor in an encounter is justified in using a reasonable amount of force against his adversary when he reasonably believes (a) that he is in immediate danger of unlawful bodily harm from his adversary and (b) that the use of such force is necessary to avoid this danger. Most importantly, however, the case law and statutory law on self-defense generally requires that the defendant's belief in the necessity of using force to prevent harm to himself (or herself) be a reasonable one, so that **one who honestly though unreasonably believes in the necessity of using force in self-protection loses the defense.** Since Samantha's belief was unreasonable, choice (A) is correct according to the weight of authority. See **LaFave,** p. 391–393.

**57. (C)**

Zeke and Grover would be guilty of larceny which at common law may be defined as the (1) trespassory (2) taking and (3) carrying away of the (4) personal property (5) of another (6) with intent to steal it. In the present example, the defendants committed larceny by taking (caption) and carrying away (asportation) the package containing the baked bread. With respect to the crime of burglary, students should note that at common law burglary consisted of (1) breaking and (2) entering of (3) a dwelling house (4) of another (5) in the nighttime (6) with the intent to commit a felony therein. Here, the defendants would be guilty of attempted burglary (rather than the completed crime) because they did not gain *entry* into Kettle's structure. Students should note that at common law the dwelling home requirement would extend to a place of business if it was usually slept in by the proprietor or one of his employees. See LaFave, **Criminal Law,** p. 712.

**58. (A)**

In accordance with the felony murder rule, at common law one whose conduct brought about an unintended death in the commission or attempted commission of a felony was guilty of murder.

**59. (D)**

In accordance with the Model Penal Code, murder cannot be based upon a shooting which constitutes justifiable homicide (e.g., where the police officer or felony victim shoots the felon to prevent the commission of the felony). See *Commonwealth* v. *Redline,* 137 A.2d 472 (1958). Thus, **the Redline limitation on the felony-murder doctrine holds that a felon is not liable for the death, which the felon did not intend, of a co-felon participating in criminal activity. Examination Tip:** As of 1988, the *Redline* view should now be followed on the MBE.

According to LaFave, **Criminal Law,** 2nd Ed. p. 629, "it is now generally accepted that there is *no* felony-murder liability when one of the felons is shot and killed by the victim, a police officer, or a bystander." Although this is contrary to the common law rule, Redline is now the prevailing view in a majority of jurisdictions.

## 60. (D)

Choice (D) is correct. Clearly, alternative (A) is incorrect since Goldman did not commit larceny when he fraudulently converted the watch which he was lawfully in possession of. Choice (B) is wrong because one who takes another's property intending at the time he takes it to use it temporarily and then return it unconditionally within a reasonable time (and having the substantial ability to do so) lacks the intent to steal required for larceny. Choice (C) is also wrong because one may take the property of another honestly, but mistakenly, believing that it is his own property. In such an event, defendant lacks the intent to steal required for larceny, even though his mistaken, but honest, belief was unreasonable. A similar result was reached in *People v. Rosen* 78 P.2d 727 (1938) where defendant used a pistol to recapture money which he had lost by illegal gambling, honestly believing the money still belonged to him; conviction of larceny held *reversed* for lack of intent to steal. Consequently, choice (D) is correct since it is no defense to larceny that the taker intended to return it (i.e., the stolen property) only if he should receive a reward for its return.

## 61. (C)

It should be pointed out that no area of the substantive criminal law has traditionally been surrounded by more confusion than that of ignorance or mistake of fact or law. As a result, ignorance or mistake of fact of law is a *favorite* Multistate testing area. As a general rule, ignorance or mistake as to a matter of fact or law is a defense ***if it negates a mental state required to establish a material element of the crime.*** For example, to take the classic case of the man who takes another's umbrella out of a restaurant (because he mistakenly believes that the umbrella is his) is not guilty of larceny because he does not have the mental state (intent to steal the property of another) required for the crime. However, LaFave states that a "quite different kind of mistake of law, whereby the defendant believes that his conduct is not proscribed by the criminal law is generally not a defense." LaFave, p. 356. Students should be aware that choice (A) is wrong because the Columbia statute may be violated in either of two ways. First, anyone who gives, sells, or furnishes an air gun (or firearm) to a minor is guilty of violating the statute. Second, anyone who is the owner or in control of a firearm who knowingly permits it to be used by a minor is also in violation of the statute (which imposes strict criminal liability). In the present case, Mrs. King violated the first section of the statute by giving the air rifle to her son who was under the statutory age.

### 62. (A)

Statutory extortion (or blackmail) covers threats to do *future* bodily harm. On the contrary, the crime of robbery by intimidation requires that the threat be to do *immediate* harm. In the present example, since Duneberry threatened Kirksey with future bodily harm, the former would be found guilty of extortion, not robbery. In addition, Duneberry should be found guilty of criminal battery which may be defined as the unlawful application of force. Assault, on the other hand, does not require such physical contact.

### 63. (A)

Commission of the crime of larceny requires a taking (caption) and carrying away (asportation) of another's property. A taking occurs when the offender secures dominion over the property, while carrying away requires some slight movement of the property.

### 64. (B)

Robbery consists of all the six elements of larceny: a (1) trespassory (2) taking and (3) carrying away of the (4) personal property (5) of another (6) with intent to steal it plus two additional elements: (7) that the property be taken away from the person or presence of another and (8) that the taking be accomplished by means of force or "putting in fear." Choice (B) is correct, since the defendant should only be found guilty of the crime of larceny, not robbery. Defendant took Gloria's stereo system from her house without any force or intimidation. Therefore, since the "taking" and "asportation" elements of robbery did not coincide with the violence or intimidation elements, defendant would not be guilty of robbery. All eight elements are necessary for a robbery conviction. Choice (A) is incorrect since defendant robbed Lee of the ring which belonged to Herman. Here, students should note that to prove robbery it is unnecessary to show that the personal property belonged to the victim at the time of the taking with force

---

**Multistate Nuance Chart**

**CRIMINAL LAW**

**ROBBERY = LARCENY + BATTERY**

**or**

**ROBBERY = LARCENY + ASSAULT**

} Which depends on whether victim is intimidated (assault) or victim suffers bodily injury or physical harm (battery).

Larceny and battery (or assault) merge into robbery. They are lesser included offenses. For bar exam purposes, a defendant cannot be guilty of robbery *and* larceny for the same criminal offense.

---

or intimidation. Choice (C) is obviously wrong since the "taking" of the gold chain was directly from Mary's person. Choice (D) is also incorrect, since defendant entered Jerry's home, overpowered him, and then forced him to reveal where he had hidden the money. Thus the taking was accompanied by violence and defendant would be found guilty of robbery.

## 65. (C)

According to LaFave, "A is guilty of murder if he is actually the agent of B's death, notwithstanding the fact that he acted at B's request—as where A shoots and kills B upon B's insistence that he wants to die now rather than continue to suffer from a serious illness." **Criminal Law,** p. 650. Choice (A) is therefore incorrect since mercy killing would not result in Butler's acquittal of the first degree murder charge. Choice (B) is also incorrect because the lack of premeditation and deliberation (subjective mental states determined from the defendant's conduct in light of the surrounding circumstances) does not preclude the fact that defendant's conduct in firing the gun at Hadley could still have been knowing and/or willful. Choice (D) is incorrect because Butler's intent to kill Orlando, the intended victim, will be transferred to Hadley, the actual victim, under the doctrine of transferred intent. By process of elimination, choice (C) is correct. Suicide is not murder under the statute since Butler would be required to have knowingly or willfully caused the death of *another human being,* not of himself. By attempting suicide, Butler did not knowingly or willfully cause the death of Hadley.

## 66. (C)

This Multistate question deals with statutory interpretation. Here, it is necessary to carefully read the facts to see that the Mariposa statute makes it a crime to *sell* condoms to anyone under the age of 17. In the present example, Al Key did not violate the statute because he didn't sell the condoms to Young. As a result, we know the correct answer must be either choice (C) or (D). Note that (D) is wrong because if Al Key is *not* criminally liable, then no vicarious liability will be imposed on the owner of the drug store.

## 67. (D)

This is another extremely popular Multistate Criminal Law example dealing with **legislative intent.** As noted in the previous answer, the Mariposa statute is interpreted to make the sale, not the purchase, of condoms (to minors) a criminal offense. As such, only sellers of condoms and other contraceptive devices may be convicted under the statute.

## 68. (A)

Most importantly, the agreement is all important in conspiracy. In order to have a conspiracy, there must be an agreement between two or more persons to engage in a criminal act. Since Calvin was an undercover police officer, he never intended to really purchase the narcotics. Rather he feigned agreement because he wanted to trap Emmette. Therefore, no agreement (or "meeting of the minds") existed. Choice (A) is preferred over (B) because in a conspiracy you need the **requisite plurality** of two or more persons entering into an agreement. On the other hand, Emmette can be convicted of sale of narcotics because sale does not require an agreement between two or more persons.

## 69. (D)

This rather simple Criminal Law question provides two very important "tips" for MBE success. First, **reading comprehension** is equally as important as your knowledge of the law. Second, you must always be on the lookout for "red herring" answer choices and Pavlov dog responses. In this question, for example, the facts clearly indicate that Marcus was the aggressor. When Caveman caught Marcus in bed with his wife, Caveman calmly remarked, "put your pants on and get the hell out of here." **Caveman did not threaten Marcus with bodily harm or injury.** It was only after Marcus brandished his weapon that Caveman acted in self-defense and killed him. This type of question frequently appears on the Multistate because many students will skim the facts and go for the Pavlovian answer (B) since they have been trained for that response anytime they see an apparent "heat of passion" killing.

## 70. (C)

The common law definition of burglary requires that there be a (1) breaking and (2) entering of (3) a dwelling house (4) of another (5) in the nighttime (6) with the intent to commit a felony within. Although Foster originally broke into the cabin at night, his breaking and entering was not accompanied by the requisite felonious intent. As a consequence, defense statement III is correct. Similarly, defense I is correct because since burglary is a specific-intent crime, intoxication is a defense to the crime if it negates a required element of the crime, and this is so whether the intoxication is voluntary or involuntary.

## 71. (D)

Foster would not be guilty of arson under the common law, in that arson requires the presence of "malice," which is not satisfied by a mere showing of criminal negligence.

## 72. (C)

As noted earlier, the crime of **attempt** consists of (1) an **intent** to do an act or bring about certain consequences which would in law amount to a crime; and (2) an **act in furtherance of that intent** which, as it is most commonly put, goes beyond mere preparation. Robbery, on the other hand, consists of all six elements of larceny—a (1) trespassory (2) taking and (3) carrying away of the (4) personal property (5) of another (6) with intent to steal it—plus two additional requirements: (7) that the property be taken from the person or presence of the other and (8) that the taking be accomplished by means of force or intimidation. In the present case, Fanny will be guilty of ***attempted robbery*** because she acted with the requisite intent to commit a robbery and performed an overt act (or "substantial step") in furtherance of that goal. Her act of reaching into her pocketbook and her statement accompanying this action would constitute an "act toward the commission" of the crime. It is important to point out that attempted robbery (choice [C]) is a better answer than robbery (choice [B]) because Juan was not intimidated or deceived by her ruse. Although Fanny is not guilty of robbery, she, nevertheless, may be convicted of attempt.

## 73. (C)

At common law, burglary consisted of breaking and entering the dwelling house of another at nighttime with intent of committing a felony. In the instant case, Dunebar and Russ did not intend to commit a felony at the time they entered Will's house. They did not formulate their criminal intent (e.g., to steal the puppies) until after they had entered the house. Choice (B) is incorrect since it is irrelevant whether they intended to hold the puppies for ransom. With respect to the question of burglary, it is necessary for the defendant to formulate his intent to commit a felony *prior* to the breaking and entering. Therefore, alternates (A) and (D) are incorrect.

## 74. (A)

First, Russ is guilty of larceny, not robbery. Robbery requires that ***the taking be done by means of violence or intimidation.*** Larceny from the person or presence of the victim is not robbery without this added element of force or fear. The commonest sort of fear in robbery is the fear, engendered by the robber's intentional threat, of immediate bodily injury or death to the property owner himself (as where the robber points a gun, loaded or unloaded, at the owner with a threat to shoot unless the latter hands over his property). In this example, neither Russ nor Dunebar actually threatened Will with bodily injury. As a result, choice (D) is wrong because no robbery took place. Note that choice (C) is also incorrect because practically all extortion statutes cover the demand for (or acquisition of) money. Here, however, the defendants never extorted or actually demanded money (even though "they had the idea" of doing so).

## 75. (A)

Rookie would be guilty of killing Dunebar since a person may not use deadly force in the defense of personal property. A person may use deadly force in the defense of property generally only in conjunction with another privileged use of force, i.e., self-defense or defense of another individual. Furthermore, the modern view is that deadly force may be used only to prevent the commission of dangerous felonies (e.g., those involving a substantial risk of death or serious bodily harm). As a consequence, choices (B), (C), and (D) are incorrect.

### 76. (D)

At common law, burglary required the breaking and entering of the dwelling house of another at nighttime with intent to commit a *felony* therein. **REMEMBER:** Assault and battery were two separate common law misdemeanors. Consequently, Leslie could not be found guilty of burglary (at common law) because she intended to commit a misdemeanor only.

### 77. (B)

At common law, burglary consisted of (1) breaking and (2) entering (3) a dwelling house (4) of another (5) in the nighttime (6) with the intent to commit a felony therein. As a consequence, choice (B) is correct because hurling the rock through the window of Smith's home would constitute an effective breaking and entering. Moreover, since Defendant intended to kill Smith, requirement (6) would also be met. Students should be aware that at common law assault and battery were misdemeanors. Therefore, if Defendant only attempted to hit or injure Smith, he technically would not be found guilty of burglary at common law. Lastly, at common law, the crime of burglary could be committed in a hotel or any place of human habitation or occupancy. In this context choice (D) is incorrect because the nighttime requirement was not met.

### 78. (A)

At common law, arson was defined as the malicious burning of the dwelling of another. The mens rea denoted by the term "malicious" includes both *intentional* conduct and *reckless* conduct. Choice (A) is correct. If the jury determines that Swenson was reckless in his act of damaging the restaurant, such conduct will be sufficient for the crime of arson inasmuch as a piece of the ceiling was charred. The requisite degree of "burning" for arson is *charring,* i.e., more than blackening by smoke. Choice (C) is incorrect because reckless burning without additional intent is sufficient for arson. Choice (D) is incorrect because any attempted arson would have merged into the completed crime of arson.

### 79. (A)

Choice (A) would least likely relieve Frankie of liability for felony murder. The common law felony murder rule provides that one whose conduct brought about an unintended death in the commission of a felony was guilty of murder. For a defendant to be found guilty of felony murder, he need *not* have the *intent* to kill the victim. Thus, choice (A) would not be a good defense. Alternatives (B) and (C) state the respective defenses of insanity and duress to the underlying felony (here arson). Thus, if Frankie is not found guilty of the underlying felony, he cannot be convicted of felony murder. Choice (D) is incorrect, because of the absence of the causation factor which is generally a requirement in felony murder cases.

## 80. (D)

Generally, one has no legal duty to aid another person in peril. For criminal liability to be based upon a failure to act, it must first be found that there is a legal duty to act. Such an affirmative act is placed upon persons standing in certain personal relationships to the persons—upon parents to aid their small children, upon husbands to aid their wives, upon ship captains to aid their crews, upon masters to aid their servants. LaFave, p. 203. Choice (A) states this general rule; however, it is not the best answer. Professor LaFave points out that "(j)ust as one cannot be criminally liable on account of a bodily movement which is involuntary, so one cannot be criminally liable for failing to do an act which he is physically incapable of performing." *Ibid.* p. 209. In our question, if Husband is physically unable to assist his wife, then he will not be guilty of manslaughter for failing to aid her from bleeding to death. Choice (D) is correct.

## 81. (C)

The key words in this question are that Harry "was playing a practical joke on Mr. Scylla and was trying to scare him." The mental state described by these words falls short of that necessary under the given Ames Penal Code. The Ames statute requires for assault an unlawful *"attempt"*—i.e., an *intent* plus an act to commit an unlawful application of force (i.e., a battery). If Harry did not **intend** to commit any application of force on Mr. Scylla, which is what the facts state, then, if the jury believes him, he will be not guilty due to lack of intent to cause physical injury. Therefore, choice (C) is correct. Without a specific-intent to unlawfully apply force, Harry cannot be guilty, so choices (A) and (B) are incorrect. Choice (D) is incorrect since fright is not required for criminal assault under the given statute.

## 82. (C)

As a general rule, whenever an intentional battery or assault results in an un-intended death, the defendant is guilty of involuntary manslaughter. LaFave notes that a criminal assault, like a criminal battery, is an unlawful act malum in se. Therefore, if the defendant approaches close to another person intending to strike him but not to kill him, and the latter, who unknown to the defendant possesses a weak heart, has a heart seizure, and dies as a result of fright produced by the threatened attack, the defendant is guilty of manslaughter, *though he never touched the victim.* See *Regina v. Dugal,* 4 Que. L.R. 350 (Q.B. 1878), referred to by LaFave in **Criminal Law,** p. 601.

## 83. (D)

Students must be aware of the distinction between larceny and embezzlement. Whenever a master (employer) hands his property to his servant (employee), the servant acquires only custody (as the owner-master retains "constructive possession" of the property), so that the servant who misappropriates the property is guilty of larceny. However, whenever the servant acquires possession of his employer's property and misappropriates it, he is guilty of embezzlement. In sum, misappropriating employees who have *possession* of their employer's property are guilty of embezzlement, those with *custody* are guilty of larceny. For this reason, if Hayden had possession when he misappropriated the book, his crime would be embezzlement, not larceny. Therefore, choice (D) would LEAST aid him in his defense for the crime of larceny. Students are advised to refer to CAVEAT 30 for a more detailed analysis of misappropriating employees (an area which gives rise to a great deal of confusion and difficulty for law students).

## Multistate Nuance Chart
## CRIMINAL LAW

| LARCENY | EMBEZZLEMENT |
|---|---|
| 1. *trespassory* taking and carrying away the property of another | 1. property must be in the embezzler's *lawful* possession when he misappropriates it |
| 2. requires only a taking and an asportation | 2. requires a conversion (i.e., a serious act of interference with the owner's rights) |
| 3. moving the property a short distance (i.e., the asportation) will do | 3. the mere act of moving the property a short distance (the asportation for larceny) will *not* do |
| 4. requires an intent to steal (or, as stated in Latin, an animus furandi) which must concur with the larcenous conduct | 4. requires a specific-intent to defraud |

### 4. illustrative distinctions:

| | |
|---|---|
| (a) an employer who hands his property to his servant (employee) retains possession of it, the servant having mere *custody*, so that the servant who misappropriates the property is guilty of larceny; | (a) an employee who receives his employer's property from a third person (to return to his employer) acquires *possession,* so that the servant who misappropriates the property is guilty of embezzlement; |
| (b) generally minor employees (such as caretakers, janitors, nightwatchmen) are considered as having custody of their employers' property, and so guilty of larceny when they steal. | (b) employees delegated with greater authority (such as office managers, corporate officials, public officials) are deemed to have possession, and so guilty of embezzlement when they fraudulently convert. |

## 84. (A)

At common law, larceny may be defined as the (1) trespassory (2) taking and (3) carrying away of the (4) personal property (5) of another (6) with intent to steal it. Students should note that common law larceny was limited to the taking of *tangible personal property*. Scott and LaFave in their hornbook **Criminal Law** note that modern statutes in all jurisdictions have broadened the scope of larceny to include such intangible personal property as written instruments embodying choices in action or other intangible rights. However, students must be aware that in the *absence* of a specific statutory provision, it has been held *not to be* larceny to make use of the factory, or of the labor and services, of another. In this regard, note that sometimes the property which X owns is in the lawful possession of Y, who has a pledge or lien interest in the property to secure a debt which X owes Y. From X's viewpoint such property is considered the "property of another" for purposes of larceny, so that if X takes it from Y's possession with intent to deprive him of his pledge or lien interest therein, X is guilty of larceny.

## 85. (C)

One source of continuing confusion for law students (and lawyers as well) is whether the doctrines concerning complicity and conspiracy are essentially the same, so that liability as a conspirator and as an accomplice may be based upon essentially the same facts. Is one who is a member of a conspiracy of necessity a party to any crime committed in the course of the conspiracy? On the other hand, is one who qualifies as an accomplice to a crime of necessity part of a conspiracy to commit that crime? According to LaFave, both of these questions must be answered in the negative. In the present case, Marvin should be found guilty of conspiracy (to commit larceny) which is an agreement between two or more persons, which constitutes the act and an intent to do either an unlawful act or a lawful act by unlawful means. Since Marvin suggested that Kimberly recover her car (without paying for the parking charge) with a spare set of keys and then drove her to the parking lot (after it had closed), he would be found guilty of conspiracy to commit larceny. On the other hand, should Marvin also be found guilty of the crime of larceny itself? The answer is yes. Generally, one is liable as an accomplice to the crime of another if he (a) gave assistance or encouragement or failed to perform a legal duty to prevent it (b) with the intent thereby to promote or facilitate commission of the crime. Several terms have been employed by courts and state legislatures in describing the kinds of acts which will suffice for accomplice liability. LaFave notes that the most common are "aid," "assist," "cause," "command," "counsel," "encourage," "hire," "induce," and "procure." Clearly, in the case at bar, Marvin "aided" and "assisted" Kimberly in recovering her car (without paying for the service charge) to be criminally liable for larceny under the state statute.

### 86. (D)

Most importantly, Jill is not guilty of larceny because there was no trespassory taking. Simply stated, trespassory means the taking (or caption) must be without the owner's permission. In the present case, Morris gave Jill permission to take his fur coat. As a result, choices (A), (B), and (C) are incorrect. Moreover, no conspiracy occurred because Morris obviously did not manifest an intention to steal his own coat.

### 87. (D)

In the area of Criminal Law, students experience a great deal of difficulty concerning the inchoate crime of attempt. Let's first review the elements of attempt which consist of (1) an **intent** to do an act or bring about certain consequences which would in law amount to a crime and (2) an **act in furtherance of that intent** which goes beyond mere preparation. In the case at hand, Johnstone, the defendant, possessed the requisite state of mind inasmuch as he intended to defraud the victim. Next, by handing the counterfeit replica of the 1933 Ruth card to Liver to carry out his scheme, that ipso facto would constitute a **substantial step** toward the commission of the offense. Choices (A), (B), and (C) are simply diversions that have no legal relevancy.

### 88. (A)

For the crime of solicitation to be completed, it is only necessary that the actor, with intent that another person commit a crime, have enticed, advised, incited, ordered, or otherwise encouraged that person to commit a crime. The crime solicited need not be committed. LaFave notes that it is *not* a defense to a solicitation charge that, unknown to the solicitor, the person solicited could not commit the crime. **Criminal Law,** p. 422. Similarly, it is also *no defense* that the person solicited is an undercover agent and under no circumstances would have committed the crime solicited. See *State v. Davis*, 319 Mo. 1222, 6 S.W.2d 609 (1928). It is important to point out that Wife is not guilty of conspiracy because an essential element of the crime is an agreement (for an unlawful purpose) between two or more persons. For example, assume that A wants to burglarize a store and thus approaches B to solicit his assistance in the commission of a crime, that upon hearing A's plan B manifests his complete concurrence in the scheme and expresses his willingness to participate, but that B secretly intends not to go through with the plan and has merely feigned agreement because he wishes to trap A. Under these circumstances there is no conspiracy because there is no agreement since B obviously does not have the required intent-to-burglarize mental state. Although A has the requisite mental state, *he may not be convicted of conspiracy because there has been no agreement and thus no criminal act.* LaFave, p. 459.

**89. (A)**

According to the holding in *United States v. Veola* (1975), the U.S. Supreme Court held that with respect to the federal statutory offense of conspiracy to commit an assault on a federal officer, defendant's knowledge that the intended victim was a federal officer was held not to be a material element of the crime.

**90. (A)**

The usual definition of the crime requires (1) the receiving of (2) stolen property, (3) knowing it to be stolen property, and (4) done with intent to deprive the owner of his property. Most jurisdictions properly hold that an *actual belief* the property is stolen is required for guilt. As such, it would appear as though both choices (A) or (B) are arguably correct. Regarding the crime of receiving stolen property, however, students are required to know the **modern trend** for Multistate testing purposes. In the past few years, many jurisdictions have in their statutes abolished the requirement of actual knowledge and imposed guilt if the receiver "had reasonable grounds for believing" or "has reason to know" that the goods were stolen. Under the modern view, choice (A) is the preferred best argument.

**91. (B)**

Whenever the crimes of assault or battery result in an unintended death, the defendant is guilty of involuntary manslaughter. In the present case, Defendant committed a (criminal) battery by nicking Bartender with his penknife. Remember that **criminal battery is simply the unlawful application of force to the person of another.** As with rape, battery is a "general-intent" crime (which means that the crime is completed by the unlawful act and no specific mens rea is necessary).

**92. (A)**

In the famous case of *People v. Jaffe*, 78 N.E. 169 (1906), the defendant was convicted of an attempt to violate a section of the criminal code which made it an offense for a person to buy or receive any stolen property knowing the same to have been stolen. Unknown to the defendant, the property in question had been restored to the owners and was within their control when he purchased it, and thus no longer had the character of stolen goods. The appellate court reversed Jaffe's conviction on the ground that "if the accused had completed the act which he attempted to do, he would not be guilty of a criminal offense." In other words, since Jaffe had done everything he had intended to do—in the sense that he had already received the goods in question—and had not thereby committed the crime of receiving stolen property, he could not be found guilty of attempting to commit that crime under a legal impossibility theory. Conversely, choices (B), (C), and (D) are examples of factual impossibility which do not constitute a defense for attempt.

## 93. (D)

Generally, it may be said that accomplice liability exists when the accomplice intentionally encourages or assists, in the sense that his purpose is to encourage or assist, another in the commission of a crime as to which the accomplice has the requisite mental state. As a consequence, defendants in situations (A), (B), and (C) would incur accomplice liability since their actions or nonaction served to promote or facilitate criminal activity. Choice (D) is, therefore, correct since under the principle of accomplice liability one does not become an accomplice by an intentional act of assistance or encouragement merely because he knows that such an act might facilitate a crime. This is not to say, however, that an owner (of an automobile) by permitting an intoxicated person to drive his car will necessarily escape liability. Owner could very well be found guilty of criminal negligence involuntary manslaughter without being declared an accomplice of the intoxicated driver.

## 94. (D)

The "key" to this question is recognizing that Priscilla is being prosecuted for *felony-murder*, not murder. Choice (A) is incorrect because even though Priscilla was acquitted of the crime of murder, she could still be prosecuted for felony-murder. This is true because felony-murder is a distinct and separate form of murder in that the crime requires proof of a fact that murder does not (namely, commission of the underlying felony). Therefore, choice (A) is incorrect because **res judicata,** the doctrine of claim preclusion, bars the retrial of the *same cause of action.* **Exam Tip:** As a general rule, the res judicata doctrine is applicable in civil, not criminal, cases. Choice (B) is wrong because Bobby's effort to free himself would clearly be foreseeable. By the same token, choice (C) is incorrect inasmuch as changing one's mind is never sufficient grounds for withdrawal from a crime. By process of elimination, choice (D) is therefore correct.

## 95. (B)

A principal in the first degree may simply be defined as the criminal actor. He is the one who, with the requisite mental state (mens rea), engages in the act which causes the criminal result. One who uses an intermediary to commit a crime is not ordinarily a principal in the first degree. It is otherwise, however, when the crime is accomplished by the use of an innocent party (e.g., as in the present example) or irresponsible agent, as where the defendant causes a child or mentally incompetent to engage in conduct. In such a case, the intermediary is regarded as a mere instrument and the originating actor is the principal in the first degree.

## 96. (D)

Choice (D) is correct because an innocent agent, without a criminal state of mind, would not be held responsible where he/she merely left an instrument which caused the criminal result. In this regard, when an actor leaves poison for another who later drinks it, he is a first degree principal, as is the person whose unwitting agent acts for him in his absence. It should be pointed out that although it has been said that a principal in the first degree must be present at the commission of the offense, this is not literally so.

## 97. (D)

First, it is necessary to determine upon the available facts whether the necessary elements of an attempt are present. That is, looking at all of the facts may it be said that there existed both (1) the requisite mental state of an intent to commit a murder, and (2) an act in furtherance of that intent beyond mere preparation. Since the facts to not indicate that Steve intended to kill either Reggie or Lavender (in fact Steve believed that Reggie was in an upstairs bedroom), the requisite mens rea is lacking, and therefore Steve would not be guilty of attempted murder. Note, however, that if Lavender died from the gunshot, Steve would probably be guilty of "depraved-heart" murder. LaFave and Scott note that "extremely negligent conduct, which creates what a reasonable man would realize to be not only an unjustifiable but also a very high degree of risk of death or serious bodily injury to another or to others (although unaccompanied by any intent to kill or do serious bodily injury) and which actually causes the death of another, may constitute 'depraved-heart' murder."

## 98. (D)

This question deals with a very tricky hornbook area, namely, finders of lost property. According to LaFave, the owner of lost property has "constructive possession" of it as long as actual possession is vacant; therefore, a finder who misappropriates property may be viewed as taking it by a trespass from the owner's possession. Such conduct constitutes *larceny if*, at the time of the finding, *the finder 1) intends to steal and 2) either knows who the true owner is or has reason to believe that he can ascertain the owner's identity.* LaFave, p. 711–712. Nevertheless, it is not larceny for the finder to pick up the property with knowledge of its ownership, intending to return it to the owner, even though later the finder converts it to his own use. *Ibid.* p. 712. This situation fits the facts in our question. Penny found Mullins's gold Rolex watch with knowledge of its ownership, but with the intent to return it. Her intent to keep the watch did not concur with the taking. No larceny has been committed. Therefore, choices (A) and (C) are incorrect. Choice (B) is incorrect because "constructive possession" of the watch was still in the owner, Mullins. Embezzlement requires a fraudulent conversion of the personal property of another by one in *lawful possession.* By process of elimination, choice (D) is correct.

## 99. (A)

Students should recognize that "guilty" is not an alternative. Even though you may believe that Harry is guilty, this question forces you to say "not guilty."

What this question is really asking is, "Why is he not guilty?" The reason is that Sue consented to Harry's actions and there is a question whether Harry committed enough acts to result in an attempt. If the elements of the crime are not present, the issue of entrapment is not even reached. Choice (B) is incorrect because it reads solely because he was entrapped, and it would not be the only reason he is not guilty. Alternative (D) is intended to confuse and lead unwary students into thinking that the point of the question is to test their ability to define entrapment. If entrapment were the issue and if Harry was predisposed, then he would be "guilty." Note that if you were to assume that choices (D) and (B) were both correct (which, in fact, they are not), then (B) would be preferred as a statement of law as opposed to (D)'s statement of fact. In addition, alternative (C) is incorrect because there is no alibi defense under the given facts.

### 100. (D)

Even though Bob did not tell Harry that the TV is stolen, there are enough circumstances present to indicate to Harry that the TV is stolen. Even if one considers choice (D) as only possibly correct, the other three alternatives are wrong. There was no larceny of the ring, since Harry intended to return it. Choice (A) is incorrect because there is no larceny and there was obviously consent to the battery. In addition, there was no embezzlement of the ring since Harry was not in lawful possession of it. Thus, choice (C) is incorrect.

### 101. (C)

The correct answer is (C) as Harry would only be guilty of perjury.

### 102. (B)

Choice (B) is the only correct choice since Harvey was merely in possession of the stolen guns when the police raided the warehouse. The burglary was committed by members of the Purple Gang. From the given facts, we may not infer that Harvey was a member of the gang or that he participated in the burglary.

### 103. (A)

Malicious destruction of property is a separate criminal offense apart from larceny. Therefore, choice (B) is wrong. Certainly, Grayson was guilty of larceny for stealing Keefe's vehicle. But the theft by itself will **not** satisfy the malice requirement for destruction of property. In order to be guilty of the crime of malicious destruction of property, there must be evidence presented that Grayson acted maliciously (thus satisfying the mens rea requirement). Choice (D) is incorrect because "general-intent" crimes still require a mens rea whether it be malice, criminal negligence, or recklessness instead of a "specific" intent (e.g., intent to steal). Here, Grayson did not maliciously destroy Evert's property. Rather the damage to Evert's home resulted from the car brakes malfunctioning.

## 104. (A)

Criminal battery is defined as the unlawful application of force to the person of another which results in bodily harm or an offensive touching. Battery is a "general-intent" crime where the offensive or unpermitted contact results from the defendant's negligent or reckless conduct. On the other hand, if the defendant intends to injure the victim, then the criminal offense is of a "specific-intent" nature. According to LaFave, one of the defenses to criminal battery is defense of property. LaFave states that "one whose *lawful* possession of property is threatened by the unlawful conduct of another, and who has no time to resort to the law for its protection, may take reasonable steps to protect the property." Note, however, that LaFave does not discuss whether a person *un*lawfully in possession may use reasonable force to protect her property from trespass or theft. In the present situation, Zoe obviously was not the rightful owner of the umbrella when she tried to regain possession from Wesley. Nonetheless, the question of whether Zoe was privileged to use reasonable force becomes moot because she actually used *excessive force* under the circumstances. The facts state that "Zoe grabbed for the umbrella with one hand and pushed Wesley with the other." Thus, even if Zoe was privileged to grab the umbrella she was not privileged to push Wesley. That's why she remains liable for the criminal offense of battery. In this regard, LaFave states that "one may not use more than reasonable force or the amount of force that reasonably appears necessary to prevent the threatened interference with the property." For that reason, choice (A) is a more preferable answer than (D). See LaFave, pp. 399–400.

## 105. (B)

Involuntary manslaughter consists of two types: (1) *criminal-negligence manslaughter* which requires conduct creating an unreasonable and high degree of risk of death or serious bodily injury (i.e., more than ordinary tort negligence); (2) *unlawful act manslaughter* where the death-causing conduct occurs during the commission or attempted commission of an unlawful act (generally a malum in se misdemeanor) involving a danger of death or serious bodily injury. LaFave, **Criminal Law,** p. 594. Malum in se crimes generally include morality offenses and serious traffic offenses, as well as criminal assault or intentional battery. By unlawfully passing another car on the right, Dodge committed a traffic violation (i.e., a misdemeanor) which resulted in Wesley's death. Dodge may be found guilty of involuntary manslaughter based on the fact that his unlawful act directly and proximately caused Wesley's death. Therefore, choice (B) is correct. Choice (A) is insufficient since the motor vehicle violation will merge into misdemeanor manslaughter. Choice (C) is incorrect since voluntary manslaughter always involves an intentional killing. Choice (D) is incorrect because Dodge's conduct was not of a high enough degree to constitute depraved or wanton recklessness sufficient for depraved-heart murder.

## 106. (B)

The "alter ego" rule holds that the right to defend another is extensive with the other's right to defend himself. Thus, the defender A who intervenes to protect B against C takes the risk that B is not in fact privileged to defend himself in the manner he employs so that, where B is not privileged, A is guilty of assault and battery or murder of C in spite of his reasonable belief that B is privileged. The other view (i.e., statement I) is that, so long as the defendant *reasonably* believes that the other is being unlawfully attacked, he is justified in using reasonable force to defend him. Although there is a split of authority as to which view should be followed, LaFave does state that the latter view is the better rule.

## 107. (C)

In Criminal Law, students must distinguish between actus reus and mens rea. The Meridian statute given in the facts is similar to the **A.L.I. Model Penal Code** test for insanity. As a defense it will negate the mens rea of the crime committed. Kermit was charged with involuntary manslaughter, a crime requiring criminal negligence. Choices (A) and (B) address the statutory language in that Kermit could not "conform his conduct (volitionally) to the requirements of law" because he was so shocked that he froze. Although a good argument, note that both choices use the *defense* of insanity to negate the mens rea of the crime. Choice (C) is even stronger, however, because an actus reus must have occurred before a proper defense is even relevant. A person may be criminally liable for his omission to act when (1) there is a legal duty to act under the circumstances, and (2) *he can physically perform the act.* LaFave, **Criminal Law,** p. 182. If Kermit's failure to act—where he was babysitting his nephew and had a legal duty to act (based on either relationship or contract)—was not deemed to be *voluntary,* due to the fact that he was so shocked that he was unable to move, then he cannot be criminally responsible for lack of an actus reus. This argument is more basic than the other alternatives because it negates an element of the crime itself rather than using a defense to the crime; therefore, choice (C) is Kermit's *best* defense and the correct answer.

## 108. (A)

Attempt is a heavily tested area on the Multistate. On the February 1997 MBE there were five questions dealing with the inchoate crime of attempt. The crime of attempt consists of *(1) an intent to commit the "target" offense and (2) a "substantial step" in the furtherance of the crime.* At common law, legal impossibility (but not factual impossibility) was a defense to attempt. The "key" to this question, however, is recognizing that *legal impossibility is not a valid defense* under this jurisdiction's attempt statute. Therefore, Tupac can be found guilty of attempt despite the fact that the "target" offense (i.e., the anti-noise statute) has been ruled unconstitutional. Note that choices (B) and (C) are wrong because double jeopardy does not attach. Double jeopardy prohibits reprosecution for a crime after there has been a final judgment (such as a conviction or acquittal). A dismissal of the initial charge does not constitute a final judgment.

## 109. (A)

The prevailing American view is that **bigamy is an offense of absolute liability.** Even in the minority jurisdictions, a defendant remarrying under a bona fide mistake of fact may be guilty if the belief in the spouse's death was based on lack of due diligence in determining the facts. See *Gillum v. State*, 147 S.W.2d 778.

## 110. (C)

Students should note that Dineen's intoxication may have at first negated his willful failure to return to prison. However, when he finally sobered up on January 17 and then (intentionally) decided not to return to prison for another couple of days, he would violate criminal offense (C) by willfully failing to return to prison and remaining out of custody for more than 14 days.

## 111. (A)

The facts do not indicate that Howe willfully failed to return to prison at the prescribed time. Rather, he was shot two hours before his prescribed return, and then treated at a hospital for his wounds (which resulted in his late return to prison).

## 112. (C)

Regardless of his attorney's advice, Liddy did in fact willfully remain out of federal custody over 14 days. Therefore, choice (C) is the best alternative.

## 113. (A)

Under the present circumstances, the facts do not indicate that Squealy intentionally (or willfully) stayed out of federal custody. He lost track of time because of his mescaline, or narcotic, intoxication. Under the prevailing view, voluntary or involuntary intoxication (whether brought about by alcohol or by narcotic drugs) is a defense to crime when it negatives the existence of an element of the crime. Generally intoxication when it negates an element of the crime does so by negativing some mental element (intent or knowledge) which the crime requires.

## 114. (A)

It is important to note that Veasey did *not* willfully or purposely fail to return to prison on time. Rather, he was coerced into participating in the bank robbery. A person's unlawful threat (1) which causes the defendant reasonably to believe that the only way to avoid imminent death or serious bodily injury to himself or to another is to engage in conduct which violates the literal terms of the criminal law, and (2) which causes the defendant to engage in that conduct, gives the defendant the defense of duress.

## 115. (D)

Students should note the distinction between specific and general-intent crimes. According to LaFave in his **Criminal Law** hornbook, it is sometimes stated that intoxication can negate a specific-intent which the crime in question may require (meaning some intent in addition to the intent to do the physical act which the crime requires), but it cannot negate a crime's general-intent. In this regard, the crimes of (a) assault with intent to commit rape, (b) assault with intent to commit battery, and (c) conspiracy are all specific-intent crimes. Therefore, intoxication may serve as a defense to the specific-intent crimes enumerated in choices (A), (B), and (C). However, intoxication will not negate the criminal culpability of Defendant in alternative (D) because statutory rape is a crime which imposes "absolute" criminal liability (i.e., no available defense).

## 116. (A)

The majority of jurisdictions hold that while voluntary intoxication may be so great as to negate premeditation and deliberation, this fact serves only to reduce the homicide from first degree to second degree murder. A basic tenet of criminal law is that one may not use more force, in self-defense, than is reasonably necessary. Choice (B) is incorrect since one who can safely retreat need not do so before using nondeadly force. Thus, the question of retreat is a problem only when deadly force is employed in self-defense. The prevailing view is that the defender who was not the original aggressor need not retreat, even though he can do so safely, before using deadly force upon an assailant whom he reasonably believes will kill him or inflict serious bodily harm.

## 117. (D)

Students must be aware that intoxication can negate a "specific-intent" crime but it cannot negate a "general-intent" crime. So-called "specific-intent" crimes require two elements: (1) an actus reus (or the criminal act) + (2) the mens rea (or "guilty mind"). Common law larceny, for example, requires the taking and carrying away of the property of another, but in addition it must be shown that there was an *intent to steal* the property. Similarly, common law burglary requires a breaking and entry into the dwelling of another, but it must also be established that the defendant acted with the *intent to commit a larceny or felony therein*. On the other hand, so-called "general-intent" crimes require only an actus reus. In this regard, the crimes of (1) rape, (2) battery, and (3) arson are commonly referred to as "general-intent" crimes. These crimes are completed by the criminal act *without regard to the defendant's intention*. The crime of rape, for example, is committed by the act of non-consensual sexual intercourse irrespective of the defendant's intention. A *key* Multistate testing area deals with the distinction between crimes of rape and assault with intent to commit rape. Note that although rape is a "general-intent" crime, assault with intent to commit rape is a "specific-intent" crime. Similarly, while battery is a "general-intent" crime, assault with intent to commit battery is a "specific-intent" crime.

## 118. (D)

Students should be aware that many statutes defining conduct which is criminal employ words or phrases indicating some type of bad-mind requirement: e.g., "intentionally"; "knowingly"; "purposely"; or "fraudulently." In this regard, LaFave points out that such crimes require "subjective fault"—actually a bad mind of some sort. For example, the statutory crime of receiving stolen property is generally worded in terms of receiving stolen property "knowing the property to be stolen." Such wording requires that the defendant, to be guilty, *must know* in his own mind (i.e., subjectively) that the property he receives is stolen. Similarly, in the present example, since Sellers did not (subjectively) know that he was selling contraceptives to a minor, he did not possess the requisite mens rea.

## 119. (B)

Generally, the defense of necessity is limited to those situations where the pressure comes from the physical forces of nature (i.e., storms, hurricanes, earthquakes, etc.) rather than from other human beings. Usually, when the pressure is from human beings, the defense, if applicable, is called duress rather than necessity. However, alternative (C) is incorrect because it has been held that duress cannot justify an intentional killing. As a result, choice (B) is preferred in light of the Model Penal Code commentaries which suggest that the defense (of necessity) should be available in the situation where a person intentionally kills one person in order to save two or more. Alternative (D) is wrong because the facts do not indicate that Lucy was acting in self-defense.

## 120. (B)

Dr. Bortion is guilty of criminal-negligence involuntary manslaughter. For criminal-negligence manslaughter most jurisdictions require that the defendant's death-producing conduct involve a higher degree of negligence than ordinary (tort) negligence. In addition, most jurisdictions require that the defendant's conduct create an unreasonable and a high degree of risk of death or serious bodily injury to another. Clearly, Dr. Bortion's conduct (in performing a surgical operation on a woman who wasn't pregnant) was grossly or criminally negligent. He would therefore be guilty of manslaughter because Miss Period's death was causally connected to the unnecessary operation. Also, Dr. Bortion would be guilty of false pretenses since he defrauded Miss Period of $500. False pretenses, although defined in slightly different ways in the various jurisdictions, consists of these five elements: (1) a false representation of a material fact (2) which causes the victim (3) to pass title to (4) his property to the wrongdoer, (5) who knows his representation to be false and intends to defraud the victim.

**121. (B)**

The correct alternative is (B). Neither Boozer's mistake of fact regarding Billy's age nor Fishco's mistake of fact regarding the nature of the stolen property would suffice to exonerate. In case summary (B) Boozer is found guilty of the offense of selling liquor to a minor. It is important to note that such an offense is of the strict liability variety since there is no mental state to be negated and, thus, no mistake or ignorance of fact will relieve defendant of liability. Under such a strict liability rule, it is no defense that Defendant believed the minor was of age, and this is true even if the minor appeared to be of age, represented himself as having reached the requisite age or produced false credentials showing he was of age. In this case, Fishco would be found guilty of receiving stolen property since he knew the goods were stolen. Although Fishco believed them to be shrimp when they were in fact clams, it is apparent that this mistake of fact would be no defense because it does not negate the mental element of the crime.

**122. (B)**

The correct choice is (B). In the majority of jurisdictions, bigamy is a crime of strict, or absolute, liability. The prevailing view of the crime of bigamy is that none of the following constitutes a valid defense: reasonable belief that the first spouse is dead; reasonable belief that the first marriage was illegal; reasonable belief that a decree concerning the first marriage was a divorce decree; or reasonable belief that a foreign divorce would be recognized in the jurisdiction. Therefore, Thelma's mistake of fact regarding her first husband's death would not relieve her of criminal liability for her bigamous union with Wade.

**123. (A)**

It is a well-established proposition of the common law that ignorance or mistake of law, which results in the defendant's not knowing that his conduct is illegal, generally provides no defense to a criminal charge. There are situations, however, where the proposition requires modification. Such a situation is where the defendant is unaware of the legal duty in question. In this regard, alternative (A) is correct since Maloney and Spack were both ignorant of their legal duties—in Maloney the duty not to sell a firearm to a convicted felon, and in Spack the duty to obtain licensing for the sale of securities.

**124. (D)**

Redneck's mistake of law, regarding the age of consent in Omega, would not constitute a valid defense. Similarly, Maybelle's ignorance of law, whereby she honestly believed that her taking of the Elvis records was not proscribed by criminal law, would not excuse her for the larceny.

**125. (C)**

Clearly, in case summary (C) Dineen would not be guilty of larceny since his honest mistake regarding ownership of the raincoat would negate the intent-to-steal mental state required for the crime of larceny. By analogy, Eddie's mistake of fact as to what his uncle had said (he mistakenly thought his uncle was giving him the car) would similarly negate his intent to steal the T-Bird.

**126. (C)**

Voluntary intoxication is a defense only if it disproves the existence of a specific-intent required for the crime. Choice (C) is the correct alternative since voluntary intoxication cannot be a defense to battery, a general-intent crime. Choices (A) and (B) are both incorrect statements of law. Choice (D) is irrelevant because Drew's belief that the gun was unloaded would not affect his intoxication defense.

**127. (D)**

Conspiracy may be defined as (1) an ***agreement*** between two or more persons, which constitutes the act; and (2) an ***intent*** to thereby achieve a certain objective which, under the common law definition, is the doing of either an unlawful act or a lawful act by unlawful means. The agreement between Gilbert, Emmanuel, and Smith to take part in the bank robbery formed the conspiracy. The fact that Smith was an undercover police officer is irrelevant because the ***plurality requirement*** of two or more persons was satisfied. In addition, Gilbert is guilty of automobile theft because he stole the Toyota. Furthermore, Gilbert is guilty of attempted robbery because he (1) intended to rob the bank and (2) performed an act in furtherance of the crime by stealing the car which he intended to use in the bank robbery. Although many students will incorrectly choose (C), choice (D) is a better answer because the ***"substantial step"*** requirement was satisfied, thereby making Gilbert guilty of attempt as well as conspiracy.

**128. (A)**

An important Multistate maxim is always choose an answer that is absolutely correct over one that may be correct. Obviously, Renee committed a battery when she grabbed the necklace from Roxanne's neck. Criminal battery is defined as the unlawful application of force to the person of another. On the other hand, there are two types of criminal assaults: (1) the attempted-battery type, and (2) the intent-to-frighten type. The attempted-battery type of assault requires an intent to commit a battery, i.e., an intent to cause physical injury to the victim. Since Renee did *not* intend to injure Roxanne, she would not be guilty of the attempted-battery–type of assault (even though she is guilty of the second type). Note that a majority of jurisdictions follow the attempted-battery type of assault, while only a minority of states recognize the intent-to-frighten type. Furthermore, choice (C) is wrong because robbery requires an intent to steal. Since Renee did not intend to steal Roxanne's necklace, she cannot be convicted of robbery.

**Multistate Nuance Chart:**
**CRIMINAL LAW**

## INCHOATE CRIMES

| SOLICITATION | CONSPIRACY | ATTEMPT |
|---|---|---|
| 1. defendant entices, advises, encourages, orders, or re-quests another to commit a crime; | 1. consists of (a) an agreement between two or more persons to commit a crime *and* (b) an intent to achieve the criminal objective; | 1. consists of (a) an intent to commit a crime and (b) an act in furtherance or a "substantial step" toward the commission of the offense; |
| 2. the crime solic-ited need *not* be committed; | 2. the agreement is the "essence" or "gist" of the crime; | 2. the act in furtherance of the crime must go beyond mere preparation; |
| 3. the crime requires no agreement or action by the person solicited; | 3. unlike attempt, the crime does *not* require a "substantial step" in the commission of the crime; | 3. "specific-intent" crime, i.e., the defendant must have the specific-intent to commit the designated crime; |
| 4. defenses: at common law no defenses were recog-nized; under Model Penal Code, however, renunciation is an affirmative defense; | 4. solicitation *merges* into conspiracy; <br><br>5. if the conspiracy is successful, a conspirator may be subject to conviction for both the conspiracy and the completed crime; | 4. defenses: at common law legal impossibility but not factual impossibility was a defense to a charge of attempt; under the modern view, however, impossibility is *no* defense when the defendant's actual intent (not limited by the true facts unknown to him) was to do an act proscribed by law. |
| 5. merges with the target felony. | 6. defenses: at common law with-drawal was not a valid defense; under the Model Penal Code, however, withdrawal is recog-nized as an affirmative defense *if* the defendant "thwarted the success of the conspiracy." | |

**129. (A)**

Another extremely popular Multistate testing area deals with federal statutory crimes. Why? Simply because this is one of the "gaps" or areas not adequately covered in the "general outline" courses. With respect to federal criminal law, the national government of the United States has very broad "police powers" to create crimes over conduct in federally owned or controlled territory not within the jurisdiction of any state. Thus, the federal government has territorial jurisdiction over (a) conduct on federal land areas not located within the states, such as the District of Columbia and Territories; (b) conduct on federal enclaves (islands of federal territory located within the states), such as army posts, naval bases, post offices, and national parks; (c) conduct on ships and aircraft of American nationality when outside the jurisdiction of the states, as on the high seas or even in foreign waters; and (d) conduct by U.S. citizens which takes place outside the jurisdiction of any state. For the most part, LaFave points out that federal criminal laws define offenses in terms of substantive misbehavior (e.g., theft) and the matter of jurisdictional requirements are dealt with separately. In fact, under the Federal Criminal Code technical issues of jurisdiction are not prominent "and the government is relieved of any burden of showing that the defendant knew of the special fact which results in federal jurisdiction." LaFave, **Criminal Law,** p. 113. By the same token, since federal conspiracy laws do not require the mental retainment of jurisdictional requirements, choice (A) is correct.

## 130. (B)

At early common law one whose conduct brought about an unintended death in the commission or attempted commission of a felony was guilty of (felony) murder. American jurisdictions, however, have limited the rule in one or more of the following ways: (1) by permitting its use only as to certain types of felonies; (2) by stricter interpretation of the requirement of proximate or legal cause; and (3) by a narrower construction of the time period during which the felony is in the process of commission. LaFave, **Criminal Law,** p. 545. With respect to the proximate or legal cause limitation, it is often said that the death must be a *foreseeable* consequence of the felony. That is to say, the death must have been the "natural and probable consequence" of the defendant's conduct. Therefore, choice (B) is the best answer because looking at the matter with hindsight, it seems extraordinary that a death would actually come about in such an unforeseeable manner.

## 131. (C)

Obviously, to constitute a conspiracy there "must be a combination of two or more persons." LaFave notes that this plurality requirement might be restated in terms of at least two guilty parties, *for acquittal of all persons with whom the defendant is alleged to have conspired precludes his (or her) conviction.* **Criminal Law,** p. 488. Thus, if A and B are jointly charged with a conspiracy not alleged to involve any other parties and the jury returns a verdict of guilty as to A and not guilty as to B, A's conviction may not stand. *Martinez v. People,* 267 P.2d 654 (1954).

## 132. (A)

This question is testing students on the scope of liability for conspiracy. First, it is important to realize that a conspiracy existed. According to LaFave, a ***conspiracy*** requires "1) an agreement between two or more persons which constitutes the act, and 2) an intent thereby to achieve a certain objective which is the doing of either an unlawful act or a lawful act by unlawful means." LaFave, p. 525. As part of Clyde's plan to rob the bank, he enlisted Bonnie to drive the getaway car, and she agreed. Her subsequent decision not to go through with it is an insufficient basis for **withdrawal,** since she did not "thwart the success" of the conspiracy. Choice (D) is incorrect. The general rule regarding the scope of the conspiracy is that a co-conspirator will be liable for **all crimes committed in furtherance of the conspiracy.** Since the killing of Walker occurred during the commission of the robbery, Bonnie will be liable to the same extent as Clyde. She will be guilty of murder. Choice (A) is correct.

### 133. (D)

Cindy's death was unintentional and did not occur as a **foreseeable result during the commission** of the robbery. Unlike the killing of Walker, the death of Cindy occurred an **hour** later, and Clyde was not speeding at the time. Her act of suddenly darting in front of Clyde's car was not a foreseeable consequence of his get away from the robbery. Therefore, choice (A) is incorrect. Choice (B) is incorrect because Clyde lacked the requisite mental state for involuntary manslaughter, namely, gross or criminal negligence. He was driving slowly and applied his brakes at the time of the accident. Choice (C) is incorrect since the killing was not intentional. By process of elimination, choice (D) is correct: Clyde will be guilty of no crime.

### 134. (D)

In order to be liable as an **accomplice** to the crime of another, one must (a) **aid, abet, or encourage the perpetrator** (b) **with the intent** thereby to promote or facilitate the commission of the crime. Several terms have been employed by courts and legislatures in describing the kinds of acts which will suffice for accomplice liability. The most common are "aid," "abet," "advise," "assist," "cause," "command," "counsel," "encourage," "hire," and "induce." In this Multistate hypo, Blauser is not subject to accomplice liability because he was unaware that Tyson and Waxman were burglarizing Slocum's home. The "red herring" or "distractor" is the fact that the perpetrators gave Blauser $500 after pawning the jewels. Taking the money (two weeks afterwards) does not subject Blauser to accomplice liability because he didn't specifically intend to facilitate the commission of the crime at the moment of its inception. If anything, Blauser would be viewed as an **accessory after the fact** for accepting the money.

### 135. (B)

A *classic* Multistate example that has trapped many students in the past few years. Here, the *test maker* knows that most students will incorrectly choose choice (A) because they are aware that under the modern view impossibility is *not* a defense (to a charge of attempt) when the defendant's actual intent—not limited by the true facts unknown to him—was to do an act or bring about a result proscribed by law. Although this is true, choice (B) is the preferred answer because Carlos is an accomplice (or principal in the second degree) because he *aided and abetted* Jose by supplying him the gun to kill Jesus. LaFave notes that to be a principal in the second degree, **one must be present at the commission of a criminal offense and aid, counsel, command, or encourage the principal in the first degree in the commission of that offense.** Choice (B) is correct because a principal in the second degree is subject to and accountable for the same crime(s) committed by the principal in first degree.

## 136. (A)

Clearly, Thad is guilty of violating the New Jersey "bomb" statute because he built and transported the bombing device. By the same token, Jeremie is guilty as an accomplice (or accessory before the fact). An individual is criminally liable as an accomplice if he gives assistance or encouragement, or fails to act where he has a legal duty to oppose the crime of another. Certainly, both Thad and Jeremie were responsible for the commission of the crime.

## 137. (A)

Thad and Jeremie would both be guilty of felony-murder. By constructing the bomb and placing it in the hotel, they would be criminally liable for the explosion even though it prematurely detonated. At common law one whose conduct brought about an unintended death in the commission or attempted commission of a felony was guilty of (felony) murder. Note that today many jurisdictions limit the rule by requiring that the felony must be dangerous to life (e.g., arson, burglary, robbery, or kidnapping). Certainly, placing a bomb (that was activated to detonate) would be dangerous to human life. On the contrary, neither Thad nor Jeremie is guilty of conspiracy to commit murder because they did not intend to kill anyone. Thus, there was no agreement to commit murder.

## 138. (B)

Choice (A) is incorrect because in order to be an accomplice to a crime, one must (1) give assistance and (2) have the intent to promote or facilitate commission of a crime. Obviously, Regis lacked the requisite mens rea since he didn't intend or knowingly encourage Jose to commit a homicide. Choice (C) is wrong because joint venture is a torts principle and does not extend criminal liability. Similarly, choice (D) is not the best answer because it is a general principle of criminal law that one is not criminally liable for how someone else acts, unless he directs or encourages or aids the other so to act. Thus, unlike the case of torts, an employer is not generally liable for the criminal acts of his employee even though the latter does them in furtherance of his employer's business (except in the case of a statutory crime where the legislature has provided otherwise). By process of elimination, choice (B) is the best answer.

### 139. (D)

Some crimes are defined in such a way that they may be directly committed only by a person who has a particular characteristic or occupies a particular position, as with *adultery, which can be committed only by a married person.* LaFave observes, however, that this has not prevented courts from concluding that others outside the legislative class may be guilty of these crimes (commonly referred to as Wharton rule crimes) on an accomplice theory, or that other persons may likewise be guilty of a conspiracy to commit such crimes. Thus, for example, an unmarried man may be convicted of conspiring with a married man that the latter commit adultery. See LaFave, p. 491–492. It is important, however, to distinguish the above situation from the present example in which Brooke is a member of a *legislatively protected class.* In accordance with the rule enunciated in *Gebarbi v. United States*, 287 U.S. 112, 53 S.Ct. 35 (1932), *one who may not be deemed an accomplice to a crime* (because a contrary holding would conflict with the legislative purpose) *may likewise not be found to be a member of a conspiracy to commit that crime.* In *Gebarbi* the U.S. Supreme Court held that a woman could not be convicted of conspiracy to violate the Mann Act in that the man transported the woman from one state to another for immoral purposes because the *Mann Act was designed to protect women.* Likewise, in the present example, Brooke cannot be prosecuted as an accomplice to the crime of contributing to the delinquency of minors, because the crime is designed to protect minors.

### 140–143.

This set of questions is constructed in a case precedent format. In answering questions of this type, students must follow a two-step approach: (1) ascertain the rule of law or the precedent in each of the case summaries (i.e., A–D) and then (2) determine which precedent is most applicable to the given questions. This case precedent series deals with felony murder. In case precedent (A) we have a situation where someone is killed by a bullet fired from the gun of someone other than the robber. It was held that the robbers were guilty of felony murder, since their conduct in firing at the policemen, knowing that their fire would be returned, was the "proximate cause" of the victim's death. In case precedent (B) it is the victim of the robbery who is shot and killed by one of the robbers during the attempted felony. Here, too, the robbers are guilty of felony murder since it is foreseeable that robberies by armed robbers are likely to result in unintended deaths. Conversely, case summary (C) is an example of the Redline limitation to the felony murder rule. Under the Redline limitation, a felon is not liable for felony murder of the shooting of a co-felon by a policeman since it is "justifiable" homicide. On the other hand, in case summary (D) the defendant was held not guilty of felony murder because his conduct (namely, driving while intoxicated) was not the "proximate" or "legal" cause of the resulting death. Now let's link up the precedents with the questions.

**140. (A)**

Here, we have a situation where someone (an interceding policeman) is killed by someone other than the robber during the attempted robbery. Under these circumstances, the robbers will be found guilty of felony murder. Therefore, choice (A) is correct.

**141. (D)**

In this example, the defendant will not be liable for felony murder because Porky's death was not "proximately" or "legally" caused by Ozzie's felonious conduct. In fact, it is highly unlikely that Ozzie's failure to renew his gun permit would even constitute a felony.

**142. (B)**

This a classic example of felony murder in which a kidnapping victim dies as a result of the defendants' felonious conduct. Under the felony murder rule, one whose conduct has brought about an unintended death in the commission or attempted commission of a felony is guilty of felony murder.

**143. (C)**

According to LaFave in the situation where one co-felon becomes angry at his confederate during the commission of a robbery, and intentionally shoots and kills him, the former will be liable for intent-to-kill murder, but not felony murder. LaFave notes that the co-felon's intentional shooting of his cohort is so far removed from the common plan as not to make the co-felon guilty of felony murder. By analogy, in this example Rod would be liable for depraved-heart murder, not felony murder, because he recklessly fired the bullet at Stewart even though he didn't intend to kill him. As a consequence, precedent (C) is the best answer because the "true basis of the Redline limitation is the feeling that it is not justice to hold the felon liable for murder on account of the death, which the felon did not intend, of a co-felon willingly participating in the risky venture." LaFave, **Criminal Law,** p. 552.

**144. (B)**

Keep in mind that the warrant requirement is central to the Fourth Amendment protection against unreasonable searches and seizures. As a basic rule, all warrantless searches are unconstitutional unless they fall into one of the following seven exceptions to the warrant requirement: (1) search incident to a lawful arrest, (2) the "automobile" exception, (3) plain view, (4) "stop and frisk," (5) consent, (6) hot pursuit, and (7) other emergencies. A valid warrantless search must meet the requirements of at least one of the above exceptions. With respect to the "automobile" exception, the police must have probable cause to suspect or reasonably believe that the vehicle contains evidence of crime. In the present example, the police did not have a reasonable or articulable suspicion to believe that the Pointer sisters' car contained evidence of the crime. According to the facts, Belushi merely overheard the robbers remark that they "still got 10 minutes left." At no time, however, did the robbers mention anything about the ferry. Rather, Belushi simply surmised (without any concrete foundation) that they were returning to the mainland on the next ferry. As a result, choice (B) is correct because the police did not have probable cause to conduct a warrantless search of the auto. Choice (A) is wrong because if the police had probable cause to suspect that the vehicle contained evidence of the crime, then no warrant would have been necessary. Note that choice (D) is incorrect because the mere fact the police observed the women "fidgeting nervously" would not by itself give the officers probable cause to suspect that the defendants' car contained evidence of the crime.

## 145. (C)

At common law, robbery consisted of all six elements of larceny—a (1) trespassory (2) taking and (3) carrying away of the (4) personal property (5) of another (6) with intent to steal it—plus two additional requirements: (7) that the property be taken from the person or from the victim's presence and (8) that the taking be accomplished by force or intimidation. In addition, robbery may be considered a greater crime than the sum of the two lesser crimes of larceny and assault (or battery). Therefore, since larceny and assault (or battery) merge into robbery, choices (A) and (B) are incorrect. Next, we must consider whether the Pointer sisters are guilty of burglary which at common law consisted of—the (1) breaking and (2) entering of (3) a dwelling house (4) of another (5) in the nighttime (6) with the intent to commit a larceny or felony therein. In order to constitute a breaking at common law, there had to be the creation of a breach or opening. According to LaFave, "if the occupant of the dwelling had created the opening, it was felt that he had not entitled himself to the protection of the law, as he had not properly secured his dwelling." **Criminal Law,** p. 708. With this in mind, many students will choose choice (D) as correct basing their answer on the fact that Belushi opened the door for the intruders. However, this is incorrect because a "constructive breaking" occurred. LaFave points out that when entry is gained by (1) fraud, (2) threat of force, or (3) through a chimney, then a "constructive breaking" is deemed to have occurred. See **Criminal Law,** p. 709. As a consequence, since the robbers fraudulently gained entry by masquerading in their "Mr. T" costumes on Halloween, this constituted a "constructive breaking." As a result, choice (C) is correct because the Pointer sisters are guilty of burglary.

## 146. (B)

Choice (A) is wrong because it is well settled in criminal law that under the doctrine of *transferred intent* in the unintended-victim (or bad-aim) situation—where A aims at B but misses, hitting C—it is the accepted view that A is just as guilty as if his aim had been accurate. Thus, where A aims at B with a murderous intent to kill, but because of a bad aim he hits and kills C, A is uniformly held guilty of the murder of C. Choice (C) is likewise erroneous because as a general rule it is frequently said that ignorance of the law is no excuse. Note that ignorance or mistake as to a matter of fact or law is a defense if it is shown that the defendant does not have the mental state required by law for the commission of that particular offense. Obviously, in the present case Manning did have the requisite mens rea because he intended to inflict serious bodily injury on Thomas. Choice (D) is incorrect because it is commonly said in civil and in criminal cases that one is presumed to intend the natural and probable consequences of his (or her) acts. Thus, LaFave points out if one carefully aims a gun at his enemy and pulls the trigger and the bullet strikes the enemy in the heart and kills him, we ought to conclude, in the absence of some other facts, that he intended to kill (though he spoke no words of intent at the time). Similarly, a special application of the presumption that one intends to produce the natural results of his actions is found in the *deadly-weapon doctrine* applicable to homicide cases: *one who intentionally uses a deadly weapon on another human being and thereby kills him presumably intends to kill him.* In this regard, LaFave states that the deadly weapon doctrine is not a category of murder separate from the intent-to-kill category, but rather, *the intentional use of a deadly weapon authorizes the drawing of an inference that the user intends to kill.* It should be noted that the intentional use of a deadly weapon which produces death is not necessarily murder since we still allow the user (defendant) a chance to convince the jury that in spite of his intentional use of a deadly weapon he actually did not intend to kill. In light of this explanation, choice (D) is wrong because there is a presumption that Manning intended to kill Thomas under the deadly-weapon doctrine. Consequently, by process of elimination alternative (B) is the best answer.

## 147. (D)

This is an extremely tricky Multistate example. It typifies how complex and difficult even a singular question can be. In answering this question, it is necessary to interrelate the following four rules of law: (1) burglary, (2) attempt, (3) legal impossibility, and (4) mistake of law. First choice (A) is wrong because burglary is defined at common law as breaking and entering another's dwelling house at night with intent to commit a felony (a misdemeanor will not do) therein. Consequently, Palmer would not be guilty of burglary because he did not have the required mental state (i.e., intent to commit a felony). Therefore, his mistake of law will be a valid defense since it negates a mental state required for the crime. Second, choice (B) is incorrect because legal impossibility would constitute a valid defense to the inchoate crime of attempted violation of the "flashing" statute. Legal impossibility is commonly defined as the case in which the defendant did everything he intended to do but yet had not committed the completed crime. In effect, Palmer is not guilty of attempt because what he set out to do was not a crime. See LaFave, pp. 438–443.

### 148. (A)

There is a great deal of confusion in the substantive criminal law **between strict liability crimes and vicarious liability crimes.** A vicarious liability crime is one wherein one person, though without personal fault, is made liable for the conduct of another (usually his employee). It is common, however, for a vicarious liability statute to also impose strict liability; in such an instance there is no need to prove an act or omission by the defendant-employer (one by his employee will do), and there is no need to prove mental fault by anyone. Some criminal statutes, for example, specifically impose criminal liability upon the employer for the bad conduct of his employee (e.g., "whoever, by himself or by his agent, sells articles at short weight shall be punished by . . . ," or "whoever sells liquor to a minor is punishable by . . ."). In construing statutes of this type, courts often jump to the unwarranted conclusion that a statute which imposes strict liability must of necessity also impose vicarious liability. LaFave notes, however, that *there is no basis for assuming that vicarious liability necessarily follows from strict liability.* Rather, the better view, according to LaFave, is that an employer does not "allow" or "permit" his employee to do an act *unless he knows of or authorizes it.* Based on this analysis, the correct answer is choice (A).

### 149. (A)

As with other common law and statutory crimes which are defined in terms of conduct producing a specified result, a person may be criminally liable when his omission to act produces that result, *but only if* (1) he has, under the circumstances, a legal duty to act, and (2) he can physically perform the act. For criminal liability to be based upon a failure to act it must first be found that there is a duty to act—a legal duty and not simply a moral duty. According to LaFave, there are seven situations which do give rise to a duty to act: (1) duty based upon relationship; (2) duty based upon statute; (3) duty based upon contract; (4) duty based upon voluntary assumption of care; (5) duty based upon creation of peril; (6) duty to control conduct of others; and (7) duty of landowner. In this example, choice (A) is correct because the Defendant's duty to act to protect Marnie probably would arise out of contract. Since the Defendant was a guide at Yellowstone National Park he was employed to take affirmative action to protect hikers from such foreseeable dangers. This situation is analogous to a lifeguard employed to watch over swimmers at a beach. The lifeguard cannot sit idly by while a swimmer at his beach drowns off shore. Omission to do so may make the lifeguard liable for criminal homicide. Note that for a duty to act, by virtue of contract, the victim need not be one of the contracting parties. LaFave, **Criminal Law,** pp. 182–186.

### 150. (B)

This same issue was tested on both July 2005 and February 2006 administrations of the MBE. This question covers two important elements regarding robbery.

At common law robbery consists of all six elements of larceny: *(1) trespassory (2) taking (3) and carrying away (4) the personal property (5) of another (6) with intent to steal, plus two additional requirements: (7) the taking be accomplished by force, violence, or intimidation and (8) the taking must be from the victim's person or presence.* First, one may commit robbery by rendering his victim helpless by administering intoxicating liquors or drugs to produce unconsciousness as a means of force. LaFave, **Criminal Law,** p. 782. Second, choices (A), (C), and (D) are wrong because larceny is a "lesser included" crime and merges into robbery. A defendant cannot be guilty of both larceny and robbery for the same criminal transaction.

# Flowchart 1   ELEMENTS OF CRIMES

**ACT (ACTUS REUS)** — law does not punish for thought alone; D must do some criminally cognizable act.

**VOLITIONAL ACT** — normally D must cause a criminally proscribed result by some *voluntary affirmative act*; look for indicia of lack of volition or control such as (1) *epilepsy*, (2) *automatism*, or (3) *hypnotism* (duress *is not* a volitional act defense).

**OMISSION** — if D has a *legal duty*, failure to act *is sufficient.*

- **STATUTE** — duty explicitly imposed by a statute (e.g., file tax returns).
- **CONTRACT** — duty imposed by agreement (e.g., lifeguard, nurse).
- **SPECIAL DEPENDENCY** — strong moral duty *plus* knowledge that person is *dependent and relying on D* (e.g., aged relative, young child, seamen–sea captain).
- **DETRIMENTAL UNDERTAKING** — if D commences to aid and leaves victim in worse position (some states make the mere undertaking a basis for duty even without detriment).
- **CAUSATION** — if D causes victim's plight, even without fault, some states require D to aid.

**VICARIOUS LIABILITY** — D may be responsible for act of another.

- **RESPONDEAT SUPERIOR** — acts of employees in strict liability regulatory crimes.
- **UNRESPONSIBLE AGENT** — acts of unresponsible agent (e.g., a child or insane person) caused by D.
- **ACCOMPLICE CONDUCT** — reasonably foreseeable acts of an accomplice.
- **CO-CONSPIRATOR CONDUCT** — acts of co-conspirators done to further the conspiratorial goal.

**INTENT (MENS REA)** — criminal law focuses on the *culpability* (e.g., blameworthiness) of D by examining his *state of mind with regard to the criminal consequence* (see Mens Rea JIG).

- **PURPOSEFUL** — if D does an act with the *conscious object of causing the criminal result.*
- **KNOWING** — if D does an act consciously aware of the fact that a criminal result is practically certain.
- **RECKLESS** — if D is consciously aware of the fact that his act creates a substantial and unjustifiable risk that a criminal result will occur.
- **NEGLIGENT** — if D creates an unreasonable risk that a criminal result will occur.
- **VOLUNTARY** — if D does a volitional act which causes a criminal result (i.e., strict liability).

**CAUSATION** — D's act must cause the particular result proscribed by the definition of the crime.

**PROXIMATE CAUSE** — must be the cause-in-fact with no unforeseeable intervening causes.

**CAUSE-IN-FACT**
- **"But For"** — but for D's act the result would not have occurred when it occurred.
- **Substantial Factor** — even if not "but for," D's act was a *substantial factor* or an *independently sufficient cause* of the result.

**INTERVENING CAUSES** — D normally acts on a "set stage" including unforeseeable abnormalities of victim, but if an *unforeseeable independent act intervenes* between D's act and the criminal result, *D is not responsible.*

**APPLICATION OF PRINCIPLE**
- **HOMICIDE** — D must cause the death of another human being within one year of act.
- **FALSE PRETENSES** — D's misrepresentation must cause V to give up title to property (i.e., V must *rely* on misrepresentation).
- **ATTEMPT** — D need *not* cause intended result, manifested culpability is sufficient.
- **SOLICITATION** — D need *not* be successful in inducing another, act of encouraging is sufficient.
- **CONSPIRACY** — formation of criminal combination is social harm, intended crime need *not* be carried out.
- **BURGLARY** — D must actually break and enter with the requisite criminal intent, intended crime need *not* be committed.
- **POSSESSION CRIMES** — D must knowingly possess illegal item (e.g., concealed weapon, drugs, burglary tool) but he need *not* use them.

*multistate issue graph*

# Flowchart 2 MENS REA

## ISSUE SPOTTING SEQUENCE

(1) *What state of mind is required by the crime charged?*

(2) *What was D's state of mind with regard to the criminally proscribed consequence at the time he did the act causing that consequence?*

(3) *Are there any special facts negating D's culpability (i.e., any mens rea defenses)?*

**REQUIRED MENTAL STATE**

**SPECIFIC-INTENT** — *purpose or knowledge that act will cause a particular criminal result.*

**INDICATIVE LANGUAGE**

**Intentional, Deliberate, Willful (Purposeful)** — words requiring an act with the *conscious object* to cause a particular result (regardless of the likelihood of achieving result).

**Knowingly, With Knowledge** — requiring *conscious awareness* that conduct is *practically certain* to cause a particular result (regardless of D's desire to cause result).

**THE BIG 7: BAM ACTS** — (1) Burglary; (2) Assault — intent to batter or to frighten; (3) Murder — *intent-to-kill forms only;* (4) Attempt; (5) Conspiracy; (6) Theft; (7) Solicitation.

**MEN'S REA DEFENSES** — (1) *insanity;* (2) *diminished capacity;* (3) *intoxication* (voluntary or involuntary); (4) *mistake of fact* (ever if unreasonable).

**GENERAL-INTENT** — D must be at least *grossly and culpably negligent* with regard to causing the criminal result.

**INDICATIVE LANGUAGE**

**Recklessly, Maliciously** — requiring that D is *consciously aware* that his act creates a *substantial* and *unjustifiable risk* that a particular result will be caused.

**Criminal Negligence** — more than "*mere negligence*," requiring that D's conduct manifest a *gross and culpable departure from standards of reasonableness* with regard to a particular result (D need *not* be aware of risk). Normally, only used in homicide cases dealing with autos, guns, drugs, or risk of fire.

**Statutory Construction** — a statute proscribing conduct without specifying level of mens rea is normally *construed to require recklessness.*

**THE LITTLE 4: BRIM** — (1) Battery; (2) Rape; (3) Involuntary Manslaughter; (4) Murder — *other than intent-to-kill forms.*

**MENS REA DEFENSES** — (1) *insanity;* (2) *involuntary intoxication;* (3) *reasonable mistake of material fact.*

**STRICT LIABILITY** — D may be convicted if his *voluntary act* caused the criminally proscribed result.

**MORALITY CRIMES: CABS** — (1) Contributing to delinquency of a minor; (2) Adultery; (3) Bigamy; (4) Statutory Rape.

**TRAFFIC, SAFETY, AND WELFARE REGULATIONS** — where normal punishment is quasi-crime (e.g., fine or revocation of license), administrative necessity justifies liability without culpability.

**ULTRAHAZARDOUS ACTIVITIES** — persons dealing with firearms, explosives, food, alcohol and drugs held to maximum standard of care by imposition of strict liability.

**MENS REA DEFENSES** — none, strict liability requires only a voluntary act.

**DETERMINING MENTAL STATE**

**PRESUMPTION** — D is *presumed* to intend to cause the *natural and probable consequences* of his conduct.

**EVIDENCE OF INTENT** — look for direct statements by D or circumstantial evidence (such as motive) which tend to indicate D's state of mind with respect to the criminally proscribed consequences.

*(continued below)*

# Flowchart 2   MENS REA *(continued)*

**MENS REA DEFENSES**

**INSANITY**

**M'NAGHTEN TEST (majority rule)** — D not criminally responsible if (1) *at the time of the offense D was* (2) *laboring under such a defect of reason from a disease of the mind as* (3) *not to know* (a) *the nature and quality of his act or, if he did not know it,* (b) *he did not know that the act was wrong.*

**IRRESISTIBLE IMPULSE (supplementary M'Naghten in many states)** — D not criminally responsible if (1) *at the time of the offense,* D (2) *was unable to control his conduct* (3) *as a result of mental disease.*

**ALI/MPC TEST** — D not criminally responsible if (1) *at the time of the offense,* (2) *as a result of mental disease or defect,* she (3) *lacks substantial capacity to either* (a) *appreciate the criminality of her conduct, or* (b) *to conform her conduct to the requirements of the law.*

**PROOF** — insanity is an affirmative defense, but once D introduces evidence of insanity, burden of proof shifts to prosecutor to show D is not insane.

**COMPETENCY** — regardless of D's mental state at the time of the offense, an accused *cannot be tried* for a crime if (1) *at the time of trial,* she is (2) (a) *incapable of understanding the nature of the proceedings, or* (b) *of assisting in her defense in a rational or reasonable manner.*

**MENTAL DEFICIENCY** — about 12 states permit evidence of mental deficiency short of insanity to negate deliberation requirements of first degree murder; California allows mental illness to negate malice aforethought and reduce an intentional murder to voluntary manslaughter.

**DIMINISHED RESPONSIBILITY**

**INTOXICATION** — *involuntary intoxication* is a defense to any crime; it may negate a required mental state if D is so intoxicated that *he did not understand the criminal nature of his conduct; voluntary intoxication* may (1) negate specific-intent element of an offense if (2) before he formulates the criminal intent he (3) becomes so intoxicated that he lacked the capacity for culpability.

**INFANCY** — children under 7 cannot crimes; 7–14, child presumed incapable of crime, but prosecution can rebut with evidence that child actually understood his conduct was wrong; over 14 children may be treated as adults (subject to state juvenile laws).

**MISTAKE OF FACT**

**SPECIFIC-INTENT CRIMES** — any material mistake of fact (whether reasonable or unreasonable) negates specific-intent.

**GENERAL-INTENT CRIMES** — a reasonable mistake of material fact negates recklessness or negligence required by general-intent crime.

**MISTAKE OF LAW** — generally no defense, but MPC allows defense if (1) D *reasonably relied upon official interpretation of a law which was later declared invalid;* (2) *without fault, D was not apprised of administrative rule;* (3) *if knowledge of legal status is an element of the offense; or* (4) *where statute requires an affirmative act.*

*multistate issue graph*

KAPLAN) **pmbr**

# Flowchart 3   ATTEMPTS

D is guilty of an attempt to commit a crime if: (1) with the *specific-intent to cause a criminal result*, he (2) *does some legally sufficient act toward the commission of* the intended crime.

**SPECIFIC-INTENT** — D must be either purposeful or knowing with regard to causing the result proscribed by the underlying crime; always look for specific-intent defenses, especially intoxication and exculpating mistake. Remember, specific-intent is required for all attempts, even if substantive crime is strict liability (e.g., attempted bigamy).

**SUFFICIENT ACT** — must be beyond mere preparation; a question of law for the judge.

**LAST ACT** — the *last act* required of D is always sufficient, even if subsequent acts of another are necessary (e.g., P puts poison in V's pills on nightstand).

**UNEQUIVOCAL ACT** — if D's act *unequivocally manifests criminal intent* it is sufficient (very often even the last act does not do this, however).

**CORROBORATING ACT** — best view focuses upon the significance of D's act in *demonstrating that D had the firm and present intent to commit the crime* (under this view the act must corroborate the existence of firm intent).

**IMPOSSIBILITY**

**FACTUAL IMPOSSIBILITY** — *if crime would have resulted had the facts been as D thought they were, impossibility is no defense:* (1) *inherently inadequate instrumentality* (D mistakes sugar for poison); (2) *error in time or place* (D attempts to "pick" an empty pocket, or kill a person already dead). Factual impossibility is based upon a mistake which does *not* negate culpability (i.e., D is worse than he appears).

**STATUS OF GOODS** — some courts hold that D cannot be guilty of an attempt to possess stolen property if property possessed is not in fact "stolen" (i.e., true owner consented to use of property to apprehend D). Under this view, a mistake as to the legal status of a thing provides a valid defense. Most courts and MPC treat this as factual impossibility (rather than legal impossibility) and deny the defense.

**LEGAL IMPOSSIBILITY**

**INTENDED RESULT IS NOT ILLEGAL** — if D believes an act is illegal but it is not, he cannot be guilty of an attempt simply by doing that act since the conduct actually intended is not regarded as socially harmful, thus, D must manifest a willingness to do an act actually proscribed by law.

**DEFINITION OF CRIME EXCLUDES D** — if, according to the definition of a crime, it is impossible for D to commit the substantive offense, there can be no attempt by D.

**ABANDONMENT** — crime of attempt is complete once a legally sufficient act has been committed, but some courts and MPC allow a defense if D (1) *voluntarily abandons the criminal act* (2) *prior to completion of the substantive crime* (3) *under circumstances manifesting a complete renunciation of criminal intent.* Look for extrinsic causes of withdrawal which are *not defenses* (e.g., fear of apprehension, selection of a different victim, etc.)

*multistate issue graph*

# Flowchart 4 CONSPIRACY

*(1) Agreement between (2) two or more persons (3) who have the specific-intent (4) to either (a) commit a crime or (b) to engage in dishonest, fraudulent, or immoral conduct injurious to public health or morals.*

**AGREEMENT**
— there must be a *true agreement* to promote or facilitate a particular objective

- **AGREEMENT SUFFICIENT** — at common law, the agreement itself is the only act required to complete the crime; federal and about half of states now require some *additional overt act* in furtherance of the conspiracy (although the act need not be illegal in itself and only one conspirator need do an act).

- **PROOF** — agreement may be inferred from concert of action (look for mutual adoption of a common purpose).

- **FALSE AGREEMENT** — secret police agent or other "false agreement" situations are not conspiracies — there must be true actual intent to carry out unlawful objective by at least two parties. (MPC is contra; party with true intent is still liable.)

- **UNKNOWN CONSPIRATORS** — D must agree with at least one other person but need *not* agree with (or even know identity of) all other members of the conspiracy.

- **SINGLE OR MULTIPLE CONSPIRACY** — the agreement is the essence of conspiracy; thus, there is only one conspiracy even if agreement encompasses separate diverse criminal acts and even if agreement entails a continuous course of criminal conduct.

- **STATUS DEFENSE TO SUBSTANTIVE CRIME** — if D conspires with B, it is no defense to either party that D may not be capable under the legal definition to commit underlying crime himself (e.g., a man cannot rape his own wife).

- **DIPLOMATIC IMMUNITY** — that one party is immune from prosecution is no defense to other party.

- **DIMINISHED CAPACITY DEFENSES** — if B, the only other conspirator, possesses a diminished capacity defense negating specific-intent (e.g., intoxication, infancy, insanity), a few courts preclude conviction of D as well as B; better view including MPC permits convictions of D regardless of B's *personal mens rea defenses*.

- **ACQUITTAL ON MERITS** — if B, the *only* other conspirator, is acquitted *on the merits* (i.e., not because of procedural or personal mens rea defenses), D may not be convicted.

**TWO OR MORE PERSONS**

- **HUSBAND-WIFE** — today, D may conspire with a spouse (not so at old common law).

  - **Consent Crimes** — if crime logically requires the voluntary participation of another (e.g., bribery, incest, adultery, gambling), there is no conspiracy unless agreement involves *an additional person not logically essential*.

- **WHARTON'S RULE**
  - **Plurality Required by Substantive Crime** — if substantive crime requires a number of participants (e.g., 5 or more conducting gambling operations), there can be no separate charge of conspiracy *unless* agreement involves persons who are not guilty of the substantive crime itself.

  - **Model Penal Code** — abandons Wharton's Rule.

- **MENS REA DEFENSES APPLY** — D may assert any mens rea defenses which negate specific-intent.

**SPECIFIC-INTENT**
— D must have the specific-intent with regard to a criminal objective.

- **PURPOSEFUL AGREEMENT** — it is always sufficient that D enters the agreement with the conscious object of causing, promoting, or facilitating a result which he knows to be criminal.

- **CORRUPT MOTIVE DOCTRINE** — many states require that D actually had a *corrupt motive* (that he knew that intended conduct was illegal) except where the act is inherently wrong.

  - **Mere Knowledge** — normally not sufficient, but conviction is possible if: (1) goods supplied are *highly dangerous* (e.g., explosives), or *highly regulated* (e.g., drugs); (2) the crime is *very serious* (e.g., homicide, kidnapping); (3) there is *continuous involvement*, or (4) if D *affirmatively encouraged* use more of his goods when he had reason to know that the use was illegal.

  - **Knowledge Plus Stake** — D may be convicted if he *knows* that his goods or services are used for a criminal purpose *and* he has a "stake" *in the success of the criminal objective* (e.g., D charges an inflated price).

*(continued below)*

# Flowchart 4  CONSPIRACY  *(continued)*

**CONSPIRATORIAL OBJECTIVE**

**CRIME** — it is a conspiracy to agree to commit any crime, including a misdemeanor.

**PUBLICLY INJURIOUS ACT** — it is a conspiracy to agree with another to do any act (even if lawful) which is injurious to public health or morals and is accomplished by dishonest, fraudulent, corrupt, or immoral means (MPC and some states are *contra* limiting conspiracies to "crimes").

**DEFENSES**

**ABANDONMENT** — once a conspiracy has been formed, it is no defense that D subsequently withdrew, even if done prior to the completion of the underlying crime. (MPC and some states *contra*, but only if D: (1) completely renounces criminal purpose, *and* (2) makes substantial efforts to prevent the commission of the underlying crime.)

**IMPOSSIBILITY** — factual impossibility is not a defense though D may prevail if the conspiratorial objective is simply not illegal, regardless of D's contrary belief.

**SEPARATE OFFENSE** — conspiracy is a separate offense, distinct from the underlying crime (i.e., there is no merger).

**VENUE** — a criminal charge may be brought in any county where some act in furtherance was committed by any party, *or* where the agreement was made.

**HEARSAY EVIDENCE** — in a trial for conspiracy, otherwise inadmissable hearsay statements of co-conspirators are admissible against D if *made in furtherance of the conspiracy.*

**SPECIAL CONSEQUENCES**

**VICARIOUS LIABILITY**

**General Rule** — in addition to conspiracy and the substantive crime intended, D may be convicted of other crimes committed by members of conspiracy *in furtherance of conspiratorial goal* (it is no defense that D did not intend nor know of the acts.)

**Chain Conspiracy** — if D is part of a "chain" of known illegal acts (e.g., smuggling–wholesaling–retailing of drugs), he is liable for all crimes committed to further the conspiratorial goal (look for *"community of interest"*).

**Wheel Conspiracy** — if D conspires with B and B enters into similar separate and unrelated agreements for similar crimes with X and Y, B is the "hub" of a "wheel conspiracy"; if there is a *community of interest* so that D, X, and Y are interested in the success of each other's agreements with B, there is a "rim" connecting all the "spokes" in *one conspiracy* and all parties are liable for the criminal acts of the others. If there is no community of interest, there are 3 separate conspiracies and only B is liable for the acts of all others (as well as for 3 conspiracies).

**ATTEMPTED CONSPIRACY (SOLICITATION)** — one who attempts to induce, encourage, or command another to commit a crime is guilty of solicitation; if the other person agrees there is conspiracy.

**DURATION** — vicarious liability lasts until the goal of the conspiracy is achieved (including *immediate escape*) or D withdraws by informing all co-conspirators. (In many states, D must make some substantial effort to prevent the crime.)

# Flowchart 5a   CRIMINAL HOMICIDE ISSUES

**Issue Spotting Sequence:** (1) Is D responsible for an *act* causing the death? (2) Was D's act the of the death? (3) Was the act directed at *another* person? (4) Was the person *living* at the time of the act? (5) Did D possess a *criminal intent* with respect to the death? (6) Was there any *legal justification?*

**ACT**
- **Voluntary Affirmative Act** — act is sufficient even if it is itself lawful and/or inherently non dangerous. If immediate killing act was involuntary due to epileptic seizure or sudden unconsciousness, look to see whether the last voluntary act done by D was done with awareness of possibility of loss of control.
- **Omission** — death caused by D's failure to do an act he had a *legal duty* to do as the result of: (1) special statute, (2) contractual delegation, (3) special relationship of dependency, (4) voluntary undertaking (if abandonment puts victim in worse position), or (5) D's innocent act imperils victim.
- **Vicarious Liability** — D is responsible for homicidal acts of: (1) unresponsible agents put into motion by D, (2) accomplices—if act was reasonably foreseeable, and (3) co-conspirators—if act was done in furtherance of the conspiratorial goal (whether it was foreseeable or not).

**CAUSE**
- **Cause-in-fact**
  - **But For** — D's act was a necessary condition of result; "but for" the act, the victim would have lived longer.
  - **Independently Sufficient** — even if not the "but for" cause, D's act was sufficient in itself to produce result.
  - **Substantial Factor** — even if not either the "but for" cause or an independently sufficient cause, D's act was at least a substantial factor in producing result.
  - **Outside Time Limit** — at common law, the victim must die within a year and a day of the injury inflicted by D. Modern states extend time up to 3 years.
- **Proximate Cause**
  - **Pre-existing Conditions** — D "takes his victim as he finds him" and acts on a "set stage"; therefore, even unknown and unforeseeable pre-existing conditions which contribute to V's death do *not* intervene to break the chain of causations. Though D is criminally responsible for the direct results of his conduct from a causation stand point, unusually unforeseeable conditions may create a mens rea defense.
  - **Intervening Causes** — a separate event or act which occurs between D's cause-in-fact conduct and the death will *supersede* D's act and break the chain of causation if the intervening act or event was: (1) *independently sufficient* to cause the death, (2) *unforeseeable,* and (3) an *independent* act of God or another person not directly and logically flowing from D's act. (Some courts will also relieve D of responsibility if the intervening rescue force was *dependent.*) Failure of intervening rescue does *not* break the chain of causation.

**DEATH OF ANOTHER** — suicidal acts and attempts are not sufficient for homicide though many states separately punish attempted suicides especially if they endanger or injure innocent persons.

**LIVING PERSON**
- **Unborn Infants** — a victim has to be "born alive" and separated from its mother before homicide responsibility can arise. Some courts hold that a "viable" unborn fetus is a person for homicide purposes if it was sufficiently developed to be capable of living independently from its mother. State has right to declare a fetus "alive" after the first trimester of pregnancy. *Roe v. Wade*
- **Comatose Victims** — death occurs at the moment all bodily functions permanently cease, and not before. Because of live sustaining equipment that can support biological life and minimal body functions long after irreparable deterioration of the brain, the notion of "brain death" is a possible alternative.

*(continued below)*

# Flowchart 5a   CRIMINAL HOMICIDE ISSUES (continued)

**CRIMINAL INTENT** — homicide crimes are "graded" in terms of the culpability of D with respect to the death (see Flowchart 5b) but the following mental states are sufficient for some form of criminal homicide.

**Specific-Intent to Kill** — D has the specific-intent to kill if he is either *knowing* or *purposeful* with regard to the death. This includes willful, deliberate, premeditated, and deliberate killings. Unless justified, all intentional killings are either murder or voluntary manslaughter. Intent to kill is an express form of malice aforethought.

**Unintentional Killings** — D can be guilty of criminal homicide even if there was no intent to kill at the time of the death-causing act. Unintentional killings may either be murder or manslaughter but intent is criminal if D: (1) *intends to cause great bodily harm, a forcible felony, or resist a known lawful arrest*, (sufficient states for implied malice aforethought and, therefore, murder), (2) was *reckless* with regard to the death (wanton reckless disregard for human life is an extreme form sufficient for murder), (3) was *criminally negligent* with regard to the death, or (4) *intends to commit a malum in se unlawful act* (or inherently dangerous crime) not amounting to a forcible felony.

**LEGAL JUSTIFICATION (See MIG 7)**

**Self-Defense** — at the time of the act D (1) *reasonably believed* (2) that the *amount of force used was necessary* to protect himself from (3) *imminent* (4) *great bodily harm or death.* D may not be aggressor and, in minority of states, he must retreat before using deadly force if he knows he can do so with complete safety (except in his own home).

**Defense of Other** — D's act was (1) done *in defense of another person* and (2) the *person defended had a legal right to use the same amount of force used by D.* D "stands in the shoes" of the person defended and his conduct is judged in terms of actual facts. MPC, N.Y., and modern view permit defense if D reasonably believed that person defended would have been legally justified in using the force employed by D. Some states require person defended to be a close relative.

**Prevention of Crime** — D's act was intended to (1) *prevent commission of a forcible felony* (e.g., burglary, arson, robbery, rape, kidnapping, felonius assault) which (2) *was actually being committed* and (3) the *force used was reasonably believed necessary.* MPC, N.Y., and modern view judge D in terms of his reasonable belief about the commission of the felony, not the actual facts.

**Apprehension of Dangerous Felon** — D's act was (1) *done to effectuate an arrest or prevent escape* of a person who had (2) *actually* (3) had committed a *forcile felony,* (4) the *force used reasonably appeared to be necessary,* and (5) *the act did not unreasonably endanger innocent bystanders.* If D is a peace officer his conduct will be judged in terms of his reasonable belief as to the commission of the underlying felony, not by the actual facts.

**Necessity** — D's act was (1) *done to prevent imminent loss of life* (2) under circumstances where *according to ordinary standards of intelligence and morality* (3) the *harm sought to be avoided outweighed the harm caused by the act.*

**Defenses Not Available** — deadly force is *not justified* on a theory of *duress, entrapment, defense of property* (although if victim was committing a burglary or robbery prevention of a forcible felony justifies a killing), or *consent* ("mercy killing" or euthanasia is not a recognized defense but it can mitigate sentencing).

*multistate issue graph*

# Flowchart 5b  HOMICIDE CRIMES

**MURDER** —
Unlawful killing
with malice
aforethought,
no degrees
of murder at
common law.

**Intent to Kill** — Includes both *purposeful* (conscious object) and *knowing* (practically certain) killings. Specific-intent defenses available to negate mens rea. Under modern statutes, if intent to kill is supplemented by *deliberation and premeditation* (mental states revealing a relatively calm, "cold-blooded," reflective killing as opposed to a sudden, impulsive, or spontaneous killing). If victim does not die, D is guilty of attempted murder.

**Unintentional Killing — Wanton Reckless Disregard for Life** — Unintended killing resulting from an act done with a *conscious and knowing* disregard of a *plain and strong likelihood* that an *unjustified death or serious injury will result.* Any facts which negate conscious awareness of the risk may prevent mens rea (but voluntary intoxication may not negate recklessness). More than "mere recklessness"; act must reveal a wanton depraved indifference to human life. If victim does not die, no attempted murder since no specific-intent to kill.

**Unintentional Killing — Intent to Cause Great Bodily Harm (GBH)** — Unintended killing resulting from an act done with the purpose or knowledge that it cause *serious protracted injury* or create a *substantial risk of death* (very similar to recklessness). Includes any intentional wounding with a gun or knife, breaking of bones, clubbing, poisoning, or an act designed to produce unconsciousness by drugs or violence. Intent to do GBH may be negated by mistake, extreme intoxication, and in minority, by diminished mental capacity. If victim does not die, no attempted murder. Under modern statutes unintended death resulting from *intentional use of poison or explosives, torture,* or *ambush* (lying in wait) is first degree.

**Unintentional Killing — Intent to Resist Known Lawful Arrest** — Unintended killing resulting from act done in resistance of a *known lawful arrest.* D must actually know that the arrest is under lawful authority and mens rea defenses may negate that knowledge. If victim does not die, no attempted murder.

**Unintentional Killing — Intent to Commit a Felony** — Unintended killing proximately caused by and during the commission of a felony or an attempted felony. Wide state variations as to the *nature of the underlying felony* (most limit to forcible felonies—burglary, arson, robbery, rape, kidnapping), the *degree of offense* (usually first degree), and *special limitations* (usually as to the status of the killer or victim). *No attempted murder if victim does not die.*

**Special Limitations** — modern view permits felony murder (FM) only if D or a criminal accomplice directly kills the victim and where victim is an innocent person (not an accomplice).

**Underlying Felony Must Be Proved** — any defense to the underlying felony (e.g., claim of right to a burglary or robbery) absolves D of FM responsibility.

**Perpetration** — felony includes period from attempt (i.e., act beyond preparation) through immediate flight until final rest.

*(continued below)*

# Flowchart 5b   HOMICIDE CRIMES (continued)

**VOLUNTARY MANSLAUGHTER**
An intentional murder "mitigated" by facts negating malice aforethought.

**Intentional Killing — Provocation —** Intentional killing done in the *heat of passion caused by legally sufficient provocation* (actual or threatened battery or perceived infidelity — *not mere words*). Provocation must be such that it might render a reasonable ordinary person to lose self control and act rashly. "Cooling off" period between provocation and killing act destroys defense. Normal range of physical and temperamental defects are *not* taken into account but extreme disabilities of a permanent nature *may* be considered by a liberal court. Modern trend is to liberalize types of legally sufficient provocation and focus on culpability; MPC allows any "extreme emotional disturbance" regardless of cause. If victim does not die, some courts hold D for *attempted voluntary manslaughter*; others only for felonious assault.

**Intentional Killing — Mistaken Justification —** Intentional killing done with an *actual but unreasonable or erroneous* belief that the act was legally justified. Includes use of excessive force, unreasonable belief that harm was imminent, error as to the rights of a person being defended, etc. — called *imperfect defense*. If victim does not die, some convict of attempted voluntary manslaughter; others felonious assault.

**Intentional Killing — Diminished Capacity —** While most states allow evidence of mental defect short of insanity and extreme intoxication to negate the "premeditation" aspect (reducing a charge to second degree murder), a small minority go further and permit a showing of diminished mental capacity to *negate malice aforethought* and reduce the charge to voluntary manslaughter. Diminished capacity applies only to homicide charges.

**INVOLUNTARY MANSLAUGHTER**
An unintentional unlawful killing without malice aforethought.

**Unintentional Killing — Ordinary Recklessness —** Unintended killing resulting from an act done with a *conscious disregard* for a *substantial and unjustifiable risk of death or serious injury* but one that does *not* demonstrate a wanton depraved indifference to human life. The distinction between ordinary recklessness resulting in involuntary manslaughter and depraved recklessness resulting in murder is merely a question of degree to be determined as an issue of fact.

**Unintentional Killing — Gross and Culpable Negligence —** Unintended killing resulting from a negligent act which reveals a wanton disregard of the risk of death or serious injury. More than ordinary negligence, it must be *gross* and *culpable* but it is *not* required that the prosecutor prove that D was consciously aware of the risk (compare to recklessness). Normally deals with mishandling of an *inherently dangerous instrumentality* (e.g., guns, explosives, automobiles), *product* (e.g., food and drugs), or *situation* (e.g., risk of fire in a public place).

**Unintentional Killing — Unlawful Act Rule —** Unintended killing proximately caused by and during the commission or attempted commission of a malum in se (i.e., wrong in itself) misdemeanor or felony (if jurisdiction limits FM rule to forcible felonies). Sometimes called the misdemeanor-manslaughter rule. Many states apply rule only to *inherently dangerous crimes* or *non-dangerous crimes committed in an unusual and inherently dangerous manner*. Look for this possibility whenever FM fails.

**Unintentional Killing — Provocation and Mistaken Justification —** Unintended killing resulting from an *act only intended to wound or frighten* done in the heat of passion with *legally sufficient provocation* or in *an honest but erroneous belief that the force used was legally justified* (compare to voluntary manslaughter where the intent was to kill).

*multistate issue graph*

# Flowchart 6    COMMON LAW BURGLARY

(1) Trespassory (2) breaking and (3) entering (4) a dwelling (5) in the nighttime (6) with specific-intent to (a) commit a larceny or (b) any felony (7) therein.

**TRESPASSORY** — entry must be without consent, but entry gained by misrepresentation of identity or other trick is trespassory.

**BREAKING** — D must create or enlarge the opening for his entry; includes opening an unlocked door or raising a partially open window, but D need not actually "break." In many states, unlawful "remaining" in a store after closing is a constructive breaking, though common law requires that the breaking must be done to gain entry, not to exit. Some states abandon the breaking requirement entirely.

**ENTERING** — D must physically intrude victim's property.

    ┌ **D'S BODY** — any portion of D's body is sufficient.

    └ **INSTRUMENT** — any tool or hook invading the property is sufficient if it is used to achieve the criminal purpose (as opposed to using it to merely gain entry).

**DWELLING** — structure must be a place where one *normally* sleeps (although it need not be occupied at the time of entry).

    ┌ **INCLUDES CURTILAGE** — structures immediately surrounding the dwelling (e.g., enclosed in the area of the "yard") and physically connected buildings.

    ├ **INCLUDES BOATS AND TRAILERS WHERE PEOPLE SLEEP**

    └ **MODERN STATUTES EXTEND TO ALL "ENCLOSED STRUCTURES" ABANDONING THE DWELLING REQUIREMENT**

**NIGHTTIME** — entry must occur 30 minutes before sunset or after sunrise. This requirement is *abandoned under modern "breaking and entering" statutes.*

**SPECIFIC-INTENT**

    ┌ **LARCENY** — **Intent to Commit Any Larceny Is Sufficient (even if petty larceny)**

         **Be Sure All Elements of Larceny Are Specifically Intended:** (1) trespassory taking, (2) carrying away, (3) personal property, (4) known to be owned by another, (5) intent to permanently deprive. The claim of right defense is particularly likely to arise; if it does, there is no burglary.

    └ **ANY FELONY** — intent to commit *any* felony is sufficient, but look for defenses to the underlying felony.

**THEREIN** — D must intend to commit the crime *in the dwelling* (or enclosed structure); it is not sufficient that D broke and entered only to get to another place.

*multistate issue graph*

# Flowchart 7   JUSTIFICATION FOR THE USE OF FORCE

**REASONABLE FEAR** — D must *actually and reasonably* believe that D is threatening imminent bodily harm (belief need not be correct).

**IMMINENT HARM** — *D must believe harm is imminent* although D may seize last reasonable opportunity to defend himself if V attempts to deprive him of the capacity for self-defense (as where V attempts to tie D up and torture him later). Note: If threat of harm is past, D has no right of self-defense.

**BODILY HARM** — "self-defense" is not available to prevent or respond to insults regardless of how offensive or vile, *use of force justified only to prevent a reasonably anticipated battery.*

**DEADLY FORCE** — (1) *force intended to cause death or* (2) *force creating a substantial likelihood of causing great bodily harm* (including death).

**RECIPROCITY** — D may only use deadly force to respond to deadly force.

**RETREAT RULE (minority)** — D may not use deadly force if he *actually knew he could have prevented the harm by retreating.*

**D must subjectively believe that he could retreat in complete safety.**

**D need not retreat from his own home (many states include any place of nightly repose and some include offices and automobile).**

## SELF-DEFENSE
— if D has a (1) *reasonable fear of* (2) *imminent* (3) *bodily harm* he may use (4) that amount of force which is *reasonably necessary* to prevent the harm (5) unless D is an *aggressor.*

**NECESSARY FORCE** — *short of deadly force*, D may use that amount of force that is *reasonably necessary to prevent the threatened harm;* if D uses excessive force, he becomes an aggressor and loses the right of self-defense.

**AGGRESSOR** — D is an aggressor if (1) *he strikes the first blow or* (2) *commits a crime against V.*

**REGAINING RIGHTS OF SELF-DEFENSE** — aggressor regains the right to use force in self-defense if (1) *he abandons aggression completely and V actually perceives the abandonment,* or (2) *V uses excessive force.*

**AGGRESSOR LIMITATION**

**DEFENSE AGAINST UNLAWFUL ARREST** — D may use reasonable, non-deadly force to prevent an unlawful arrest or unlawful attachment of her property, but she acts at her own risk; the arrest or attachment must, in fact, be unlawful or the defense is denied. (Modern view prevents all use of force to resist any arrest, even if unlawful.)

**DEFENSE OF OTHERS** — in defending another person (V) from imminent injury, D is justified in using only the amount of force which V could use in his own defense; D stands in the shoes of V and if V was, in fact, the aggressor, the force used by D is not privileged. (MPC and modern trend allow D's conduct to be measured by the reasonable person standard — if D reasonably believed the force used was justified, the defense is valid.)

**DEFENSE OF PROPERTY** — modern *non-deadly* force may be used to prevent theft, destruction, or trespass of property. If deadly force was used, look to see whether it could be justified as *self-defense* (e.g., as where D shot an armed robber) or *to prevent a dangerous forcible felony* (e.g., as where D shot a burglar intruding into his home).

**LAW ENFORCEMENT DEFENSES** — police officers and private citizens may use force in preventing crimes and effectuating an arrest. Normally, courts are more liberal in allowing force to *prevent* a crime (especially a felony) than in an after-the-crime arrest.

**POLICE** — may use amount of force, *including deadly force, which reasonably appears necessary* as long as force is *not disproportionate* to the offense involved or the resistance offered, (Some states limit use of deadly force to prevent commission of a dangerous forcible felony or apprehension of a dangerous fleeing felon.)

**CITIZEN** — may use the same amount of force as police officer except *D acts at his own risk;* defense is denied if D is mistaken about the commission of the crime. (MPC and modern trend test D's conduct by reasonable person standard.)

**NECESSITY** — force, including deadly force, is justified to avoid an (1) imminent public or private injury, (2) resulting from natural physical forces, (3) which injury is about to occur through no fault of the actor and which is (4) of such gravity that (5) according to ordinary standards of intelligence and morality (6) the desirability of avoiding the injury clearly outweighs the state's interest in preventing the proscribed conduct.

*multistate issue graph*

# Flowchart 8 CRIMINAL LAW

## ACQUISITION BY STEALTH, FORCE, OR THREAT

**TRESPASSORY** — taking by stealth or force.

**TAKING OF POSSESSION (caption)** — D must take possession and acquire dominion and control; there can be no larceny if D already has lawful possession.

**CARRYING AWAY (asportation)** — larceny complete when D carries the property away from the point of taking; slight movement is sufficient.

**PERSONAL PROPERTY** — D must take tangible personal property at common law, but most states have special statutes for theft of services and other intangibles.

**OF ANOTHER** — D must specifically know the property is owned by another; any bona fide claim of right is a complete defense. Also look for mens rea defenses of mistake or intoxication.

**INTENT TO PERMANENTLY DEPRIVE** — D must intend to *permanently* deprive the owner of the property *at the time of the taking*; no larceny if D intends to restore the identical property taken but intent is sufficient if D: (1) intends to pay a cash equivalent at a later time, (2) intends to return only if a reward is paid, or (3) recklessly exposes property to loss.

**LARCENY** — (1) trespassory (2) taking and (3) carrying away of (4) personal property (5) known to be another's with (6) the intent to permanently deprive.

**FROM A PERSON** — taking from the "presence" of a person is sufficient if force or threat was needed to sever the property from the person's control.

**FORCE OR THREAT** — must precede or accompany the taking. *Armed robbery* is an aggravated form where D uses a weapon or an article designed to look like a weapon.

**ROBBERY** — (1) larceny (be sure all elements are present) (2) from a person (3) accomplished by force or putting in fear (i.e., threat). Includes threat to person, his family, or his property.

**INJURY** — includes threats to injure V or his family or to injure V's property.

**ACCUSATION** — includes threats to charge or prosecute V with a crime (whether or not V actually committed the crime) if used to cause V to do an act or pay money; claim of right is no defense.

**DISGRACE** — includes threats to expose V to disgrace or extreme humiliation.

**NEED NOT BE IMMEDIATE** — unlike robbery, the threat need not relate to an immediate harm.

**EXTORTION** — statutory extension of common law robbery consisting of (1) the use of malicious threats with the (2) specific intent to (3) compel a person to either (a) pay money, or (b) do or refrain from doing any act against his will (commonly referred to as "blackmail").

## ACQUISITION BY FRAUD OR TRICK

**TITLE** — the owner must intend to convey permanent unfettered possession (i.e., title) to D in a *sale or trade* transaction.

**REPRESENTATION** — unlike larceny by trick, it is *not* sufficient that D makes a false promise; there must be misrepresentation of a present or past *fact* or there is no crime.

**SCIENTER** — D must know of the falsity of the representation at the time of acquisition.

**RELIANCE** — owner must actually rely on D's misrepresentation.

**OBTAINING PROPERTY BY FALSE PRETENSES** — (1) *acquisition of title* (not mere possession) of (2) personal property (3) by means of a representation of fact (*not* a promise of future performance) (4) known by D to be false (5) at the time of acquisition.

**POSSESSION** — the owner must intend to convey only temporary possession to D in a *rental, loan, or bailment* transaction.

**REPRESENTATION** — includes misrepresentation of past or present facts *and* a false promise to return the property.

**SCIENTER** — D must actually know the representation or promise was false at the time of the taking.

**RELIANCE** — owner must actually rely on D's misrepresentation or D is only liable for attempt.

**LARCENY BY TRICK** — (1) taking of possession (not title) of (2) personal property (3) known to be owned by another (4) with the intent to permanently deprive (5) where such taking is accomplished by means of a representation or promise (6) known by D to be false (7) at the time of the taking.

## CONVERSION

**CONVERSION** — D need only apply the property to a *personal use* to be guilty, regardless of the intent to restore or even the actual restoration of the property.

**PROPERTY** — by some statutes includes title to real property.

**LARCENY BY CONVERSION** — same as larceny by trick except that there is *no false representation*; the intent to permanently convert the property for D's own exclusive use must be formed *after* the lawful acquisition of possession in a rental, loan, or bailment situation.

**ENTRUSTMENT** — D must have acquired custody of the property as a result of a special fiduciary relationship (e.g., trustee, agent, employee).

**EMBEZZLEMENT** — a variation of larceny by conversion developed to deal with (1) the improper use (i.e., conversion) of (2) property (3) entrusted to D's custody; there is no need for the intent to permanently deprive and no need for a misrepresentation.

*multistate issue graph*

# NOTES

# NOTES

KAPLAN) *pmbr*

# NOTES

KAPLAN) *pmbr*